High-Performance
CHEVY SMALL-BLOCK
Cams & Valvetrains

GRAHAM HANSEN

S·A DESIGN

CarTech®
Auto Books & Manuals

INTRODUCTION TO SMALL-BLOCK CHEVY CAMS AND VALVETRAINS

The first generation small-block Chevy should certainly be considered one of the most important automotive designs of the last half of the 20th century. It has powered more performance machines and won more races than any engine in the history of man. No wonder so much has been written on the subject.

In the grand scheme of things, the internal combustion engine is a relatively simple device. It pulls air and fuel into a cylinder, squeezes it, ignites the mixture, turns a crank, and then pushes the oxidized material out — suck-squeeze-bang-blow. Yet as simple as this operation seems on the surface, man has been tinkering with these same four strokes for over 100 years. For performance enthusiasts who subscribe to the notion that the first-generation small-block Chevy is among the top ten creations of the last 50 years, you have the makings of an obsession of sorts.

Much has been written, espoused, preached, immortalized, and misunderstood about performance-building the small-block Chevy. You can now add this effort to that mountainous list. We are not here to let you in on any long-lost secrets kept hidden in the lockers of eccentric engine builders. While there may be some data squirreled away deep underneath mountains of flow-bench numbers and dyno sheets in a forgotten Smokey Yunick notebook, the reality is that the best engine builders in the business deal with the same impediments to performance that the average street enthusiast faces. Both are challenged by the same question: How do I stuff more air and fuel into the cylinder to make more power? The valvetrain side of that question is addressed in this book.

Basics

In order to really understand how high-performance engines work, we have to start with the basics. The problem is that few enthusiasts are willing to make the time to learn even the most rudimentary information. They're too caught up in all the glamour of big carburetors, gargantuan camshafts, and stratospheric compression ratios all placed at the altar of the omniscient god of horsepower. The good news is that those guys probably aren't reading this book.

So those of you who are starting at the beginning with this effort must be different. You're willing to take the time

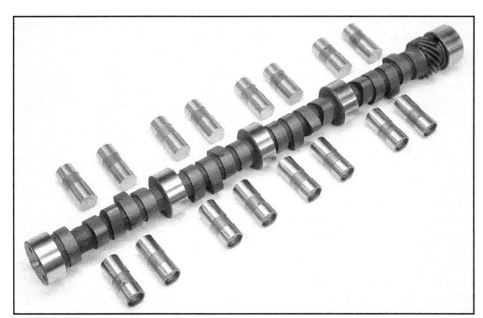

Looking at a typical flat-tappet small-block Chevy camshaft, it doesn't look that complex. Add a few lifters, pushrods, and rocker arms and you have a complete valvetrain. But in order to really make these parts work, it's important to know how all these components work individually and in concert with each other.

to read these carefully presented lines of information in hopes of grasping the nuances of the valvetrain side of the four-stroke cycle as it relates to the small-block Chevy. We leave the radical notions of exotic rod-length-to-stroke ratio theories and hypersensitive swirl-enhancing carburetors to our longhaired friends with endless time on their hands. Instead, we concentrate on what works, what is proven to work, and perhaps even present some ideas you may not have heard before. If it makes you think and has you scratching the back of your head wondering how it all relates, then we've done our job.

Despite the fact that the small-block Chevy is a man-made machine, it does appear that even the venerable Mouse motor has, at mostly inopportune occasions, a mind of its own. It is subject to the laws of nature and physics and often those actions seem to be counter-intuitive. That's the challenge and the beauty of dyno testing. One reason we enjoy beating on the little Mouse motor is because the results usually require us to think about what's happening inside those cylinders. The more we understand, the more efficiently the engine performs. Eventually, that process results in more power.

In this book, we're going to concentrate on the brains of the small-block Chevy – the camshaft and valvetrain. The camshaft triggers the onset of induction and exhaust, essentially predetermining the torque and horsepower curve even before the engine ever fires.

A good engine builder can look at the cam specs along with the cylinder head flow and a few other small yet important details and can tell you, within an amazingly narrow window, what that engine makes for power. That's because these men have been building these engines for years and have the experience to know what works.

By merely changing the camshaft and match building the proper valvetrain, you can transform an otherwise docile street engine into a high-RPM performer capable (assuming decent flow potential) of making much more horsepower. This game's rules on where power is often produced comes at a price. This goes well beyond the cost of the parts; it has more to do with the change in the power curve shape resulting from the modifications made to the cam timing. You might make more horsepower at a higher RPM, but at the expense of torque at lower engine speeds. The more educated players in this game are skilled at improving the power throughout the entire power curve without sacrificing gains made at lower engine speeds. Pull off that torque-enhancing hat trick and the performance world is going to beat a path to your shop door.

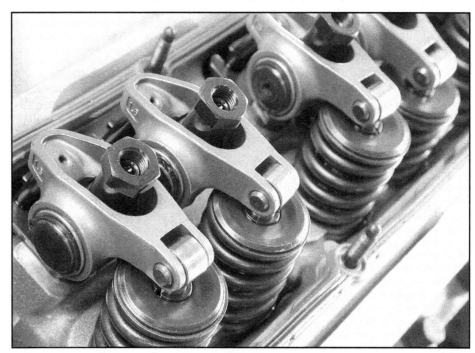

This is what you see when you pull the valve cover off of a typical performance small-block Chevy. This book explains how each of these components assists the engine in making enough power to impress your friends and transform rear tires into smoke.

Many enthusiasts play the horsepower game mainly in a one-dimensional sense of "how high?" They make changes to the engine, but concentrate their evaluation only on peak horsepower. If it went up, then it was a positive move. Sounds simple enough. While that approach has its merits, it is often limited and shortsighted and often does not result in a lower elapsed time at the drag strip or local circle track. We'd like to

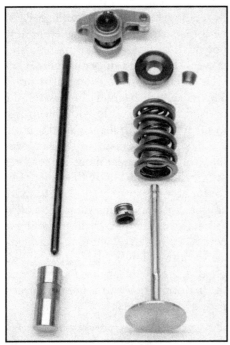

The valvetrain should really be considered as a whole when optimizing a specific engine package. Cam lobe profile, spring pressures, valvetrain weight, rocker ratio, and a raft of other considerations are all part of the dance that allows your engine to make its best power.

suggest taking a broader, two-dimensional approach to power that asks both "how high?" and "how wide?"

Most dyno tests are performed over a wide power band encompassing 3,000 or 4,000 rpm. Smart engine tuners look not just at the peak horsepower number but also the shape of the power curve. Did the engine also increase power below the peak horsepower point? Did the engine merely trade torque at the lower end of the RPM scale to deliver additional peak horsepower gain, or did the modification raise the power curve along the entire breadth of the test? The answers to these questions

are one key to engine tuning. Frankly, it's very easy to build an engine with impressive peak horsepower numbers if you don't pay attention to, or care about, the shape of rest of the power curve. These peaky engines operate like a light switch—or a two-stroke that's "up on the pipe"—the power is either on or off.

The more challenging approach is to create an engine that not only delivers impressive peak horsepower, but can also grunt down at lower engine speeds. At the same time, it must crank out massive torque that helps accelerate the engine off a slow corner or pull out of the bottom of the shift recovery RPM. Mixing and matching components that deliver both a solid torque curve and impressive peak horsepower numbers is the mark of a truly accomplished performance engine builder. The goal of this book is to help you understand the basics behind how the cam and valvetrain contribute to that success.

Where We're Headed

To begin, we dive head first into the basics of how camshafts work. On the surface, a cam lobe is a very simple device. It converts rotary or spinning motion into vertical or linear motion. But within that is a tremendous body of knowledge. This book stays away from the serious geometry and polynomial picnic math that's involved with cam lobe design, and sticks with the material that best benefits the enthusiast. Besides, we don't understand much of that highbrow number crunching anyway.

Chapter 3 deals with the valvetrain, or all the components that accompany the camshaft. We then break each one of those pieces down into separate chapters to get into each component on an in-depth basis. This is the kind of information you won't get in an abbreviated magazine article, simply because there isn't room in those stories to address everything you need to know. We have canvassed the industry experts, manufacturers, and racers to pull out the best information and bring it to you.

Once we've delineated all the separate components, we then get into how to install and degree a camshaft. This is critical information because if the camshaft is

There's much more to the story of rocker arms than just ratio. Proper pushrod length can make or break a good valvetrain.

to operate as the designer intended, proper installation is important. There's much more to degreeing a cam than just lining up the dots on the cam and crank gears.

Choosing the correct camshaft for your particular application requires an important body of knowledge. This literally begins and ends with being honest about exactly what you want out of your engine. It goes far beyond demanding maximum power. The key is to decide on precisely how the engine is going to be used and how it is expected to perform. Once those decisions are made, this narrows the selection process down to a few cams with the best lobe profiles. Once you begin to understand how camshafts operate, the chapter on choosing a cam may be one of the most important chapters in this book. Every

Shaft rocker systems used to be in the exotic drag-race engine realm. But now for a little more than the cost of a good stud-mounted roller rocker system, you can have a race-bred shaft-mounted system. Shaft systems eliminate many problems associated with high spring-pressures and stud-mounted rockers.

Roller cams are the new darlings of the performance world. Hydraulic and mechanical rollers run the entire spectrum from pure OEM pieces to 10,000 rpm drag-race screamers. More importantly, there's a ton of selection in between for the street enthusiast.

It doesn't make any sense to put all that effort into choosing the right cam if you're not going to install it precisely where it should be. Accurately degreeing a cam is not difficult, nor are the tools that expensive.

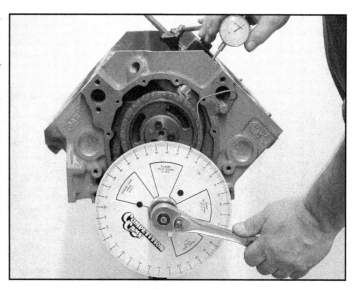

Valve float isn't just the scourge of drag racers running in the stratospheric RPM ranges. Match the wrong valvesprings with an aggressive cam and the valves can float at speeds as low as 4,000 rpm!

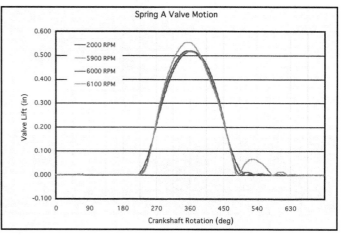

camshaft is a compromise and within each cam selection, you could probably choose 8 to 10 more cams that merely move the numbers around slightly to better optimize its operation.

We also venture into the intriguing territory of valvetrain dynamics and the often-used but rarely understood term of "valve float." This book shows that most enthusiasts' idea of valve float may only be partially correct. Many of the major cam companies have invested in valvetrain machines called Spintrons. Spintrons use hyper-accurate pressure transducers to record what happens to the valvetrain and especially the valvespring during high-RPM operation. If you've ever seen any of those short video clips at a trade show, they are fascinating slow-motion documentaries on the gyrations the valvespring experiences during high-speed operation. You come away from the experience wondering how your valvetrain survives all this and still works consistently. It is amazing!

The end of this book also touches on matching camshafts and cylinder heads. Here the information becomes less science and more Kentucky windage and best guesstimates. The relationship of the intake and exhaust port flow numbers plays a significant role in this inter-component dance. Selecting the ideal lift and duration for both the intake and exhaust lobes and optimizing the lobe separation angle become very complicated. Ultimately, this is where trial-

Engine dyno testing is where we discover just how much we really know about matching cams with the rest of the engine. Many enthusiasts see a dyno as answering the question: "How much power does it make?" However, most engine builders realize that the dyno more often creates many more questions than it answers.

and-error testing creates the ideal combination. But with all the variables involved with just the camshaft separate from the rest of the engine, you can begin to see how complex this all becomes when you're searching for that

last push to pump up your power curve.

Finally, we take all these words and pictures and condense them down to a few engine combinations. A few small-block Chevys are twisted up and we see what kind of numbers these powerplants

This is the new LS7 small-block that makes 500 SAE net horsepower and 475 ft-lbs of torque from 427 ci. This is also the first Detroit production engine sporting titanium valves.

can create. We cover the entire spectrum of engines from extremely mild and torquey small-blocks that you can drive every day on the street, up through some crazy stuff that spins to the moon making astounding power.

If you manage to make it through this entire book, we're not promising you a PhD in cam design—far from it. What we can offer is a better understanding of the complex operation involved with all the monkey motion that accompanies a rocker arm-motivated small-block Chevy. Then you can use the information to launch into your own doctorate power program in the quest for more horsepower from our beloved small-block Chevy.

FUTURE SHOCK

This book is all about camshaft and valvetrain parts for the first-generation small-block, since that's the engine that most enthusiasts have in their garage. But we would be remiss if we didn't at least acknowledge the GEN III and now GEN IV small-block and the technology that it represents. Why bother with these newest small-blocks? Because they represent the latest technology in small-block design and what the factory is doing now for production engines only a few years ago would have been considered efforts reserved for pure race engines. Does that sound like journalistic hype? Read on.

The latest version of the small-block Chevy is now called the GEN IV, and the new high-water mark is the new 2006 LS7 engine. Let's start with a GEN IV that is 7.0 liters, that's 427 ci using a 4.125-inch bore and a 4.00-inch stroke. The engine sports an 11:1 compression ratio that it uses to make 500 hp at 6,200 and

475 ft-lbs of torque at 4,800 rpm. To keep reciprocating weight down, the connecting rods are titanium while a dry sump lubrication system uses scavenge and pressure systems along with a separate oil tank that carries 8 quarts of oil.

You don't make 500 hp from a production engine without an aggressive valvetrain. We're adding this information just before this book goes to press, so we don't have any camshaft duration figures as yet, but the intake valve lift figure is a whopping 0.591 inches, and the heads flow some pretty serious airflow since they are completely CNC-machined castings with raised intake and exhaust ports to match the fully CNC-machined combustion chambers. In addition, the valve angle has been tilted from the GEN III's 15-degree valve angle to an even more vertical 12 degrees. Plus, the heads are fitted with monstrous 2.20-inch intake and 1.61-inch exhaust valves, and because

the intake valves are so big, GM opted for titanium valves to keep the weight manageable up to the engine's 7,000-rpm redline! That's right, this engine has titanium intake valves, which also means it uses captured lash caps on the intake valve tip to prevent wear from the dedicated 1.8:1 investment cast roller rockers arms.

See if this description doesn't sound like a race engine—we have a big-bore, long-stoke 427 ci engine with 11:1 compression, titanium connecting rods, titanium intake valves, a dry sump, offset rocker arms to clear the intake ports and heads with a 12-degree valve angle, and 1.8:1 rocker arms. So given the state of the art of the LS7 production ZO6 Corvette engine, we can take many cues from this effort to apply to the venerable first generation small-block. And for those of you who bemoan all this technology—how much horsepower does your small-block make?

CAMSHAFT BASICS

A camshaft may look like a simple device, but those little eccentrics hide a roller coaster-like world of velocity, acceleration rates, and complex polynomial equations. For a simpler start, camshafts come in several configurations. The cam on the left is a cast-iron flat-tappet hydraulic while the cam on the right is a steel hydraulic roller.

The most basic shape in nature is the circle. While each lobe on a camshaft is actually an eccentric, it begins and ends with a circle, which is where we start. A camshaft lobe really has only one job – to convert rotary or spinning motion into linear or back-and-forth motion, which is what the eccentric does. Place a follower against the base circle of a cam. Now spin the lobe and watch the follower move up and down in its bore. How quickly that follower creates lift and how long it creates lift before returning to the lobe's base circle is what we are investigating in this chapter. We then take that information and combine it with the rest of the lobes on the cam and see how they all work together to make the combustion process more powerful.

Camshaft Types

Before we get too deeply into this, let's first look at the two basic types of camshafts used in the typical small-block Chevy—the flat tappet and roller lifter style. Flat tappet cams are the senior members of this exclusive club. They were the first type of cam used in the earliest 265-ci Mouse motor. In this case, the face portion of the lifter slides along the lobe as the camshaft turns. The second style of cam is the roller lifter version. Those without a historical perspective may assume that the roller lifter and cam design is a relatively new invention. But in reality, some of the earliest known internal combustion engines used roller cams and lifters, dating at least as far back as the 1911 Stearns flat-head engine and probably even earlier.

Within each of these two cam families are subsets of mechanical and hydraulic lifter cams and lifters. Mechanical cams (whether flat tappet or roller) use a very simple lifter. They are solid with just a radius cup in the top of the lifter for the pushrod. These cams require a designed-in clearance into the system to account for growth as the engine expands on its way to its normal operating temperature. This is one reason for the clearance or "lash" spec that accompanies any solid lifter camshaft.

The second style, the hydraulic, is far more popular for street engines. It incor-

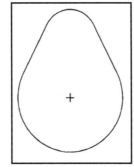

This illustration shows the basic shape of a cam lobe, generating lift from the base circle. Both lift and duration are calculated from the base circle.

As you gain knowledge of camshaft design, it should become clear that it is almost impossible to just look at a cam and tell much about it. This is why accurate cam measurement is so critical to ensure optimal performance.

porates a small piston inside the lifter body that rides on a cushion of engine oil. This small chamber is filled with engine oil, creating a pressurized area that automatically compensates for clearance changes in the engine during operation. Instead of clearance used for mechanical lifters, hydraulic cams require preloading the lifter used to compensate for these changes in clearances. We get more into that in the chapter on cam installation.

Lobe Prospecting – Duration

Now let's condense that camshaft down to one simple lobe and dissect it into its more simplistic components. A lobe has a few simple points worth mentioning, starting with the base circle. The lobe begins to rise off the radius of the base circle; this is referred to as the opening flank. The peak or top of the lobe is referred to as the nose. As the lobe continues to turn, we reach the closing flank that eventually transitions back to the base circle.

The most basic measurement of any lobe is the amount of rise, or lift, created at the nose. This is called lobe lift. Cam or lobe lift is the amount of tappet rise eventually multiplied by the rocker arm to create valve lift. Rocker arms are covered in detail in Chapter 6. When the cam designer creates

lift in a lobe, it is not created instantly. In other words, the cam lobe is not square. Instead, it has a slope that gradually pushes the lifter up to its maximum lift. The amount of time the lifter is raised off the base circle is referred to as duration and is expressed most often in crankshaft degrees.

In the small-block Chevy, and in all four-stroke engines, the camshaft is driven at exactly half of the engine speed. This is easy to see in the cam drive system in a small-block Chevy where the cam gear has exactly twice the number of teeth as the crank gear. To make it easier to work

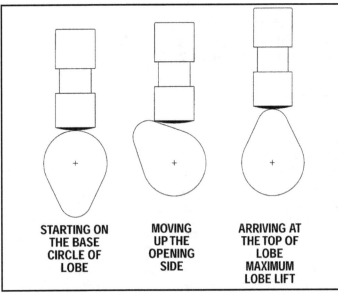

STARTING ON THE BASE CIRCLE OF LOBE — **MOVING UP THE OPENING SIDE** — **ARRIVING AT THE TOP OF LOBE MAXIMUM LOBE LIFT**

A camshaft is a simple device that converts rotary motion into linear or up and down movement. The lifter follows the shape of the lobe, imparting lift as the eccentric moves away from the radius of the base circle. (Illustration courtesy of Crane)

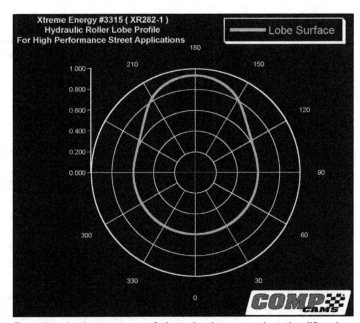

Duration is the amount of time, in degrees, that the lifter has moved away from the base circle. Duration is always listed in crankshaft degrees.

ALPHABET SOUP FOR CAMS

When you begin to dig under the surface of high-performance engines, you immediately begin to run into shortcuts and acronyms that engine builders and cam designers use to deliver information more quickly. When it comes to camshafts, an entire language is associated with this internal combustion component. In case you're not familiar with some of the acronyms, here are a few definitions:

TDC – Top Dead Center – this is when the piston has reached the exact top of its stroke. TDC is also used as a starting point for crankshaft degrees, so TDC for piston Number One is always 0 degrees.

ATDC – After Top Dead Center – this is the position of the piston (usually Num-

ber One) in relationship to TDC. This can be expressed, for example, as 12 degrees ATDC. This is generally the area where exhaust closing occurs.

BTDC – Before Top Dead Center – this is the position of the Number One piston before TDC, as in 20 degrees BTDC. This is generally the area where intake opening occurs.

BDC – Bottom Dead Center – this is the position of the piston (usually Number One) at the exact bottom of the piston stroke, 180 degrees from TDC.

ABDC – After Bottom Dead Center – this is the position of the piston expressed in degrees after the 180-degree mark, as in 52 degrees ABDC. This is generally the area where intake closing occurs.

BBDC – Before Bottom Dead Center – this is the position of the piston expressed in degrees before the 180-degree mark, as in 60 degrees BBDC. This is generally the area where the exhaust opening occurs.

LDA – Lobe Displacement Angle – this is the number of camshaft degrees that separate the intake and exhaust lobe centerlines. This is another term for lobe separation angle (LSA) or Lobe Center Angle. We use LSA in this book.

LSA – Lobe Separation Angle – see Lobe Displacement Angle. Some writers use the acronym LSA to shorten their copy. To ensure that you understand the information presented in this book, we have avoided this shortcut.

All four-stroke engines spin the camshaft at half engine speed. This small-block Chevy timing set makes that clear since the camshaft gear is twice the size of the crank gear. If the cam were to spin at engine speed, it would have to be very large and heavy. So making it smaller creates a more compact engine design.

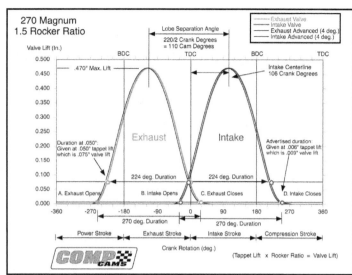

Studying this one illustration does more to help you understand how all the basic camshaft functions interrelate. Lift, duration, lobe separation, and overlap are all present in this one graph.

with the numbers, most cam specs are expressed in degrees of engine rotation. Given that, the amount of time that the lobe rises off the base circle, then is described in degrees of crankshaft rotation. For example, a typical small-block Chevy intake lobe may be expressed as having 270 degrees of advertised duration. This means that if you were to place a dial indicator on a lifter with a 360-degree wheel bolted to the nose of the crankshaft and you measured the amount of time (in engine degrees of rotation) that the lifter was off the base circle, you would see the crankshaft turn 270 degrees. It's not quite that simple because of specific checking points that must be used. We've addressed that in the accompanying sidebar on advertised duration versus duration at 0.050 tappet lift.

The important distinction to retain here is that the camshaft is turning at half engine speed yet duration is expressed in engine degrees. At first, it may appear that the intake lobe is open for 3/4 (270 of 360 degrees) of an entire rotation, so how can that work? To explain this, we have to go back to the basic four-stroke cycle. In order to have enough time to complete all four of the intake, compression, combustion, and exhaust events, the engine must rotate through two complete revolutions, or 720 degrees. So if we have a camshaft with 270 degrees of 720 degrees rotation, it is only 37.5 percent of total engine rotation per four-stroke cycle, which works very nicely.

Lobe Centerlines

So now that we've covered lift and duration, lobe centerline is next. For every lobe with a given number of degrees of duration, there is a mid-point or halfway point in that event. This can be easily expressed in a line drawing of a lobe splitting it right down the middle. Cam designers use this midpoint to help them position both the intake and exhaust lobes in relation to each other. Again, this position is expressed in crankshaft degrees. For example, the intake lobe of a typical small-block performance camshaft has an intake lobe centerline positioned at 106 degrees ATDC (after top dead center). Note that this is the position of the intake lobe centerline as positioned in the engine. This shortcut is used because it's the easiest way for a typical engine builder to ensure that his camshaft is positioned properly in the engine. If the cam is correctly ground and installed, this is the number the engine builder comes up with when he degrees the camshaft in the engine. How to degree a cam is shown in a later chapter.

As you might have already assumed, the exhaust lobe also has a lobe centerline figure, most often expressed as a given number of degrees ABDC (after bottom dead center). This figure is generally not used very much in typical installation or checking procedures, except to help determine our next detail in our somewhat complex world of camshaft information. This is something called lobe separation angle,

or lobe displacement angle. Simply put, this is the number of degrees (expressed this time in camshaft degrees) separating the intake and exhaust lobe centerlines. The easiest way to understand this is to look at the layout of the intake and exhaust lobes in the drawing. It looks like two adjacent hills or camel humps. If you study

Using a degree wheel ensures the proper positioning of a camshaft in the engine. We get into more details on this in the chapter on installation and degreeing (Chapter 9), but this is how you know where the intake lobe is in reference to TDC on piston Number One.

this drawing carefully, it does more to explain how camshafts work than literally thousands of words of explanation.

If you look at the cam graph, you can easily spot both the exhaust and intake lobe centerlines at (or near) the peak of their respective lift curves. The distance between those two centerline points is expressed in cam, not crankshaft, degrees. Of all the camshaft specs, lobe separation angle is the only camshaft spec expressed in camshaft degrees. This is because the definition takes the total number of crankshaft degrees of separation and divides it by two. By doing so, this changes the number to camshaft degrees because the cam spins at half crank speed.

An important point to make when discussing lobe separation angle is that the cam designer establishes the angle. Once that relationship is established by grinding the cam, the lobe separation angle cannot be changed unless a new camshaft is machined. This makes engine development and tuning somewhat difficult with any cam-in-block pushrod engine because changing the lobe separation angle requires a new camshaft. If we were working on a dual overhead cam (DOHC) engine, changing the lobe separation angle is merely a matter of moving either the intake cam or the exhaust cam centerlines, or both. In fact, the General Motors DOHC 4.4L Northstar V8 (among many other engines foreign and domestic) uses variable valve timing to move either or both the intake and exhaust valve cams relative to each other over an incredible range of motion.

Advance or Retard

Before we get to the next level of camshaft discussion, it's important to go over camshaft opening and closing points. Several options are available to do this. First, let's look at advance versus retard. In those classic bench-racing sessions that you've no doubt been a party to, you've probably heard a tuner talk about advancing or retarding the camshaft. Advancing a cam merely means that the engine builder desires to open both the intake and exhaust valves sooner in the four-stroke process. For example, let's say that the intake lobe centerline on a particular camshaft has an intake centerline of 110 degrees ATDC. By physically changing the position of the cam in relation to the crankshaft, the engine builder can begin the process of opening and closing the cam sooner in relationship to the Number

```
COMP CAMS
ENGINE SMALL BLOCK CHEVY 265-400
PART # 12-246-3       01/08/2003
GRIND NUMBER CS XE274H-10

                         INTAKE    EXHAUST
VALVE ADJUSTMENT        HYD        HYD
GROSS VALVE LIFT        .490       .490
DURATION AT
  .006  TAPPET LIFT     274        286
VALVE TIMING       OPEN      CLOSE
AT  .006  INT      31 BTDC   63 ABDC
         EXH       77 BBDC   29 ATDC
THESE SPECS ARE FOR CAM INSTALLED
AT  106  INTAKE CENTER LINE
                         INTAKE    EXHAUST
DURATION AT .050        230        236
LOBE LIFT               .3270      .3270
LOBE SEPARATION         110.0

981-16          SPRINGS REQUIRED.
VALVE SPRING SPECS FURNISHED WITH SPRINGS
```

All cams include a timing card. This card reveals the basic information you need to identify, properly install, and degree the camshaft in the engine. This is a COMP Cams timing card. If you happen to misplace your card, most cam companies now list all off-the-shelf cam cards on their website that you can easily print out.

One piston at TDC (top dead center). By advancing the camshaft four degrees (for example), he now has an intake centerline of 106 degrees ATDC instead of 110 degrees ATDC. This may seem backwards, but if you study the cam graph, you can see that 106 degrees ATDC actually is opening the intake valve sooner.

While we're on the subject, let's go over the effect that moving the camshaft has on engine operation. Typically, advancing a camshaft begins the process of each valve event earlier in the four-stroke cycle. By starting everything sooner, this generally improves low-speed and mid-range power while hurting high-RPM power. When you retard a camshaft, this delays the beginning of the four-stroke cycle, and typically tends to improve top-end power at the expense of low-speed and mid-range power. The most important effect of advancing or retarding the camshaft is that this moves the cam's intake closing point. Of the four intake and exhaust opening and closing points, the intake closing point is by far the most important. Establishing when the intake valve closes in relationship to TDC does more to shape the engine performance curve and the RPM point at which peak torque occurs than any other single cam factor. This is discussed in much more detail in the sidebar on the four opening and closing points.

Keep in mind that changing the intake centerline means the engine builder has also moved every other opening and clos-

ing point in the engine. This is because he has physically moved the entire camshaft in relation to the Number One piston. If he desires to move only one or two open-

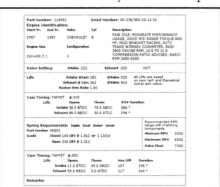

Note how this Crane timing card is different from the COMP. With no cam card standardization, each cam company reveals its basic information in different ways. For example, Crane lists valve opening and closing points at both advertised duration and at 0.050-inch tappet lift.

ing or closing points, it requires a new camshaft. The reason that engine builders may move the intake centerline is because it is a quick and easy way to evaluate if the camshaft and engine combination is close. The danger, as we mentioned, is that the tuner is moving all four of the valve events, and not all four events reinforce engine power in the same way (see the sidebar "Changing Lobe Separation Angle").

Perhaps this is also a good place to discuss the relationship of the intake centerline to the lobe separation angle.

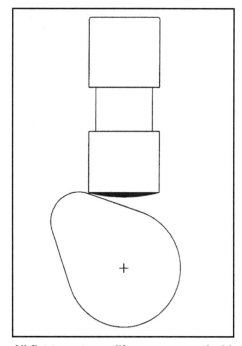

All flat tappet cam lifters are ground with a very slight convex shape on the surface that rides on the lobe of the cam. This helps ensure that the lifter spins as it moves through its lift curve. This increases lobe durability. The lobes on the cam are also ground with a slight taper. Half the lobes on a small-block Chevy cam are ground with taper in one direction, and the other half are ground with taper in the opposite direction. This positions the cam in the engine with no "thrust" in either direction. (Illustration courtesy of Crane)

Generally, if a camshaft is ground "straight up," the intake centerline position and the lobe separation angle is the same number. For example, let's say that we have a cam with a lobe separation angle of 110 degrees and an intake centerline angle of 110 degrees ATDC. More often than not, most street cam companies design their camshafts with a few degrees of advance built into their camshafts. This is easy to see on most cam cards because the cam company lists the intake centerline with a different spec than the lobe separation angle. For example, COMP Cams designs most of its street-oriented cams with four degrees of advance ground into its cams. This shows up as a 106-degree ATDC intake centerline figure on a camshaft with a 110-degree lobe separation angle. Many other cam companies do some-

thing similar because it's common for enthusiasts to order a slightly larger cam than what the engine really needs for the application. By advancing the cam four degrees, the cam company in essence advances the intake closing point, which improves low-speed torque, making the camshaft a little more livable at part-throttle engine speeds.

Overlap

Now we know what the lobe separation angle is, but what does that tell us? This is a very important camshaft specification because this angle establishes and defines a critical function of camshaft design known as overlap. Very early in the development of performance engines, way back in the flathead days, engine designers discovered that if they advanced the intake lobe in relation to the exhaust lobe, the intake stroke would begin sooner. The engine made more power. The why was less important.

Overlap is widely misunderstood and is worth investigating more closely since it helps determine many different engine characteristics. The basic idea is to open the intake valve before TDC. At first, this would seem counterproductive since it is the volume change from the piston traveling down the cylinder that

helps move the air and fuel mixture into the cylinder. That's all true, but the key to understanding the concept of overlap is to think in terms of the amount of time it requires to fill that cylinder. At low engine speeds, the intake port has sufficient time to fill the cylinder at a leisurely rate. The more efficiently it does this, the more torque the engine makes.

Peak torque occurs at the point in the engine's power curve where the engine most efficiently fills the cylinder. This is also where volumetric efficiency is at its highest. As engine speed increases after peak torque, less actual time is available for the port to fill the cylinder. So the engine builder extends the duration, allowing him more time to fill those hungry cylinders at higher engine speeds.

Another trick is to maintain the same duration and advance the intake centerline. This moves both the intake opening and intake closing points earlier in relation to TDC, creating an overlap condition where the exhaust valve is just closing. What's the advantage to doing this? First, we don't increase the total length of time the intake valve is open. Second, we actually move the intake closing point slightly earlier, which tends to improve the mid-range torque. To take it one step further, we could even increase the intake duration,

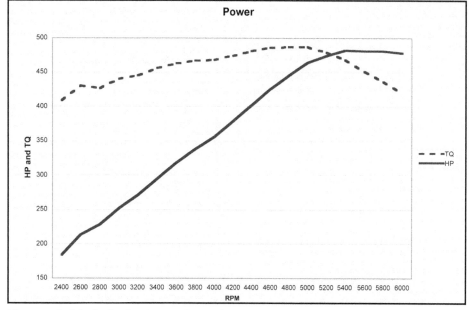

The camshaft is the brain of an engine and, more so than any other component, determines at what RPM peak torque occurs. A long-duration cam helps place peak torque at a higher engine speed, while a short-duration cam generates peak torque at a much lower RPM.

Properly matching the intake manifold with the cam helps create more overall power. Short-duration cams generally match up well with dual-plane intakes, while longer-duration cams are usually paired with single-plane intakes in search of more peak horsepower.

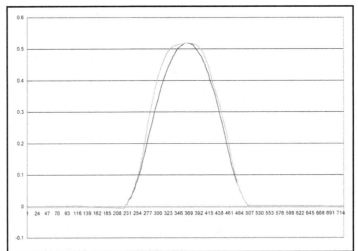

This graph comparison shows how two cams with similar advertised duration numbers can be quite different. The more aggressive lobe accelerates the lifter faster just after opening in order to create more lift with less duration.

because we started it sooner, to have an even longer duration that doesn't suffer from a very delayed intake closing.

All of this assumes that we have not moved the exhaust lobe. But what if we do move the exhaust lobe? The freedom of moving the exhaust lobe creates an opportunity to experiment with not only different intake closing points (the most important of the four valve events), but both the exhaust opening and exhaust closing events as well. Let's say we'd like to advance the exhaust lobe. This moves the exhaust lobe centerline away from the intake, increasing the lobe separation angle and decreasing the amount of overlap. This reduced overlap improves the idle quality, but also tends to hurt the top-end power slightly. This is because it also opens the exhaust valve a little sooner; perhaps before the cylinder pressure has fully expended its energy pushing on the piston.

Conversely, if we retard the exhaust lobe, the lobe separation angle comes closer together and increases the actual valve overlap. The net effect of doing this is delay in the exhaust valve opening. An increased amount of overlap tends to hurt the idle quality; plus, it generally tends to diminish low-speed torque. At higher engine speeds, this delayed opening can improve top-end power, but that may occur only at the very top of the engine power curve. This requires the engine builder to closely examine his torque curve to see if moving the lobe is truly

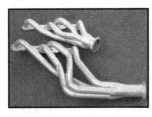

Headers must also be chosen intelligently. Long tube headers create more torque while short tube headers tend to enhance top-end power. Primary pipe diameter is also critical to extract maximum power out of a given engine combination.

beneficial. Increasing overlap by retarding the exhaust lobe may indicate that longer exhaust event duration is required in order to fully scavenge the cylinder at higher engine speeds. This is really matching the exhaust lobes of the cam to the exhaust ports, which is how you eventually make the most power on any engine.

Overlap Specialties

In car magazine ads from the late 1960s and early 1970s, Ed Iskenderian referred to the overlap portion of cam timing as the fifth cycle. This was a successful attempt to draw attention to just how critical the overlap segment of an engine's cam timing is to engine performance. For example, let's take a small-block hydraulic flat tappet cam with an advertised duration of 270 degrees at 0.006-inch tappet lift. If we add the exhaust closing (EC) of 21 degrees ATDC to the intake opening (IO) of 29 degrees BTDC (before top dead center), we get an overlap event of 50 degrees. This is close to the amount of overlap the engine actually experiences. Now let's look at a hydraulic cam with 305 degrees of adver-

tised duration also at 0.006-inch tappet lift. This cam has an EC of 43 degrees ATDC and an IO of 43 degrees BTDC for a total of 86 degrees of total overlap.

Both of these camshafts use a lobe separation angle of 110 degrees. However, we have a huge 36-degree difference in the amount of overlap between these two camshafts. This illustrates why just the lobe separation angle cannot be relied upon to truly indicate the amount of valve overlap in degrees. As you can see from this demonstration, overlap actually increases as either intake or exhaust lobe duration increases with the same lobe separation angle. That's why you see many long duration cams with wider-than-normal lobe separation angles such as 114 degrees.

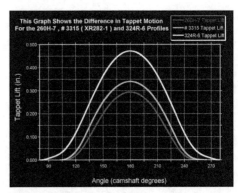

This graph reveals the different lobe profiles from mild to wild. The bottom curve is a short duration 260 advertised duration lobe. The middle curve is a plot of an XR282 roller lobe, while the top curve is a full-boogie drag race mechanical roller. The drag-race lobe has the longest duration and the steepest lift curve. The steeper the lift curve, the more violent the valve motion and the harder this type of lobe is on the valvetrain.

To further illustrate this point, if we took the longer duration 305 cam and widened the lobe separation angle to 114 degrees by moving both the intake and exhaust lobes equally, this would change the EC to 41 degrees ATDC and IO to 41 degrees BTDC, reducing the total overlap degrees from 86 degrees to 82 degrees. Remember that lobe separation angle is expressed in cam degrees, which means that cam specs are expressed in crank degrees. We can actually break overlap down into several areas and look at them closer to see how it affects engine operation.

Exhaust Closing

If we look at just the EC side of the overlap equation, it is defined as the total number of crank degrees that the engine "sees." It begins with the moment the intake valve begins to open until the exhaust valve physically closes. We can use 0.006-inch tappet lift if you'd like to define these areas.

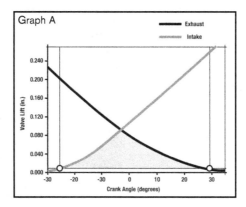

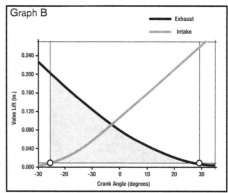

Looking at Graph A, we have a total picture of the lobe separation angle. Most attention is paid to the small triangle shape in the middle, roughly around TDC. But this diagram contains much more than just this area. Note in Graph B that we've shaded the area affected by just the EC side of the curve. This area is the point on the EC side where the intake valve first opens until the exhaust valve finally closes. The shape of this curve is dictated by the closing-side curve of the exhaust lobe profile. The valve-closing portion of the lobe, especially approaching the seat, is a critical section of the lobe design. This is because a fast closing rate can contribute to valve-bounce off the seat, especially at high RPM. This is never good for engine longevity. By advancing the exhaust lobe, you can reduce the overlap area of the curve. Retarding the exhaust lobe center-

ADVERTISED VS. DURATION AT 0.050

Bigger sells, especially to hot rodders. It didn't take performance cam grinders long to realize that if their numbers were a little bigger than their competitor's, then those crazy engine builders and hot rodders would be influenced to buy the bigger of the two. After all, the reasoning went, bigger is better.

Here's where the marketing men took over from the back-room machinists. When we talk about camshafts, duration is an important number. But the numbers can be misleading. Most often, you see camshafts expressed with two sets of duration numbers. The larger number is the advertised number, followed generally by a number expressed as duration at 0.050-inch of tappet lift. So which number is correct? Actually both of them are accurate and both refer to the same camshaft. Here's how it works.

If you look at a typical lobe, duration begins at the very instant that lift is created. So where do you start that meas-urement? At 0.0001, 0.001, or 0.010 inches of lifter rise? In the early days of performance camshafts and before the days of standards created by the Society of Automotive Engineers (SAE), every camshaft company created its own set of measurement standards. It didn't take the performance camshaft companies long to figure out that if a competitor had a 300-degree cam, it was worth increased sales to have a cam with 305 degrees of duration that was really no bigger. How do you do that? Easy – just begin the measurement process a little sooner in the lift curve. So if your competitor's advertised duration specs used 0.007 inches of tappet lift, you could start measuring an identical cam at 0.005 inches of lifter rise and you instantly have a "bigger" cam with a few more degrees of duration. As an example, COMP Cams uses 0.006 inches for its advertised duration numbers while Crane uses 0.004 inches of lifter rise.

So, if you applied Crane's advertised duration specs to any given COMP Cams lobe, it would appear longer in duration compared to COMP Cams' checking point.

It soon became apparent that the industry needed a standardized checking point in order to compare cams from different companies. Harvey Crane is the man who pushed the 0.050-inch industry standard. Harvey is the man who started Crane Cams in 1953. With this industry 0.050-inch standard checking point, which even the SAE uses, you can now compare cams from different manufacturers with a level of certainty that they are at least similar in terms of duration at that checking point. But you see as we get deeper into the asymmetrical world of lobe design, two cams with the same duration specs can be wildly different in power potential.

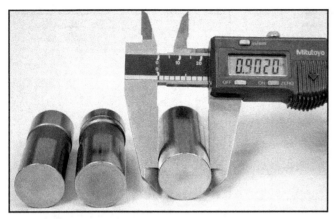

One disadvantage to the small- and big-block Chevy is its 0.842-inch diameter lifter. This is much smaller than the 0.874-inch Ford and 0.904-inch Chrysler and AMC lifter diameters that allow for a more aggressive lobe profile.

If you run into a problem when installing a cam or trying to figure out what grind would work best for your application, most of the cam companies offer technical assistance either on the telephone or on the Internet that can help you with your problem.

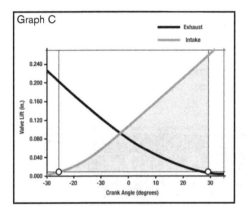

line also increases the overlap area. Changing this area of the overlap curve relates to the efficiency of your exhaust port. If the port is fairly efficient, the engine may respond favorably to decreasing the amount of time the exhaust port spends open in relation to the intake.

Some engine builders feel that increasing overlap only gives the incoming air an opportunity to flow right out the exhaust rather than being captured in the cylinder and increasing cylinder pressure in the combustion process. This is especially true if the cylinder heads offer good low-lift flow numbers as evidenced on the flow bench. An engine with excellent low-lift intake and exhaust flow numbers (relative to its valve size and flow curtain area) might desire a camshaft with less overlap. This is because intake flow ends up merely flowing right out the exhaust. Conversely, a cylinder head with somewhat poor low-lift numbers could benefit from increased overlap as a way of crutching the flow curve. It starts the flow process earli-

er to get past the poor low-lift numbers while both valves are still open.

This gets into the art of engine building and discovering exactly what the engine wants, rather than just picking an arbitrary cam duration figure and going with that number. Accomplished race-engine builders start with a cam and then experiment with different lobe separation angle variables to come up with the best overall combination.

The intake side of the overlap curve begins when the intake valve first lifts off the seat and ends when exhaust valve closes, indicated by the shaded area in Graph C. The critical nature of the overlap portion of the timing curve is also related to how well (or poorly) the exhaust system functions. All internal combustion engine exhaust systems operate around a physical operation known as wave tuning. This occurs when a finite pressure wave is created as the exhaust valve opens. The "Wave Tuning" sidebar explains this phenomenon in greater detail. You should read the sidebar now if you haven't already. Timing the arrival of the reflected wave in the cylinder creates additional cylinder filling potential and the overlap period contributes to this tuning. The arrival of this negative pressure wave timed simultaneously with both the intake and exhaust valves open creates a situation known as "scavenging." This

negative pressure not only enhances the blow-down of exhaust components in the cylinder, but also gives an early "tug" on the intake tract to improve cylinder filling. The timing of this scavenging wave is directly dependant not only on cam timing and valve overlap, but also on the configuration of the exhaust system determined by header primary pipe length, diameter, and the sizing of the remainder of the exhaust system.

As you can see, many variables play significant roles in this bed of snakes that creates power in an engine. That's

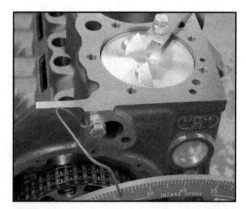

Many cam specs are referenced in relationship to TDC on the Number One piston. This is the driver side front cylinder on a small-block Chevy. Using a piston stop, you can determine the exact position of TDC on a degree wheel or use this check to ensure that the TDC mark on the engine balancer is accurate.

OPENINGS AND CLOSINGS

You can simplify the camshaft operation down to four critical points—intake opening (IO), intake closing (IC), exhaust opening (EO), and exhaust closing (EC). Let's take them in order of importance. Keep in mind that all references to these valve events are expressed in crankshaft degrees.

Intake closing (IC) is the most important position of the four because it does more to establish where peak torque occurs in the engine RPM curve than any of the other three valve events. An early intake closing in relationship to piston position improves low-speed torque, which is great for mild street engines, but this also limits high-RPM power because at higher engine speeds there is little time (in terms of crankshaft degrees) to allow for cylinder filling. This is because the engine is spinning much faster. An early IC is generally found in short duration intake lobes. Conversely, a later closing intake allows more time at higher engine speeds to fill the cylinder. This improves top-end power, but comes at the price of sacrificing low-end torque because that same later closing intake allows cylinder pressure at low speeds to be pushed back up the intake port as the piston travels upward in the bore. This doesn't happen at high speeds because inlet air is traveling at a much higher speed, so it basically shoves its way into the cylinder. This is one reason why it's possible to create volumetric efficiency numbers that exceed 100 percent on a normally aspirated engine.

We'll take intake opening (IO) next since this begins the induction cycle. This event is also a big player in the overlap game. If you open the intake valve too soon, the engine is sluggish at low speeds and suffers from greater amounts of exhaust dilution in the intake tract. An early IO also increases overlap. A later IO reduces overlap, increases idle stability, and can improve low-speed torque as long as the intake closing is not too late.

The exhaust opening (EO) point is generally considered to be the second most important point of the four valve events. EO occurs toward the end of the power stroke. Opening the exhaust too soon may sacrifice power at low- and mid-range RPM by releasing cylinder pressure that could be used to create torque, but the earlier EO also improves power at higher engine speeds by giving the exhaust port more time (again, in duration) to adequately blow down the cylinder by starting the process earlier.

The exhaust closing (EC) is the other half of the overlap game. An early EC reduces overlap, which improves idle quality by reducing the amount of time that both the intake and exhaust valves are simultaneously open. This tends to also hurt mid-range power. A later EC point increases overlap, decreasing idle quality, allowing more exhaust dilution in the intake manifold. However, at higher engine speeds, this increased overlap contributes to improved power.

why engine building continues to fascinate and attract hot rodders.

Lobe Profiling

So far we have approached the camshaft as having a somewhat generic lobe profile. This works when discussing basic camshaft configurations, but now that you have a working knowledge of how all these lobes work together on a given camshaft, we can dive deeper into camshaft technology to get more specific.

The progression of lobe design has advanced drastically in the last 20 years in terms of applying serious math to the art of designing camshaft lobes. Flat tappet lobes are discussed in this chapter, saving the more aggressive roller cam lobes for the next chapter. Several limitations on what the cam designer can do lie within the basic architecture of the flat tappet camshaft

lobe. In relationship to the lobe itself, all camshafts are limited in terms of lift by the amount of duration. Flat tappet cams, oddly enough, are limited by lifter diameter. Without getting into the complex math and geometry, as the lifter diameter grows, it is able to accommodate a more aggressive lifter acceleration rate. This unfortunately places the small-block Chevy at a distinct disadvantage in comparison to other engines. This is because the small-block (and Rat motor for that matter) is limited to a lifter diameter of only 0.842 inches. The small-block Ford uses a larger 0.874-inch diameter lifter, while the Chrysler enjoys the benefits of an even larger 0.904-inch diameter lifter. If you look at the illustration of a flat tappet lifter moving up on the opening flank of the lobe, you begin to see how a larger diameter lifter creates more lifter area to follow the lobe flank.

Within this lifter diameter situation lays the limit of lifter velocity rate. Cur-

rent camshafts often flirt with this limit in search of aggressive lobe designs, but only in the last few years. Let's compare a couple of camshafts from a historical perspective. The much-vaunted L-79 camshaft was a famous factory performance

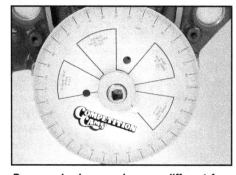

Degree wheels come in many different face configurations. Some merely indicate a 360-degree sweep, or perhaps a 0-180-0 version. This COMP Cams degree wheel indicates all four of the major valve events on the degree wheel to help you visualize what's happening.

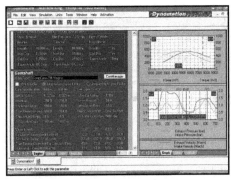

If you're really into camshafts and optimizing camshaft performance with a given engine, it might be worthwhile to invest in the Dynomation computer engine simulation program. This program employs wave-tuning effects to help predict engine performance based on these characteristics.

One professional camshaft tool found in any upscale race shop is a camshaft analyzer program like the Cam Doctor from Quadrant Scientific, which is now out of business. Another company, Audie Technology, sells a similar high-quality device called the Cam Pro. The device accurately measures and profiles each lobe. This is an excellent way to ensure that the cam grinder is doing his job and also a great way to get accurate information on the profile characteristics of a given cam lobe.

hydraulic lifter camshaft for the 1965–1967 350 hp 327ci engine used in the Chevy II, among others. This camshaft was highly regarded and an extremely popular cam with Chevy performance enthusiasts because of its single pattern offering 221 degrees of duration at 0.050-inch tappet lift at 0.447-inch lift using a 1.5:1 rocker ratio. With an advertised duration of 320 degrees, note that this cam combines an arm's length of duration with rather conservative valve lift numbers.

Now let's take a cam designed some 30 years later. We perused several cam catalogs, looking for a cam with a similar duration at 0.050-inch tappet lift, landing eventually on a COMP Cams Xtreme Energy cam with a shorter intake lobe of 218 degrees at 0.050. This cam offers a much taller 0.495-inch lift on the intake, which is a lift increase of a staggering 0.048 inches, roughly equal to using a 1.65:1 rocker ratio on the earlier cam. But the big difference is the advertised duration difference. The Xtreme Energy cam line employs a mere 270 degrees of advertised duration at 0.006-inch tappet lift. To be honest, it's not fair to compare this to the factory's massive advertised duration of 320 degrees because they start duration at initial tappet rise. But even if you subtract 20 degrees for the duration difference between the OEM's initial tappet rise checking point and COMP's 0.006-inch tappet lift spec, that still leaves a difference of 30 degrees!

This tremendous difference is due to COMP's much more aggressive lobe design. It pushes the lifter much closer to its maximum velocity rate limit. Harvey Crane, one of the great early cam designers and the man who started Crane Cams in Daytona Beach, Florida, coined a term many years ago: "hydraulic intensity." Hydraulic intensity refers to the time, in crankshaft degrees, that the lifter requires to move from its advertised duration starting point to the 0.050-inch tappet rise figure. Most cam designers use a gentle opening flank to open the valve more gradually, which makes life easier for the valvetrain. But the compromise is that it takes a toll on idle quality and low-speed torque since the valve is off its seat for a longer period of time. Most modern hydraulic flat tappet cams use around 60 degrees of hydraulic intensity duration to move the valve up to 0.050 tapppet rise, although cams that feature a shorter hydraulic intensity figure are available.

More aggressive camshafts like COMP's Xtreme Energy line of cams employ a much shorter hydraulic intensity number of 52 degrees. You can actually use this hydraulic intensity number to "fingerprint" a family of camshafts. To do this, merely subtract the 0.050-inch tappet lift duration figure from the advertised duration. However, you can only compare hydraulic intensity numbers between different cam manufacturers by using advertised duration numbers with the same checking height. Otherwise, the cam with the taller (numerically greater) advertised checking height always indicates a shorter hydraulic intensity.

One tradeoff to the more aggressive hydraulic intensity number is that the valvetrain is noisier. This tappet racket is directly attributable to the more aggressive lift curve. The advantage to this type of cam design comes in if you have a given minimum idle

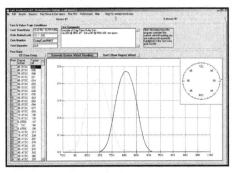

Another interesting and much more affordable camshaft profile tool is the Cam Analyzer from www.Performancetrends.com. Using this system, you measure cam lobe lift in the engine every two degrees (for example) and input this data into the Cam Analyzer program in your computer. The program then smooths the data and calculates all the pertinent data on the cam along with a decent report of the cam lobe profile.

vacuum level acceptable for street driving. With this faster ramp, you can increase the advertised duration number by a few degrees over a slower cam and still enjoy similar, if not better, idle characteristics.

Harvey Crane also coined a few other helpful terms when talking about

As you learn more about camshafts, you may discover that the cam you want is not listed in your favorite cam catalog. The best place to start is by looking in each cam company's cam lobe Master Catalog.

All cam companies stamp the basic grind information on the end of the camshaft to help them keep track of their grinds. Generally, the company stamps the grind number, the cam series, or a part number to help you identify a particular cam.

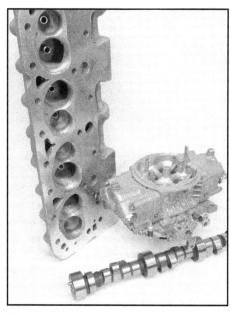

All cam companies also offer custom camshaft grinding and many, like COMP Cams, can deliver a custom ground cam in a couple of days! They do this by stocking hundreds of cam cores with the approximate lobe separation angle already machined into the cam.

It's important to remember that the camshaft may be the engine's brain, but it is still just one component in a complex interaction of many systems in an internal combustion engine. The more accurately the cam is combined with the induction and exhaust systems, the more power it makes.

cam measurement. Hydraulic intensity is useful for evaluating hydraulic cams just off their seat, but you can also judge a cam between 0.050 and 0.100-inch lift with what Harvey calls "minor intensity." Minor intensity is determined by

CAUTION: WIDE LOBES AHEAD

It's worth noting an interesting point around lobe separation angle that most of the new GEN III and now GEN IV GM engines employ. For example, if you look at the cam specs for an LS1 engine, you'll notice that the OEM cam lists lobe separation angles of 116 degrees and wider. Compared to performance cams that often use 106 to 110 degrees, this may seem like a very wide number—and it is. One of the main considerations when building any production engine is idle stability. One way to accomplish this is to decrease overlap by increasing the lobe separation angle. This does tend to sacrifice some mid-range

and upper-end power, but the interesting thing is that by not filling the cylinder quite as efficiently, it allows the designers to run a higher static compression ratio (which improves efficiency) while not encouraging the evil Dr. Detonation.

But there's more to this game than just a wide lobe separation angle. By retarding the intake centerline and decreasing overlap (assuming no change to intake duration), this also moves the intake closing later in the cycle. A later closing intake improves top-end power. Of course, this combination also relies heavily on the ability of the cylinder heads to flow copious quantities of air and

fuel, which the GEN III and GEN IV heads do exceptionally well. This is a slick little trick that the engineers play to make outstanding power with these new engines while not sacrificing idle quality. Some compromise is involved in this mix, but overall, these are very impressive numbers for stock engines. While at the time of this writing we don't have actual cam timing numbers, we do know that the new LS7 GEN IV engine makes an honest 500 normally aspirated horsepower rated using the standard SAE correction factor. When was the last time you heard of a net-500 hp production engine without a power-adder?

COMP has started placing actual cam specs with advertised duration, duration at 0.050, valve lift, lobe separation angle, grind number, and part number on the end of its cam box. This way, if you have multiple cams sitting on the shelf, you don't have to look up the part number to get the cam specs.

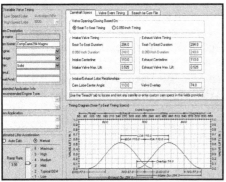

One interesting aspect of the new, redesigned Dynomation program is the Cam Manager section that allows you to either spec an existing camshaft or design your own cam. One trick portion of this section is the scale that changes the ramp rate. This doesn't change the lift or duration, but as ramp rate increases, the area under the curve increases dramatically. Of course, this faster ramp rate is much harsher on the valvetrain.

CHANGING LOBE SEPARATION ANGLE

Often, engine builders strive to improve engine performance by changing the lobe separation angle in search of more high-RPM horsepower. This is a rather simple task, since the builder can merely specify a tighter or wider lobe separation angle for a particular camshaft. But let's take a closer look at the entire function.

Let's say that we have a flat tappet hydraulic camshaft with a lobe separation angle of 114 degrees and the plan is to tighten that figure to 108 degrees. Let's say the cam company split this operation evenly between the intake and exhaust lobes. This means that the exhaust lobe is retarded by three degrees while the intake lobe needs to be advanced by the same figure. Now, let's take a look at the actual valve opening events. It would also be good here to refer to the valve event chart to help you understand how all this works.

Starting from the left side of the graph, the first effect is that the exhaust valve opening point is now delayed. If higher-RPM power is our goal, this may work in our favor since delaying the exhaust valve opening may allow combustion time to add a small amount of push to the piston. By advancing the intake lobe, we've also opened the intake valve sooner, which is a positive move since this starts the induction process earlier in the cycle. Exhaust valve closing, our third point, is also delayed with a retarded exhaust lobe, which is also a good idea since less time exists at higher engine speeds to accomplish evacuating the cylinder. Finally, the tighter lobe separation angle advances the intake lobe. This also closes the intake valve

sooner, which is in direct opposition to the goal of increasing top-end power. And since intake valve closing is the most important valve event of the four we just discussed, this points out the problem with moving the lobe separation angle in search of power in a given RPM band.

The more intelligent move for the engine tuner would be to specify where he desires the four valve events to occur, paying particular attention to intake valve closing in order to come up with a cam spec that delivers the kind of power he desires. This automatically creates a given overlap window, and then specific changes can be made to either the opening or closing points to modify the camshaft to fit the engine.

To help you with the thorny question of overlap, we've included a little chart that might help you find your way through this tangled mess of overlap and lobe separation angle ingredients.

The Lobe Separation Angle Game

Narrow	Wide
Increases Low-End Torque	Improves Top-End Power
Reduces Idle Quality	Improves Idle Quality
Increases Overlap	Reduces Overlap
Increases Cranking Compression	Reduces Cranking Compression
Decreases Piston-to-Valve Clearance	Increases Piston-to-Valve Clearance
Narrows the Power Band	Widens the Power Band

LIFT TRICKERY

When looking at the cam specs for any mechanical lifter style cam, whether flat tappet or roller, keep in mind that the valve lift spec is the gross lift based on the simple math of multiplying the lobe lift times the rocker ratio. This is gross lift because you

must subtract the valve lash from the gross valve lift to attain the actual or net valve lift. So if your cam spec card lists intake valve lift as 0.500 inches and also calls for 0.018 inches of valve lash, this means that the true, or net, maximum valve lift is really only 0.482 inches.

This is useful information if you are pushing the envelope with the valvesprings and are tight in terms of either coil bind or retainer-to-seal clearance. This 0.015 inches (roughly) can make a big difference when computing actual valve lift clearances.

WAVE TUNING

This short discussion of wave tuning that occurs within an engine must be aggressively abbreviated in order to deliver the concept in a reasonable amount of space. Simulation designer Curt Leaverton, as part of his engine simulation program called Dynomation, introduced this information into the performance engine-building community quite a few years ago. This is probably the best way to look at the very complex interactions of physical pressure excursions that occur through completion of an entire four-stroke cycle.

Let's begin with a few definitions. Sound waves are pressure pulses that create very small amplitudes, and yet even these tiny pressures can inflict hearing damage. Pressure waves that create much greater energy than acoustic waves are called finite-amplitude waves. These waves are created inside an engine and offer pressure spikes almost 10,000 times greater than acoustic waves. It is the actions of these finite-amplitude waves that dictate engine operation—good or bad.

Let's start with the exhaust stroke and exhaust valve opening (EVO). Directly after EVO, a large finite-amplitude compression wave travels down the exhaust pipe towards the atmosphere. As illustration A indicates, a positive compression wave travels down the pipe from left to right, propelling the exhaust gas in the same direction but at a much slower rate. We'll assume that this direction of travel is from the cylinder towards the atmosphere. As the compression wave exits the end of the pipe into the atmosphere, a reflected expansion wave is created. Expansion waves generate a negative pressure wave that travels from right to left, or back toward the cylinder as in illustration B. The interesting phenomenon is that this expansion wave propels the exhaust gas particles in the opposite direction, away from the cylinder. This enhances movement of exhaust gas particles out of the cylinder.

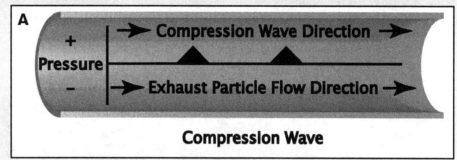

Compression Wave

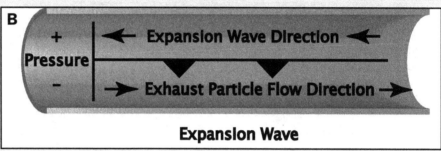

Expansion Wave

The reason this is important to know occurs as the reflected wave arrives back at the exhaust valve. All of this wave action takes time, even though it might be in hundredths of a second. With the proper length of header primary pipe at the right RPM, this reflected wave arrives back at the cylinder at the time when both the intake and exhaust valves are open during overlap. Because this is a reflected or expansion wave, its component is a significant negative pressure. This negative pressure then creates additional negative pressure in the cylinder. Since nature abhors a vacuum, atmospheric pressure pushes on the induction side of the engine to increase cylinder filling just as the piston begins to move downward.

This wave analysis technique partially explains how it is possible for a well-tuned engine to overfill a normally aspirated cylinder with a volume exceeding 100 percent. In addition, there are intake pressure waves also reflecting back and forth within the induction side. This sounds very simple, and by way of this overly simplified explanation it may appear so. But in reality, variables like cam timing (especially intake opening and exhaust valve closing), intake port cross-sectional area, header pipe diameter, port flow characteristics, intake port length, and easily a dozen or so other factors all contribute to the power curve. This is why it is so difficult to not only create a powerful engine combination, but also to predict the power that occurs.

In the old days, engine builders had to rely on trying dozens, perhaps hundreds, of engine combinations in search of that elusive all-powerful combination. Curt Leaverton's work with the Dynomation program allows the engine builder to simulate these various engine combinations and weed out the ones that don't look promising, allowing him to concentrate on those that do. The program is not simple and does require both computer power and some experience to master its intricacies. However, the Dynomation program is a great way to learn more about the incredibly complex internal combustion engine without having to spend thousands of dollars on parts. It is no replacement for actual engine experience, but it is a great tool to be used both to learn and to help make more power.

subtracting the duration at 0.050-inch cam lift from the duration at 0.100 inches. If you want to extend this kind of evaluation to mechanical cams, Harvey also came up with "major intensity." Major intensity is computed by subtracting duration at 0.050-inch cam lift from duration at 0.020-inch cam lift. In all cases, the cams with shorter intensity

figures enhance idle quality, off idle, and mid-range torque without sacrificing top-end power.

Conclusion

We've covered a large chunk of ground in this basic overview of camshaft design, but we've really only

skimmed the surface. If you really want to get into how cam profiles are designed and built, you then become immersed in concepts like acceleration rates of the lifter using terms that would take another chapter to explain.

VELOCITY, ACCELERATION, AND JERK

Throughout this book, we use terms that not everyone may understand. Because camshafts tend to be very complex components, we sometimes have to use terms that are more often reserved for discussions between cam designers and physics teachers. While that may sound terminally boring, we'll try to make it as easy to take as possible by applying these terms to real-world situations that you can use to make your engine run better.

Velocity is the rate at which a body changes position. If we think of a car moving down the road, velocity is expressed in terms of distance versus time, as in miles-per-hour or feet-per-second. With a camshaft lobe, the units of measure are typically thousandths of an inch of lifter travel per degree of camshaft rotation (in/deg). This allows the cam designer to look at the shape of the lobe independent of engine speed. You can also think of velocity as the rate of change in the lift curve of the lobe. The maximum velocity of a flat tappet cam lobe is limited by the diameter of the lifter. If the cam designer exceeds this velocity limitation, the contact point of the lifter to the lobe runs off the edge of the lifter and digs into the cam lobe—quickly destroying both. Of the main three small-block engine families of Chevy, Ford, and Mopar, the Chevrolet unfortunately suffers from the smallest lifter diameter at 0.842-inch. This means that the small-block (and big-block since they share the same lifer diameter) Chevy is much more limited in terms of tappet velocity compared to a Ford or Mopar.

Fords enjoy a lifter diameter of 0.875 inches, while the Mopar is the king of lifter diameter with a massive 0.904 inches. But also keep in mind that merely using a larger 0.875-inch lifter on a lobe designed for a 0.842-inch lifter only increases tappet contact area—it does nothing for improving valve velocity. In order to increase velocity, you must grind a lobe that can take advantage of that larger lifter diameter. It's also worth noting that many cam companies merely employ a Chevy-style lobe on a Mopar or Ford cam core, so you must first determine if a Ford or Mopar lobe is actually designed for the larger lifter diameter. If so, using its matching lifter diameter would be an advantage.

Acceleration is the second term to investigate. This is used to describe the rate at which velocity changes. It is also referred to as the first derivative of velocity. For lobe design discussion, acceleration is expressed in units of thousandths of an inch per degree^2. You may also see this expressed as thousandths of an inch/degree/degree. Tappet acceleration created by the cam designer is also limited mainly by the diameter of the lifter and the diameter of the lobe's base circle a roller follower can achieve. Manufacturing concerns also play a part in cam lobe velocity limitations.

If you dig even deeper into cam lobe design, you also hear the term "jerk." This is an engineering shorthand term used to describe the next order (or derivative) of acceleration, or how fast acceleration changes. Jerk is expressed as thousandths of an inch per degree^3. A lobe with aggres-

sive maximum acceleration rates and high jerk values is very abusive on valvetrain components. Of course, pushing this envelope is also part of the Holy Grail of cam design since higher jerk values open the valve to a given point more quickly, which can improve airflow into the cylinder. If you look into jerk values on a camshaft, the key is to investigate both the lobe's positive and negative jerk values, especially the closing side. High closing-side jerk values can cause many nasty problems.

The whole goal with designing a cam lobe is to accelerate the valve as quickly as possible without causing damage to the valvetrain components. If you've ever attended a high-performance road-race driving school, the instructors always encourage smoothness behind the wheel since that always delivers a more consistent, and quicker, lap time. We can apply this same analogy to cam lobe design—smoothness is essential. The venerable Harvey Crane went in search of smoothness by looking even deeper into the next derivative of jerk. Actually he went three levels deeper, calling them Snap, Crackle, and Pop. While the terms may be somewhat whimsical, they are merely mnemonic labels for measuring lobe motion out to the sixth position to the right of the decimal point (0.000001 inches). This requires very serious measurement equipment, far beyond what we can do with a mere dial indicator. It illustrates the lengths that cam manufacturers must employ to create modern camshaft designs—all in the search for more torque and horsepower.

ROLLER CAMS

If a chic term exists in the performance aftermarket, it is probably "roller cams." Hot rodders tend to follow the lead of the OEMs, and when GM began building hydraulic roller cam engines for the TPI Corvette and the Camaro in the late 1980s, it started a whole new trend in street hydraulic roller camshafts.

Roller cams are nothing new. In fact, roller cams are about as old as the internal combustion engine itself, which was first created over 100 years ago for diesel engines! In those early days, roller cams were created because flat tappet cams experienced excessive wear. Once metallurgy improved, flat tappet cams were preferable because they were cheaper to manufacture. But roller cams and roller followers soon became very popular with race-engine builders, and have been with us ever since.

Just like flat tappet cams, the two types of roller cams are mechanical and hydraulic. A mechanical roller tappet functions much like its mechanical flat tappet cousin and requires a lash, or clearance, in order to operate properly. The hydraulic roller tappet also has similar functions to flat tappet hydraulic tappets in that the small internal piston creates a cushion of oil that automatically compensates for growth as engine temperature expands the block and heads.

A roller cam is differentiated from a flat tappet camshaft both in strength and by the type of lifter used. Because of the smaller contact patch the roller presents to the cam, most roller cams are steel—much stronger alloy pieces than their cast-iron flat tappet cousins. The roller

Roller cams offer many advantages over flat tappet cams, but it's important to carefully evaluate the advantages versus a flat tappet cam and the application in which the cam is to be used. A flat tappet cam may be a smarter choice for many applications, both for performance and budgetary reasons.

follower employs a wheel that, as you can imagine, simply rolls over the surface of the lobe instead of sliding. This obviously reduces the friction of the two surfaces, but also requires a much harder and more durable camshaft and roller follower material. Both the camshaft and the roller itself must be very hard to be durable. The main reason for this has to do with contact area. A mild flat tappet cam design allows a relatively large portion of the lifter to contact the lobe. A roller follower, depending upon the diameter of the wheel, places a much smaller portion of the wheel against the lobe. This creates what engineers call high-unit loading pressure.

The best way to describe this is to use the analogy of a woman's high-heel shoe. With a typical flat type shoe, the

person's weight is distributed over the entire surface area of the contact portion of both shoes to the ground. When your favorite lady changes into a pair of spike high heels, a majority of her weight is now concentrated on a very small contact patch at the end of the high heel. She has trouble walking over soft ground since those heels sink right into the soft surface. A similar thing happens when you employ a roller camshaft follower – the pressure from the valvesprings is concentrated on a very small contact patch between the lifter and the cam lobe. This requires a harder, denser material like 8620 steel, which is heat-treated for increased hardness and durability. Of course, the camshaft must also be much harder as well. This is why roller cams are also made of hardened steel instead of the softer cast iron of flat tappet camshafts.

Okay, enough metallurgy 101. Compared to a flat tappet, a roller cam has many more advantages than just a harder surface and a roller that creates

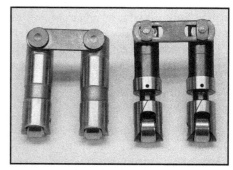

Hydraulic roller lifters (right) are generally taller and heavier than their mechanical roller tappet cousins (left).

You begin to see the problem with hydraulic roller tappets when you compare them on a gram scale. We compared this stock factory hydraulic roller tappet at 124 grams to a typical hydraulic flat tappet that weighed in much lighter at 96 grams. That's a 28 percent difference in mass.

Mechanical roller cams also require a specific amount of lash. When comparing mechanical roller to hydraulic roller cam specs, remember to subtract the lash from the mechanical roller lifter's net valve lift numbers. So if the cam has a gross valve lift of 0.550 but requires 0.020-inch lash, the net valve lift is really 0.530 inches.

slightly less friction. The true advantage of the roller over a flat tappet follower has to do with the inherent velocity or present speed limitation based on the diameter of the flat tappet. We touched on this in Chapter 2. Larger-diameter lifters are able to attain a higher lifter velocity than a smaller diameter lifter. This velocity is expressed as the number of crankshaft degrees of duration per 0.001 inches of lift. This is generally more of concern to the cam designer than the engine builder, but it is good to know if you like to impress your friends with your technical knowledge. Even with successively larger diameter lifters, you always have an inherent limitation in the lifter's maximum velocity compared to a roller follower. Ironically, flat tappet cams do have an advantage over a roller, since the flat tappet design offers a greater initial acceleration rate than can be achieved with a roller. An analogy could be to think of a flat tappet cam as having really deep gears like a set of 4.88:1s, while the roller cam is limited to something more like 3.08:1 gears. The 4.88:1s offer great jump off the line (for a cam, that means a flat tappet has great acceleration off the seat), while the roller does not accelerate as quickly. But with its analogous high-speed gears, a roller

offers outstanding velocity, especially in the opening flank area of the lobe.

This brings us to an interesting situation where a flat tappet camshaft can actually accelerate the lifter off the base circle much more aggressively in the initial portion of the lift curve than a roller cam lobe can. So, with a short-duration cam, say 210 degrees at 0.050-inch tappet lift cam, a flat tappet cam can accel-

erate the lifter to a higher lift much more quickly than a roller until the flat tappet reaches its maximum velocity. So while roller cams do offer other advantages that we get to in the coming paragraphs, short-duration cammed engines can benefit from sticking with a flat tappet design. If we were to establish a theoretical crossover point for when you convert from a flat tappet cam to a roller, it

FLAT TAPPET HYDRAULIC VS. ROLLER HYDRAULIC

Cam	Adv. Dur.	Dur. @ 0.050	Dur. @ 0.200	Lift (inches)	HIT* (degrees)
XE 268 flat hyd., Intake	268	224	137	0.477	44
Exhaust	280	230	140	0.480	
XR270 Hyd. Roller, Intake	270	218	139	0.496	52
Exhaust	276	224	152	0.502	
High Lift Lobe # 3190	266	214	141	0.530	52

* Hydraulic Intensity

All roller cams require a stronger base material than a flat tappet cam. This makes them easy to identify. The Crane billet steel roller cams can be identified by the copper color on the cam core that is left over from the hardening process.

would probably be around 210 or 215 degrees at 0.050-inch tappet lift area. Below this, a flat tappet cam is advantageous, while cams with duration figures greater than 215 degrees would begin to stack the advantages over on the roller design side of the ledger. It's not really as simple as that, but you could view this comparison in that context.

Roller lifters create what is called a pressure angle on the cam that is significantly different from a flat tappet lifter.

We touched on the limitation of the roller follower design earlier in this discussion when we mentioned that the flat tappet cam could out-accelerate the roller follower. This means that the roller cam design is inherently acceleration-limited. But conversely, rollers can produce some awesome lifter velocity rates. Our earlier reference to a roller cam having a tall gear ratio creates a top speed analogy that allows the cam designer to create steeper ramps on the cam profile. This creates greater lift for a given length of duration.

Most aftermarket street roller cams now come with an iron distributor gear pressed on the end of the camshaft. This allows the engine builder to use a stock iron distributor gear instead of those soft bronze gears, which are not very durable.

You have probably already grasped the inevitable results of this style of lobe, but it's worth investigating further. Given the roller's higher velocity rate, the cam designer can create much more lift in a shorter period of time. This is a tremendous advantage for engines with high-flowing intake and exhaust ports, since this allows the engine builder to push the valves open quickly into the lift areas where the ports can flow some serious air.

Let's investigate this idea a little deeper. Compare a typical COMP Cams XE268 Xtreme Energy flat tappet hydraulic camshaft with its closest hydraulic roller equivalent – the Xtreme Energy XR270. The accompanying chart, "Flat Tappet Hydraulic vs. Roller Hydraulic," outlines the basic specs on both cams. Plus, we also listed the specs for a more aggressive 3100–series intake lobe. The hydraulic roller XR cam is larger than the flat tappet cam in advertised duration by 2 degrees, but it still has some interesting comparisons. First, the hydraulic roller's duration at 0.050-inch tappet lift on both the intake and exhaust lobes is 6 degrees shorter in duration than the flat tappet cam.

Next, we also listed duration at 0.200-inch tappet lift. This is interesting since the intake lobe on the roller cam offers 2 more degrees of duration than the flat tappet. But it becomes a push when you subtract the difference in advertised duration. However, looking at the exhaust side, the differential is much more substantial. On the hot side

of the cam, the hydraulic roller delivers a full 12 degrees of additional duration at 0.200-inch tappet lift.

As our final point of comparison, let's look at valve lift. Here is where the hydraulic roller's lifter velocity capability shines through by offering 0.019-inch of additional valve lift on the intake side and an even larger 0.022-inch lift push on the exhaust side.

Before we jump into the analysis of our numbers, we also included another more aggressive intake lobe as further fodder for comparison. According to the COMP Cams catalog, the 3190 lobe is a more aggressive, high-lift hydraulic roller profile that requires less engine speed or more valvespring to control. But putting those points aside for the moment, the 3190 lobe does a great job of illustrating the potential advantages of a roller lobe design.

The 3190 lobe starts out at a 266-degree advertised duration lobe and immediately steps up with a 10-degree shorter duration number at 0.050 tappet lift. It does this while offering 4 degrees of additional duration at 0.200-inch tappet lift compared to the flat tappet intake lobe. Plus, the 3190 hydraulic roller also delivers a whopping 0.053 inches of additional valve lift again over the flat tappet hydraulic.

Starting in 1988, GM began using a hydraulic roller cam in their production car engines. This required a cam thrust plate on the front of the block. The step in the nose of this cam (left) identifies it as a cam intended for use in a production roller cam block.

So what does all this mean? The lift numbers should be self-evident. But let's spend a moment with the additional duration offered by the two hydraulic roller profiles. To make this comparison more interesting, let's look at how much

This is the retainer plate with the cam installed in the engine. The plate bolts to the block with two bolts. The OEM-style cam gear also has a different cam attachment pattern.

intake lobe counterpart. Since the exhaust lobe delivers 12 more degrees of duration at 0.200-inch tappet lift, it in essence looks "bigger" to the exhaust side of the engine than the flat tappet lobe. Let's say we were swapping these two cams on the dyno and the original XE 268 flat tappet cam made respectable numbers. Now, let's say that once the hydraulic roller is in place, torque fell off virtually throughout the entire curve with the smallest differential at peak horsepower. At first, this might seem perplexing, but examining the exhaust profile numbers, it could be that the cam is actually too big on the exhaust side. If

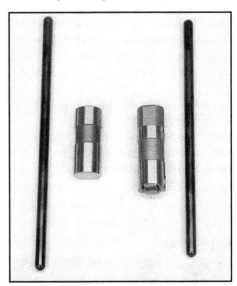

Taller hydraulic roller lifters also mean shorter-length pushrods for roller cam engines compared to either flat tappet or mechanical roller cams.

more duration we have to dial in with a flat tappet cam in order to match the aggressive 3190 lobe. In this case, the COMP Cams catalog indicates we have to jump up to an Xtreme Energy 274 cam in order to generate the same (actually 143 degrees @ 0.200) duration at 0.200-inch tappet lift.

At first, this may not seem like a big deal. But adding 6 degrees of additional duration to the intake lobe means that the engine now has a choppier idle, and less low- and mid-range torque because of the earlier opening and later closing intake valve. This cam also generates more overlap. Conversely, by employing the hydraulic roller, we enjoy the results of a shorter intake and exhaust duration, less overlap, better throttle response, and more torque in the mid-range without sacrificing top-end power. In essence, we increased the average torque, which (assuming no tire spin) always improves acceleration either on the drag strip, circle track, or street.

We should not overlook the exhaust side of this equation. The 268 Xtreme Energy exhaust lobe actually offers even more significant advantages than its

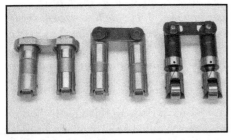

From left to right is an OEM-style hydraulic roller lifter, an aftermarket retrofit hydraulic roller lifter, and a mechanical roller lifter.

MECHANICAL FLAT TAPPET VS. ROLLER MECHANICAL

Cam	Adv. Dur.	Dur. @ 0.050	Dur. @ 0.200	Lift (inch)	Lash (inch)
Crane flat mech., Intake	288	248	155	0.500	0.022
F-288-2 Exhaust	298	258	165	0.520	0.022
Crane mech. roller, Intake	294	244	157	0.543	0.020
SR-244/362-2S-12 IG, Exhaust	302	252	166	0.561	0.020

If you are planning on using a mechanical fuel pump with a steel roller cam, you also need a special fuel pump pushrod. COMP Cams, for example, offers a fuel pump pushrod with either a bronze or a ceramic tip.

so, it would require a single-pattern cam with less duration and less overlap because the larger duration at 0.200-inch valve lift numbers indicates that this exhaust lobe could over-scavenge the engine in the mid-range area between peak torque and peak horsepower.

Conversely, if the engine responded with much stronger power numbers throughout the entire RPM band, this would indicate the engine wanted that "bigger" exhaust lobe profile to scavenge the cylinders.

Mechanical vs. Hydraulic Rollers

So far we've focused on hydraulic roller cams since these are the latest entries into the street-performance cam lineup. But in most cases, if setting lash occasionally isn't of concern, mechanical roller camshafts have many advantages over their hydraulic siblings. We can separate mechanical roller cams into two broad categories of either street or race roller cams. Street roller cams are designed with less radical velocity curves. They are designed to improve durability since the cam is used on the street with hours of idling and low-speed operation. These gentler ramps take less of a toll on valvesprings, valves, and lifters, requiring minimal maintenance.

Mechanical race rollers, on the other hand, are designed to be much more aggressive. They are designed to open and close the valves as quickly as possible. This lengthens the duration at 0.200-

inch tappet lift and opens the valve into its more useable flow window much more quickly. While this more aggressive design offers definite power opportunities, it comes at a price. Pushing the valves open and closed more rapidly means a necessity for higher spring pressures, and that increased load means valvetrain durability suffers. Higher spring pressures are not the best idea for a street engine since higher loads just mean more abuse for all the valvetrain components.

For example, several years ago, Jack Chisenhall, the owner of Vintage Air, took his 700-ci big-block Chevy-powered Studebaker on the *Hot Rod* magazine Power Tour. The car performed surprisingly well for the first portion of the Tour. However, after perhaps a thousand miles of highway cruising, the Rat motor succumbed to several broken valvesprings. At first, it appeared that weak springs were to blame, but the engine was originally designed to run 200 mph at Bonneville, so it was built around a race mechanical roller camshaft. The race roller's aggressive lift profile probably contributed more to the broken valvesprings than any other factor. Street mechanical roller cams tame much of the abuse out of the velocity curves, requiring less spring pressure since their high-RPM limit is generally lower.

If you look at "Mechanical Flat Tappet vs. Roller Mechanical," we also compared a Crane mechanical street flat tappet to one of Crane's mechanical street roller cams. Here, we tried to match the

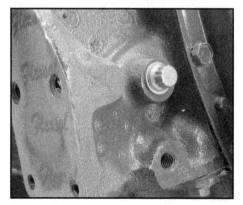

Remember on most production small-blocks that this bolt hole allows access to the fuel pump pushrod and must be plugged with a short 3/8-inch course thread bolt to prevent oil leaks.

cams based on duration at 0.050 numbers. As you can see, the roller, because of its gentler clearance ramp, actually adds 6 degrees to the intake seat timing numbers and 4 degrees to the exhaust numbers. However, when you look at the duration at 0.200-inch tappet lift, the roller has added 2 degrees on the intake and 1 degree on the exhaust side. Then, when we look at the lift numbers, the higher velocity capability of the roller creates more lift. The intake generates an additional 0.043 inches and 0.041 inches on the exhaust. You have to bump the duration of the mechanical flat tappet by 8 degrees in order to create the same lift generated by the roller cam.

Pluses and Minuses

Given these comparisons, you can see that roller cams offer significant advantages to the lift curve. But these advantages don't come without a price tag. Roller cam systems are generally much more expensive than flat tappet

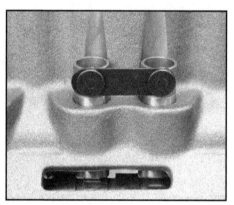

Retrofit roller lifters use an aftermarket tie-bar arrangement to maintain lifter alignment.

cams. Even assuming you don't count the high-quality pushrods, full roller rockers, and good valvesprings that you'd run either way, the price of a just the roller cam and mechanical lifters is still around $600.

One way to mitigate this heavy tariff is with factory-style hydraulic roller tappets. In 1987, Chevy began using hydraulic roller tappets in the Corvette, with the majority of small-blocks following soon after. Even trucks were running hydraulic roller tappets later in the

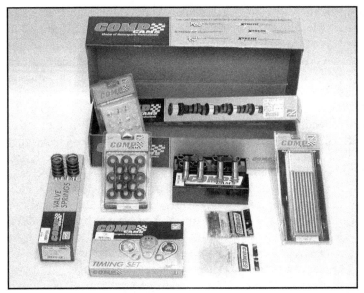

The best way to convert from a roller to a flat tappet cam is to buy an entire dedicated kit. Both COMP Cams and Crane sell complete kits that reduce the hassle but also reduce the price.

1990s. The factory hydraulic roller system made significant changes to the basic small-block Chevy's architecture which are worth noting here. To begin with, the GM system uses simple cast-aluminum tie bars that slide down over parallel flats on the hydraulic roller tappet bodies to align the roller followers with cam lobe. These tie bars are

All retrofit roller cam conversions need a cam button to prevent cam walk. The best one is this rollerized piece from COMP Cams that includes shims to optimize the thrust clearance.

retained by an eight-legged tin piece often called a spider. The spider is held in place by three bolts threaded into tapped bosses in the middle of the lifter valley.

The limitations of this design become immediately apparent when the engine experiences valve float and the lifter is no longer following the profile of the lobe. The heavy lifters can easily overpower the clamp load of the flimsy tin spider and either bend or merely push the spider out of the way. The tie-bars then easily bounce off the lifters. This allows the lifters to spin in their lifter bores with disastrous results. It shouldn't take much to imagine what happens when a roller lifter turns sideways and digs into the cam lobe. I've seen this happen, and it's ugly. The lifter immediately grinds the lobe away, pushing those metal filings throughout the engine. The engine may still run, but it creates a weird squeaking sound, eerily similar to the sound a mill creates while the feed rate is too high, which is exactly what's happening inside the engine.

The way to avoid this for production small-block hydraulic roller cam engines is to simply avoid spinning excessive engine speeds. The problem, as you probably know, is that horsepower is directly tied to engine speed. If you can create the same engine torque at 7,000 that you did at 6,000 rpm, more horsepower is produced. The problem with high engine speed is that both factory and aftermarket hydraulic roller tappets are heavy. This means that the valvespring must control this additional weight as well as the rest of the valvetrain. We address the demands placed on valvesprings in Chapter 5, but

for now let's just say that heavier components are more difficult to control and require more spring pressure to accomplish this task.

Here's the dilemma that engine builders face with higher spring pressures used with hydraulic lifters. The basic premise with hydraulic lifters is that engine oil pressure fills the cavity under the lifter piston to automatically compensate for valvetrain lash changes due to engine temperature. But if you apply too much valvespring pressure to a hydraulic tappet, it's possible to overcome the engine oil underneath the lifter piston and pump the lifter down. At high engine speeds, the combination of high valvespring pressure and lobe-acceleration forces literally pushes the oil out of the lifter. This pumps the lifter down. As soon as the engine comes down from that high-speed run, the engine immediately begins to run very rough and the engine makes a clattering sound because of the excessive lash now present in the valvetrain.

Airflow Research (AFR), a cylinder head company, designed a rev kit of sorts for small-block Chevy hydraulic roller cam engines. It places a set of springs and retainers in the lifter valley that apply pressure on the hydraulic roller lifter body. The Hydra-Rev, as AFR calls it, places the additional spring pressure on the lifter body to ensure that it stays in contact with the lobe profile. This allows the valvespring the luxury of applying its

Earlier steel roller cams required the use of a bronze distributor gear to prevent wear. Running an iron gear on a steel roller cam not only kills the iron distributor gear, but also the cam gear. The sharp edges on this gear indicate it's a candidate for the trash bin.

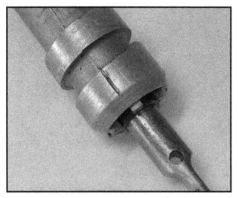

Crane recommends machining a 0.030-inch oiling slot in the distributor body to supply additional lube spray onto the cam and distributor gears.

load to control just the pushrod, rocker, and valvespring assembly. A later chapter gets into more detail on this device, but for now just know that it can allow the engine to run at higher engine speeds to make more horsepower.

Mechanical Rollers

While the Hydra-Rev solution does work, the reality with hydraulic roller tappets, whether factory or aftermarket, is that they are heavy. And any heavy component in the valvetrain is inherently bad with the possible exception of pushrods. The real question is: Why would you want to invest in a heavy valvetrain if you are trying to make high-RPM horsepower? The best solution is to convert to a mechanical roller camshaft. Mechanical rollers do not suffer from a moving lifter cup position because, as a mechanical lifter, this position is mechanically fixed. The only possible negative to mechanical roller tappets for street use is the fact that they require periodic lash adjustment. However, this is not as much work as you might imagine.

The old wives' tale here is that mechanical lifters require constant attention. The story goes that if you are running a mechanical cam on the street, you are constantly adjusting the valve lash. The reality is that this may have been the case when small-block Chevys ran mechanical lifter cams as production pieces and the rockers were retained by those flimsy, rocker-stud locking-nuts. After even just a couple of adjustments, these nuts begin to lose their

retention strength on the stud and allow the lash to change. Today, no self-respecting small-block runs these locking nuts, not even on hydraulic-cammed engines. As pervasive and inexpensive as poly locks are, there's no reason to use anything else. Once you have set the lash using a poly lock, it should not change as long as nothing bends or breaks in the valvetrain. We would recommend you check the lash, say, every 5,000 miles on a mechanical lifter engine. This may sound like a lot of work, but most street-driven mechanical lifter cams probably won't see that many miles in an entire year, so checking lash once a year shouldn't be too much of a burden. If it is, you need to find a new hobby.

Street Rollers

The advantages of a mechanical roller cam can be put to good use on the street. Mechanical street rollers offer the ability to run significant spring pressure that controls the valvetrain throughout the entire RPM curve while still not

approaching the tremendous spring pressures that brutalize the valvetrain. This creates a stable valvetrain that can easily control engine speeds up to around 7,000 rpm while not creating significant durability problems.

The obvious question when considering a roller cam is whether to go with the mechanical or the hydraulic roller cam. Much of this decision should be based on how the engine is going to be used. If this street engine sees mostly cruise-night use on the boulevard with the occasional stoplight joust, then a hydraulic roller (or even a hydraulic flat tappet) would be a better choice. But if you plan serious use for this engine with drag strip flogs and perhaps even track days on the local road course, then the mechanical roller is the obvious choice since it promises additional power with fewer compromises. Again, the overall cost may be slightly higher with the mechanical roller, but the advantages far outweigh the additional expense.

HYDRAULIC ROLLER VS. MECHANICAL ROLLER

Cam		Adv. Dur.	Dur @ 0.050	Dur. @ 0.200	Lift (inch)	Lash (inch)
COMP 280 HR	Intake	282	230	151	0.510	N/A
	Exhaust	288	236	157	0.520	N/A
COMP 268R	Intake	268	230	153	0.552	0.016
	Exhaust	274	236	159	0.564	0.018
COMP 280R	Intake	280	242	164	0.570	0.016
	Exhaust	286	248	170	0.576	0.018

All COMP mechanical roller cams are rated at an advertised duration at 0.015-inch tappet lift. All COMP hydraulic roller tappet cams are rated at an advertised duration of 0.006-inch tappet lift. This disparity is why we chose to compare cams at 0.050-inch tappet lift. But note a significant difference in lift between the hydraulic and mechanical roller cams. These are all street roller cams. Race rollers would offer even more lift. To be objective, we must subtract the 0.016-inch lash figure from the mechanical roller to compare to the hydraulic roller cam's lift. This makes the mechanical roller cam lift actually 0.536, which is still 0.026 inches more lift than the hydraulic.

It's entirely acceptable to run used roller lifters on a new roller cam as long as the lifters are in reasonable condition with no excessive wear or pit marks are on the face of the roller follower or on the lifter body itself.

GMPP Bow Tie blocks are produced with taller lifter bores. This may be a problem with certain horizontal tie-bar roller lifters. The trick when using these lifters is to machine the lifter boss for adequate clearance.

All performance camshafts, especially roller cams, must employ a smaller base circle to accommodate larger lobe profiles. This must be done to physically fit the cam lobes in the engine since lobe lift cannot exceed the radius diameter of the cam journal, or the cam doesn't fit in the engine!

Converting From Flat to Roller

One of the most important considerations you need to take into account when considering a roller cam, and especially a mechanical roller cam, is the amount of work, parts, and expense that's involved when converting from a flat tappet cam to a roller. Let's take the hydraulic roller conversion first. Then we look at the mechanical side of things.

When Chevrolet first converted its original small-block over to hydraulic roller profiles around 1988, this necessitated a new block. Several items needed to be addressed in this conversion. One of the first things to note is that the block now accommodates a thrust plate in front of the cam and behind the cam gear to prevent it from moving fore and aft. Chevy uses a simple, two-bolt thrust plate that the nose of the cam fits through on the front of the block. This is required to account for the inherent thrust created by the hypoid cam gear.

Next, hydraulic roller tappets are significantly taller when compared to a small-block flat lifter. This is mostly to accommodate the roller follower. The factory matched this with a somewhat taller lifter bore in the block to offer more support to the lifter body. Next, the factory roller cam blocks also incorporate the three threaded bosses in the middle of the lifter valley to locate the tin spider retainer plate. This tin piece places load on the tie bars that slide over the stock roller lifter body that keep the lifters from spinning in the lifter bores. These retainers keep the rollers lined up with the lobe. It should be obvious then that adding a performance-oriented hydraulic roller cam to an existing 1988 or later roller cam block is very easy. The cam companies make performance hydraulic roller cams for these applications that include a step in the front of the cam nose.

One advantage to using a later-model block with a hydraulic roller cam engine is that the factory replacement roller lifters are considerably less expensive than the

retrofit lifters intended for use with the earlier engines. It's also important to note here that it's okay to run used roller lifters on a new camshaft. While it is a major mistake with flat tappet lifters and cams, the wear pattern situation isn't quite as critical with rollers, given the much harder roller cams and rollers. So, if you have a set of used hydraulic rollers in good shape, you can reuse them with a new performance hydraulic roller cam and make it all work very nicely.

For the earlier small-blocks that were originally intended for flat tappet cams, the cam companies also make what are called retrofit hydraulic and mechanical roller cams and kits. The cams in these

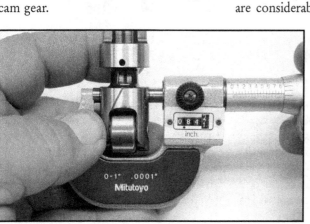

Be sure to measure the clearance between the roller lifter body and the lifter bore. A too-tight clearance quickly destroys a roller tappet and perhaps the cam, while a too-loose clearance could be equally catastrophic. The recommended lifter clearance is 0.0015 to 0.0020 inches.

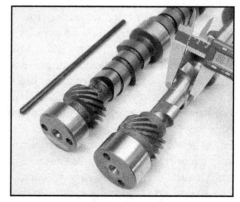

To create a more aggressive lobe profile, roller cam manufacturers often design a lobe with inverse profiles intended to create higher initial acceleration rates. These lobes require much smaller cam grinding machines that are much more expensive to produce.

16 LASHES

Lash is the clearance between the rocker arm tip and the valve stem as checked with a simple feeler gauge. Mechanical lifters require some amount of clearance in the rocker arm system to compensate for growth in engine height, especially with aluminum heads, as the engine achieves operating temperature. This clearance is also necessary to ensure that the system has sufficient clearance to prevent the valvetrain from keeping the valve open when it should be closed.

Mechanical lifter camshafts have a clearance ramp, built into the early portion of the lobe, designed to gently take up the clearance in the system before beginning the lift curve in earnest. Lash can only be checked when the valve in question is on the base circle of the lobe. Most current-generation solid lifter cams specify a relatively small amount of lash compared to camshafts from the 1960s. For example, the Duntov "30-30" Z28 mechanical flat tappet cam earned its nickname from the 0.030-inch lash spec required. This gave the camshaft a distinctive, noisy clatter that helped make it famous with hot street engines during the 1960s and early 1970s. Later model mechanical cams generally cut that lash spec in half, now with lash numbers around 0.012 to 0.020 inches.

Most cam companies specify that the lash be set with the engine hot, or at normal operating temperature. The best way to do this is with the engine up to temperature, but not running. We cover this procedure in Chapter 9. It is a simple procedure that once you learn, you can set lash on any four-stroke engine regardless of any variable.

Lash can also be used as a tuning tool. For example, by increasing the lash on a mechanical lifter camshaft, the effective duration of the cam is reduced by a few degrees. Conversely, reducing the lash increases the amount of lobe duration. Of course, these lash changes also affect the valve lift, but these changes are relatively minor compared to the changes in duration. By changing the lash, you can effectively make minor camshaft duration changes that can be used on an engine dyno to see what effect these changes have on engine power.

For example, let's say you increase the lash on all eight intake lobes on your engine and the power increases in the mid-range. What that tells you is the intake lobe is a little too long in duration and is hurting mid-range torque without affecting top-end power. On the other end of the scale, tightening the lash by a few thousandths increases the effective duration, and that generally

increases the top-end power while hurting the low-end or mid-range power. The key is to maximize the overall power curve, which means that the areas where power increases must offset the loss of power in another RPM area. If the power increase is not an overall gain, then this change is probably not in your best interest for a street engine.

It's also important to note that there are definite limitations on the amount of lash that you can change with any given mechanical camshaft. As the standard lash number is tighter, the amount of lash you can change is reduced. Most cam companies do not want you to tighten the lash on a cam with 0.020-inch lash figure by more than 0.004 inches. You can open the lash up to around 0.006 to 0.010 inches for a quick dyno test to evaluate the effect, but all the cam companies warn that this is a short-term test function only. If the engine increases power with lash numbers wider than 0.002 inches more than the published lash figure, it's recommended that you change the camshaft rather than merely run the engine in that configuration. This is because the clearance ramp in the cam lobe profile is designed to operate with a given lash. Changes beyond that designed lash clearance causes eventual and inevitable engine damage in the form of valvetrain component failures.

---

applications are identical in lobe design but employ a flat cam-face to use the standard cam drive arrangement, although you must invest in a cam button. If you are attempting this conversion for the first time, the best bet is to purchase the entire retrofit conversion kit from your favorite cam company. These kits include all the components you need to make this conversion. They usually include the following: a camshaft, valvesprings, retainers and keepers, roller lifters and tie bars, proper length shorter pushrods, cam button, timing set, and assembly lube.

With some important items to consider, we should probably go through this conversion. The first is the cam but-

ton. Roller cams require the button to prevent the cam from moving forward as engine speed increases. This is because the thrust from the distributor drive gear and the load created by the oil pump pushes the cam forward. When this happens, the helical cut of the distributor drive gear retards the ignition timing. This can represent as much as 15 to 20 degrees of ignition timing retard if the cam moves a significant distance. We get into how to set this thrust button and the clearance in Chapter 9, "How to Install and Degree a Cam."

A roller cam must also ensure the roller lifters do not spin in the lifter bore. Aftermarket roller retrofit cams

use a tie-bar that pairs lifters together to prevent them from spinning. These tie bars can be either horizontal or vertical style. If you intend to run a mechanical fuel pump with your roller cam, you also need a special fuel pump pushrod that has a tip compatible with the hardened steel cam. This can vary from a simple bronze tip to a ceramic version offered by COMP Cams.

On the other end of the cam, most street rollers now come from the cam companies with a pressed-on iron gear and rear journal. This is one reason why street roller cams cost more money. The cam company must accurately press-fit this specially designed cast-iron gear on

The cam on the right is a small-block cam with larger big-block journals. Engine builders are now building massive 55 mm journal cams for NHRA Competition Eliminator racing. The huge 2.165-inch cam journals are necessary to prevent cam journal twisting when working against the massive valvespring pressures these engines require to prevent valve float. Plus, the larger core also offers the opportunity to run a larger base circle.

the end of the steel camshaft so that you can use a stock-type distributor gear on the end of your favorite distributor. Previous to this, all street roller cams required the use of a bronze or silicon-bronze alloy gear that was intentionally softer than the hardened steel gear. The idea was that the soft bronze gear would eventually wear out, but it is easier and less expensive to replace the distributor gear than the entire camshaft. The prob-

lem with this idea is that high-pressure oil pumps place a greater load on the distributor gear, creating a premature wear problem literally within a few hours of engine time. The stock iron-drive-gear eliminates this problem. However, if you insist on running a more aggressive race-type roller cam on the street, be aware that these cams require the use of that bronze distributor gear. And it won't last as long as you think!

Other little details worth mentioning include the fact that roller lifters also require their own shorter-length pushrods since the tappets are taller than flat-face lifters. As a quick tip, it's best not to order pushrods until you can accurately measure the exact pushrod length your engine demands. Too often, "stock length" pushrods are not the proper length needed.

Conclusion

We could probably write an entire book just on all the significant advantages and disadvantages of roller cams and still not cover all the information on the subject. But the information outlined here should be enough to give you what you need to make an intelligent decision on whether or not a roller cam is in your future. Not all street small-block applications require or would even benefit from a roller cam, but the advantages are tremendous when you consider everything that a roller cam can deliver.

BASE CIRCLE BLUES

While this might pass for the title of a song you might hear on Beale Street in Memphis, the real story about base circles centers on generating lift from a roller cam. With higher lifter velocities of roller cams, it's possible to create relatively high lobe lifts from a small-block Chevy roller cam. The problem is that the stock small-block uses a 1.875-inch diameter cam journal, which means that in order to create additional lobe lift, the cam grinder is forced to make the base circle of the cam increasingly smaller in order to fit these taller lobes.

This isn't a huge problem, but it does show up most often with roller cams. The first and most obvious point with a smaller base circle is that the lifter now sits deeper in the lifter bore. This actually improves lifter contact with the bore, but a smaller base circle also immediately changes overall pushrod length, requiring a longer

pushrod. That's why professional engine builders always wait until the just before final engine assembly to spec their pushrod length. It's also not unusual to see the intake base circle diameter be different from the exhaust. So if the engine builder goes to great lengths to ensure that all the intake and exhaust valves are installed at the same height in the head, don't assume that all the lobes on the cam follow suit. It could easily happen that, like a Rat motor, you would have different length pushrods by 0.050 inches or more for the intake and exhaust valves. One advantage to smaller base circle cams is that these reduced diameters offer more clearance to clear the rods on stroker combinations.

One trick that some competition-engine builders perform is to move up to Rat motor cam journal specs. The larger Rat motor uses a stock cam journal diameter of 1.950, or 0.075 inches larger than the

small-block. This adds a little more real estate for greater lobe lifts without resorting to tiny base circles. As base circles get smaller, this also affects the cam's torsional rigidity, or its resistance to twisting against increasingly higher valvespring loads. This was obviously important to the GM engine designers, because when it came time to spec the cam journal size for the GEN III small-block, that family of engines enjoys a much larger camshaft diameter. They did not do this without just cause, since the larger cam is also much heavier than its smaller diameter small-block cousin.

Even the current generation of small-block Chevy NHRA Competition Eliminator engines have stepped up to larger 55-mm (2.165 inches) and sometimes even 60-mm cam journal cores in order to eliminate torsional twisting at those stratospheric engine speeds and incredibly high valvespring loads these engines must withstand.

VALVETRAIN OVERVIEW

The original small-block factory valvetrain layout consisted of individual stamped-steel rocker arms with a half-sphere rocker ball that located the rocker over pressed-in 3/8-inch studs. The pushrod positioned the rocker over the valve, guided by slots cast into the cylinder head.

When it comes to the camshaft on a small-block Chevy, enthusiasts tend to overlook the importance of each component in the valvetrain and its contribution to how well the entire system works. The small-block Chevy began a revolution of sorts for production engines in 1955 with its 16 individual rocker studs and spindly looking stamped-steel rocker arms. Conventional wisdom at the time subscribed to the more typical heavy shaft rocker system. At the time, Chevy's ball stud arrangement was considered radical, and many

thought it would never work. But the small-block Chevy valvetrain's utter simplicity, light weight, and simple adjustability soon won over the industry. And perhaps as much as any other design on the engine, it helped to make the small-block Chevy the most prolific and popular automotive production engine from Detroit.

The best way to understand how this simple system works, and find ways to make it work even better in today's demanding performance environment, is to take each individual component and

look at it in much finer detail. In this chapter we introduce the valves, springs, retainers, and keepers that not only help determine airflow, but also ensure that the valve religiously follows the cam profile as RPM increases. This is often not the case and is a big reason why some engines don't make the power that they should. If the devil is in the details, then we have to find a way to make sure he stays away from your small-block Chevy so it can make all the power that it should.

Let's begin with a review of the small-block's valvetrain action. The lifter takes the rotary motion of the camshaft lobe and converts the eccentric profile into vertical lift. The pushrod merely extends that lift up to the top of the cylinder head where the rocker arm operates like a simple fulcrum. The lift generated on the pushrod side of the rocker arm is multiplied by the stock small-block ratio of 1.5:1 to the valve. So, if the cam lobe generates 0.300-inch lobe lift, then, in theory, the valve sees a maximum lift of 0.450 inch. The reality of valvetrain operation rarely achieves all the goals of theoretical operation.

In the very early days of internal combustion engines, valvesprings were a major concern to engine designers. Even at low engine speeds of 3,000 rpm, it was difficult to create a valvespring that would control the valve. Some engine designers back in the 1920s even went so far as to design a desmodronic valvetrain where the rocker mechanically opened and closed the valve without the use of a spring. While innovative, these systems

We've come a long way from the original 265-ci small-block to the current 400 hp GEN IV engine in all areas, but especially in the valvetrain. The GEN III and IV engines now use a rocker shaft that ties the rocker arms together, compared to individual stud-mounted rockers of the original engine. This system has advantages and disadvantages.

were clumsy, heavy, and unreliable. The obvious solution was, and still is, the valvespring. While somewhat innocuous, the valvespring is one of the hardest working and most heavily abused components in any internal combustion engine. Chapters 5 and 12 spend a significant portion of their length on these wire-wound components and their contribution to valvetrain success.

Evolution

As simple and efficient as the small-block Chevy's original valvetrain was, it encouraged enthusiasts and racers to immediately push the engine right past its limits. The short-stroke 283 and 327 engines of the late 1950s and early 1960s allowed the small-block to spin to RPM levels that had previously been reserved for purebred race engines. The limitation then, and today, continues to be the valvetrain and specifically controlling the valve at these stratospheric engine speeds. The classic horsepower equation tells us that if you can produce the same torque at a higher engine speed, the engine makes more power. That simple formula demands that the engine be capable of not just spinning reliably, but also that the valves are doing their job of opening and closing at the precise time, every time the engine spins over. This, as engine builders and races have discovered, is a vexing proposition.

Overhead cam engine proponents have derided pushrod engines as limited by the monkey motion of all those pushrods and rocker arms flailing about inside the engine. But realistically, the

only real difference between an overhead cam engine and a typical small-block Chevy comes down to the addition of the pushrod. Perhaps more important is the question of how much the pushrod and other valvetrain components contribute to a loss of valvetrain control, since most enthusiasts acknowledge that overhead cam engines do tend to offer a certain RPM advantage.

GM engineers working on the new GEN III and now GEN IV design engines have since returned to the rocker shaft concept in an attempt to stabi-

lize the valvetrain and improve stiffness. One interesting design test for any valvetrain is to assemble a complete system for one valve and lift the valve off the seat. The system is literally struck with a hammer and measured for its structural frequency with an oscilloscope. Much like a tuning fork when struck, any valvetrain (with the valve off its seat) generates a given frequency based on its structural design. Improve the valvetrain's strength and its inherent frequency increases. While this is obviously an impractical test for the average backyard engine builder, it is an interesting test for valvetrain stability and strength.

A small design change can make a big difference in many seemingly insignificant areas. As an example, when GM Performance Parts (GMPP) designed the roller rocker arms for its street performance Hot hydraulic roller cam for the LT4 engine, GMPP specified a much tighter clearance in the upper slot in the rocker arm. By reducing the open area of the top of the rocker, this helps determine the amount of maximum valve lift the rocker can accommodate. This smaller slot limits the rocker

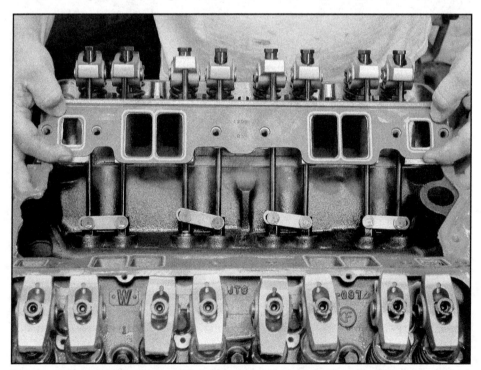

Today's performance valvetrains for the small-block Chevy are carefully integrated to match all the components in the system not only to work together, but also to create a harmonious combination that contributes to an extremely durable system that offers thousands of trouble-free street miles.

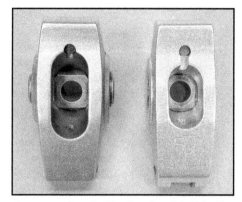

An example of attention to detail in the valvetrain is the slots cut into the GMPP 1.6:1 roller rockers used in the Hot cam hydraulic roller cams for both early small-blocks and LT1 engines. The slot is shorter in length, which limits its maximum lift, but this reduced slot length also adds strength to a rocker, reducing deflection by as much as 30 percent.

Keep in mind that the ultimate goal for your valvetrain is not just power, but also durability in the car. In a street car, your valvetrain is subjected to thousands of street miles. Aggressive cam lobes or high rocker ratios do not always react well when subjected to lots of street miles.

to a smaller net valve lift figure, but the advantage is that this change alone increases valvetrain stiffness by an amazing 30 percent.

Ironically, while the small-block originally benefited from the individual rocker stud system, most current-design high-performance valvetrains are returning to the shaft design system. The GEN III small-block employs a rocker shaft system in an effort to increase valvetrain stiffness, but that doesn't mean that the individual rocker arm should be trashed. For a typical street engine, the small-block's lightweight and inherent stability still works extremely well. Continuous improvements in rocker arm, pushrod, and certainly valvespring design are a big reason for the incredible durability that the small-block Chevy enjoys. Much of this is the trickle-down concept of components originally built for pure competition now finding their way to the street.

As an example, a mere 10 years ago, only the highest-revving drag race NHRA Competition Eliminator small-block engine builder would consider using something as exotic as a shaft rocker system conversion from companies like Jesel or T&D. Today, both companies offer shaft rocker systems for street engines that are no more expensive than a well-executed individual roller rocker set-

The original small-block Chevy valvetrain layout is incredibly simple yet amazingly strong thanks in part to newer and stronger aftermarket components.

up. Add to this the belt-drive systems finding their way onto more and more street engines and the trickle-down approach to street engines is very obvious.

This is also true with respect to valvesprings. Once considered an exotic material and spring design that were the sole dominion of the race community, valvesprings eventually found their way to the mainstream performance market. Spring design is and has always been a challenge for competition engines, but the good news is that advances in these areas in terms of design, material, and application eventually end up on the street. Integrated valvetrain performance is a major reason why it has become so easy to build 500 to 600 hp normally aspirated, big-inch small-blocks. It really comes down to a design competition between the cam designers and the valvespring engineers. As the valvespring guys come up with better springs and ways to control the violent nature of the cam profile, the cam designers merely push the envelope even further by masterfully creating increasingly aggressive lobes.

One of the biggest lessons available to the street enthusiast in terms of creating a high-performance small-block

Valvesprings and spring design are key elements in valvetrain durability and performance. Springs have evolved radically over the years from the small 1.250-inch diameter spring to monster dual springs that can measure up to 1.550-inch diameters.

Chevy valvetrain is to create an integrated system that can manage the test you intend to put it through. As we've already covered in the camshaft chapters, an ultra-aggressive drag racing cam profile valvetrain does not have the durability to survive the miles required of a street-driven engine. Conversely, to be competitive in today's professional racing environment, you must be willing to push the development of each of the components just to remain competitive. NASCAR racing is now spinning those 358-ci small blocks into the 9,500-rpm

zone for some of its short-track engine combinations. Those engines are now called upon to do this for practice, qualifying, and then muscle their way through a 500-mile, fender-banging race. The fact that these engines survive and still make power is nothing short of phenomenal.

Weight is a big consideration with the new design beehive or conical spring that reduces spring weight at the top of the spring, while also reducing retainer weight. This allows the spring to use more of its load to control the valve.

The key to these successful engine combinations is integrated components designed to work together. Professional engine builders spend lifetimes perfecting these combinations. While the average suburban garage engine builder does not have the luxury of their resources, you can still benefit by carefully researching each component and relying on the information available through the cam manufacturers like COMP Cams, Crane, Lunati, and several others. The

All early small-block Chevys relied on the placement of the pushrod through cast-in slots in the head to position the rocker arm tip over the end of the valve. Later performance additions created the pushrod guideplate, which more accurately performs this task.

One advantage to mechanical cams over hydraulics is that you can experiment with lash to improve power within a given RPM range. Increasing lash slightly reduces lift and duration, while tightening the lash has the opposite effect.

important is the fact that these aggressive acceleration rates also take their toll on valvesprings. A spring that might last thousands of very hard miles with one rocker ratio may last mere minutes with a higher rocker ratio. This leads to a gradual yet inevitable loss of top-end power and engine-speed capability.

Another useful concept in valvetrain applications is reducing the weight of the valvetrain pieces, especially in the area of the valve, retainer, and even the valvespring. Reducing weight of the spring means the top portion of the spring offers less mass to accelerate and decelerate with every valve event. This is not only worth RPM potential, but also greater "head room" between peak HP and engine valve float. What you don't want is an engine that has a valve float redline with a mere 200 or 300 rpm above peak horsepower. For most acceleration runs, shift points should be generally 500 rpm above peak horsepower. This allows the driver to shift at a slightly higher RPM so the engine speed does not drop below peak torque on the shift recovery point. This is more important in automatics with greater RPM drops between gears (especially with the 2-speed Powerglide), but is also essential,

trick is to use these companies' resources to ensure that you carefully match the valvetrain to the camshaft lobe design. This means that every component from the valve, retainers, keepers, rocker arm, pushrod, and lifter is carefully chosen to work together. If properly matched, this makes the job of accurately controlling the valve at higher engine speeds much easier. Ultimately, if the valvetrain is under control, valvetrain breakage becomes a rare occurrence rather than an unfortunate part of basic maintenance, and the engine makes more power. What could be better than that?

Part of the plan around carefully matching components has to do with a better understanding of the cam lobe designs you are employing. For example, COMP Cams has several grinds that produce such violent acceleration rates that these cams should not be used with rocker ratios beyond 1.6:1, and really should be used only with the stock 1.5:1 ratio. This is covered in more detail in the following chapter on rocker arms, but as rocker ratio increases, this radically jacks up the valve acceleration rate. As engine speed increases, these radical acceleration rates can quickly produce

uncontrolled valve motion, commonly known as valve float. Merely increasing the rocker ratio from 1.5:1 to 1.6:1 could easily contribute to a loss of 200 to 300 rpm in useable engine speed. Just as

While oil restrictors were popular in the 1970s and 1980s, they have no place in today's performance engines and should never be used with any kind of street engine since they only cause excessive heat and wear in the valvetrain. Never use oil restrictors in a small-block Chevy street engine.

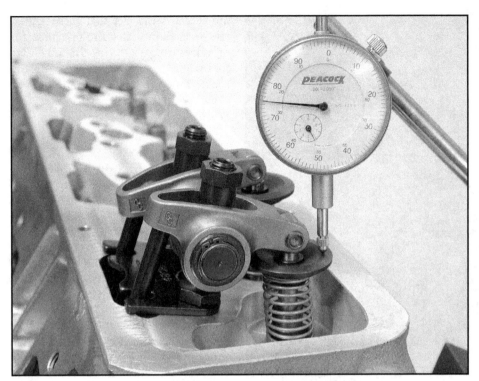

The rocker arm not only multiplies cam lift to create more valve lift, but it also multiplies the valve and spring acceleration rate.

it's easy to merely crank in more spring pressure, this is frankly the "bigger hammer" approach, and it usually just creates more problems. The more elegant solution is to lighten the components, including the valvespring itself, in an effort to reduce the weight the spring must control. Notice that we called out the pieces on the rocker side of the valvetrain. While lighter weight is important on the pushrod side, the valve side is dramatically impacted by the effect of the rocker ratio. Therefore, with a given acceleration rate created by the cam lobe, the rocker arm ratio multiplies that rate at the valve. This is then amplified by engine speed. We deal more closely with this phenomenon in Chapter 12 "Valvetrain Dynamics."

We've merely hit the high spots with this overview chapter. The real meat of the material is in the following chapters as we get into the details with each individual component. As you go through

perhaps even more so, for the narrowly spaced gears of manual 5-speed cars. Most engine builders prefer to create a power curve where the curve drops off as gradually as possible, even past peak-horsepower. Engines that drop off precipitously after peak HP are generally engines that could use further cam/intake/exhaust tuning or are experiencing valve float.

Valvetrain weight is always an issue with a strong performance engine. While

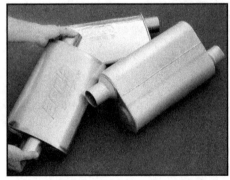

Keep in mind that any change to your exhaust system can and usually does have an effect on cam timing. A more efficient exhaust system starts with a good muffler that reduces backpressure to a minimum.

these chapters, you begin to see how each piece contributes to the entire valvetrain; just like a football or baseball team relies on each individual member to become a winning team. Think of yourself or your engine builder as the team manager, carefully choosing the right player for each position, weighing each member's strengths and weaknesses to come up with a winning formula. That's how the game is played. Do it well, and perhaps the press will write stories about you!

Any significant change to the engine, such as adding a single-plane intake over a dual plane, affects the engine's power curve. This definitely impacts your cam selection.

VALVES, SPRINGS, RETAINERS, AND KEEPERS

In a high-performance car, the suspension system is designed for the sole purpose of maintaining tire patch contact with the road surface and improving traction. When entering the world of cam and valvetrain design, the ultimate destination for all that lobe work is what occurs at the valve. This idea extends as far as expressing cam timing in figures that can be easily measured at the valve. The intake and exhaust valves are the "gatekeepers" for power. The intake valve determines how much air enters the engine, and the exhaust valve provides the portal for the oxidized combustion gases to escape. It may be flogging the obvious, but valves, rocker arms, springs, and their related components are instrumental in this symphony of power.

Valves

The original Chevy 265-ci small-block began life actuating diminutive 1.72- and 1.50-inch intake and exhaust valves. In the evolution of the small-block, now displacing as much as 454 inches out of a standard deck height block, these big-bore small-blocks can now accommodate up to impressive 2.150- and 1.625-inch valve sizes. Much of this growth is due to the larger bore sizes and massive cylinder heads that can use these larger valves. Production valves are struck from a decent forged steel material, but the OEMs have only

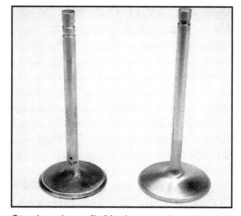

Stock valves (left) do an adequate job, but for performance applications, aftermarket stainless-steel valves like this Manley 2.05-inch intake (right) improve flow even with stock angles.

lately begun to pay attention to the major gains available with good valves and a high-quality valve job.

It is beyond the scope of this book to get into cylinder heads, but it cannot be emphasized enough that the most expensive titanium valves with NASA-researched shapes are practically useless if the guides are loose. One key to excellent flow is accurately positioning the valve relative to the seat in the cylinder head. This assumes a very tight valve guide to valve stem clearance. Without this, you can expect the best valve job to be pounded into uselessness in a very short time. It's also important to note that one way to maintain decent valveguide wear is to

pay close attention to pushrod length and rocker geometry. This limits excessive side loads imparted to the valve, which reduces wear on the guide. This is evaluated by measuring the actual amount of rocker arm tip travel across the top of the valve tip. Less travel generally means more efficient geometry.

Assuming your cylinder heads are set up properly, valve materials have dramatically improved in the last ten years. Also, you can now purchase valves and components that were once considered exotic race-only valves as off-the-shelf pieces for street engines. Companies like Childs & Albert, Manley, Ferrea, SSI, Federal-Mogul, and many others offer virtually any valve you can come up with for your small-block Chevy.

Stainless steel is the most common choice for small-block Chevy street engine valves, but within this generalized catego-

Stock valves (far right) often exhibit this ditch or undercut behind the seat area, which hurts flow. Aftermarket valves generally offer a more consistent shape along with increased strength and durability.

When choosing a performance valve, be sure to include the weight in your decision. You can often find 5 to 10 grams by shopping around with different manufacturers. This may not seem like much, but every gram reduces the mass the spring must control, especially if you are going to a larger-diameter valve.

ry is a tremendous range of materials. Heat is the big enemy of any steel, and certainly valves—especially exhaust valves—are subject to tremendous extremes in temperature. It is not uncommon for street engines to subject an exhaust valve to consistent 1,300 to 1,400 degrees F temperatures. Surface hardness suffers at these elevated temperatures and can drastically affect durability. For a performance engine, the advantages of greater strength combined with improved airflow potential are advantages that make purchasing high-quality valves an easy decision.

Since weight is commensurate with size, it's inevitable that larger valves always weigh more. But the weight penalty can generally be overcome with better springs, lighter retainers, or some combination of the two. Of course, you can step up to lighter valves with reduced stems that can cut overall weight by roughly 20 percent, but these tend to quickly become very expensive. They also demand accurate rocker and pushrod geometry because of their small stems. This is also where lash caps may be worthwhile, since

they add a slightly larger contact area. A smarter, and less expensive, move is to add titanium retainers instead, which also have the effect of reducing weight at the top of the valve. We get more in depth on titanium retainers later in this chapter.

Besides valve size, the back-side shape of the valve, including the radius between the stem and the valve face, is one of the more critical aspects of valve design. With no hard and fast rules for determining this shape, you also have the consideration of weight when it comes to creating a very gentle radius between the stem and the seat. Most of Manley's performance small-block intake valves, for example, offer an under-head angle of 10 to 12 degrees with a radius of 3/8-inch. Exhaust valves offer a gentler transition on a 15-degree angle with a 1/2-inch radius for the Race Master valves. These numbers are typical for a performance valve for the small-block Chevy.

Valve angle recommendations are difficult to pinpoint for all applications since each cylinder head ultimately prefers a certain set of angles, back cuts, margins, and seat widths. However, we can offer some general specs that can be used as guidelines for a starting point. These angles seem to have survived the test of time and most small-block heads rarely stray far from these basic dimensions. Both intake and exhaust valves seem to work best with a 45-degree seat angle. Seat widths for the intake valve seat are generally around 0.080-inch with 0.100-inch for exhaust. It's important to note that the exhaust valve prefers a wider seat, mainly to enhance heat transfer since the seat is the best source of heat migration from the valve into the head. Basically, narrower seats tend to improve airflow for a given valve lift, but these narrow seats are generally not practical for street engines since they quickly pound out after extended use.

Valve margins are another critical valve dimension and offer flow advantages for both intake and exhaust ports with specific recommendations. Most small-block intake valves prefer a wide margin of roughly 0.050-inch with a sharp edge on the chamber side of the

valve. Thicker margins increase valve weight, but don't necessarily increase flow potential. The sharp edge on the chamber side tends to help reduce reversion of exhaust gas back into the intake port during the overlap period. The exhaust valve has many theories championed, depending upon the source you choose to believe. Remember that the dominant flow direction for the exhaust is from the chamber into the port, which would tend to reinforce the concept of creating a radius on the chamber side of the margin advantageous. A 1/16-inch radius (0.0625-inch) is a popular dimension that offers some slight flow advantages. If a full radius faced valve is not to your liking, gains can still be achieved by adding a slight top angle cut that transitions between the flat face of the valve and the margin. Margins for the exhaust valve are also thicker, usually a minimum of 0.100-inch, to prevent damage to the valve from excessive cylinder temperature. Think of this thicker area as a larger heat sink that helps prevent high-temperature valve erosion.

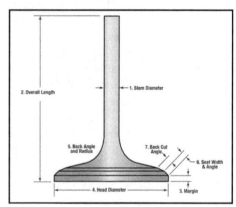

A few terms are important to know when navigating around a valve, especially if you are ordering custom valves from a manufacturer. Stem diameter (1) should be obvious, but look for the overall length (2), margin (3), head diameter (4), back angle and radius (5), seat width and angle (6), and back cut angle (7).

One increasingly popular and important step in preparing performance valves is adding a 30-degree back cut to both the intake and exhaust valves. While the advantages of these back cuts vary wildly between cylinder heads, this step is certainly worthy of discussion. Flow tests on sev-

Most performance valve jobs place the seat closer to the edge of the valve to improve flow. This is generally around 0.040 inches inboard. Another trick is to add a 30-degree back cut behind the seat to improve transitional flow, especially at lower valve lifts.

eral different heads reveal inconsistent results, which means that this 30-degree step is very application-specific. If we had to make a general statement, trend testing indicates that the 30-degree cut most often results in low-lift flow improvements, especially when used on exhaust valves. The drawback is that the back cut can often result in a loss of higher lift flow numbers. Intake flow improvements also respond best below 0.300-inch, yet we have seen several examples in which these improvements are offset by an equal or greater flow loss at higher valve lift points. The only way to know for sure if this move works with your application is to try it on a similar valve that you don't intend to run in your heads. This, obviously, also requires the services of a flow bench.

One example in which this back-cut does result in significant flow improvements, is with the increasingly popular production-iron small-block Vortec head. Early Vortec heads were produced with no back cut on either the intake or the exhaust. Later heads, especially those sold through the GMPP catalog, come with 30-degree back cut exhaust valves that made dramatic flow improvements with no other changes to the port or the valve.

Not all street-engine enthusiasts invest the time or the money to experiment with margins, valve-seat widths, and/or back-cutting valves. But considerable evidence suggests that spending the time on your heads to perform a few modifications like these can result in a much stronger flowing head, without resorting to expensive custom cylinder-head porting. If all this experimentation is more than you want to do, spend some time looking for a qualified performance machine shop involved with circle track or drag racing engines. Discussing these details with their cylinder head specialist pays off in terms of much better-flowing heads for your next great small-block street engine.

Springs

If there is one place where the classic concept of "bigger is better" is championed most often, it's with valvesprings. But before we get into the specifics of why higher spring loads work (and sometimes don't), let's spend a few moments going over basic spring design.

A radius face on the exhaust valve may help flow, especially if the port is less than optimal. Not all cylinder heads benefit from this change, so the best idea is to test this on a flow bench first and then evaluate the results.

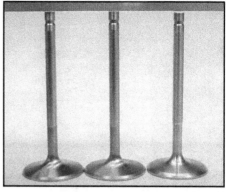

Especially in high valve lift applications, a 0.100-inch taller intake valve helps with packaging the spring to accommodate the additional valve lift without running into coil bind or retainer interference problems. Of course, a taller spring means more weight and different pushrods to maintain proper geometry.

Coil springs are far more complex than their simple shape and operation make them appear. Coil spring overall diameter, wire diameter, and the number of active coils combine to determine a given spring rate. Increase any of these values and the spring rate increases. Spring rate is rated in pounds per inch (not pounds per square inch or psi, which are pressure ratings), as in 300 pounds per inch (lbs/in). Simplified, this means that if a load of 300 pounds is placed on top of a loaded spring, it compresses exactly one inch.

The simplest coil spring is a single wire wound consistently from top to bottom. Because every spring has what is

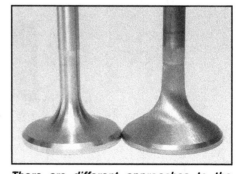

There are different approaches to the transition between the valve stem and the valve head. This gentler radius tends to be used more in exhaust applications, but adds weight in the process. This is a compromise between improved flow and additional valve weight.

Springs come in many sizes and styles. The stock small-block 1.250-inch spring (left) is okay for mild cruisers, but serious roller cams often dictate a true dual spring (center) with greater load capacity. The latest design is the beehive, or conical, spring (right) that offers reduced retainer weight and variable rate as items that are favorable to performance applications.

called a natural frequency, virtually all single-wound springs also come with a damper, a flat wire wound to fit inside the spring. This wire does just what its name implies. By fitting tightly against the coils of the spring, the damper is sized to dampen oscillations within the narrow range of the spring's natural frequency. This natural frequency can fall within a given engine speed where the spring is opening and closing at a certain rate. When these two speeds overlap, the spring quickly loses its ability to control the valve, which can result in valvetrain damage, and also loss of power since the valve could be open when it should be closed. Dual and triple springs often do not require dampers because the friction created between the different-sized springs dampens these nat-

ural frequencies. A single spring with a damper is not considered a dual spring. A dual spring is defined as having a smaller coil spring wound inside the main spring, and a triple spring obviously incorporates three springs.

It's also important to understand how springs are used in a typical internal combustion engine. To start, all springs are compressed to a given installed height and rated at what is called seat pressure. For example, a typical small-block Chevy production spring is wound at a 1.250-inch outside diameter (O.D.) and is squeezed between the retainer and the valve seat in the head at a height of around 1.750 inches. By compressing the spring slightly to attain this installed height, we can now measure the

load created by the spring. This is called the spring's seat pressure with the valve closed. A typical stock spring generally measures around 90 to 100 lbs of load at this installed height.

Let's say that we have a spring that measures 100 pounds of load at an installed height of 1.750 inches, and then we use a load-measuring tool to determine that at a height of 1.250 inches the spring now is creating 300 pounds of load. From these two measurements, we can determine the spring's rating. We moved the spring a total of 0.500 inches and the spring increased its load by 200 pounds (300 minus 100), so with a load change of 200 pounds for a half-inch, this equates to a spring rating of 400 lbs/in. This is good information to have, since a couple of simple measurements can help you determine if a spring has lost its load rating.

Coil bind is another crucial spring rating. Coil bind is the height of the spring when it is completely compressed. This is an important spec in determining if a spring can accommodate the valve lift you plan to run. We get more into depth with these specs when we show you how to set up a

The only way to know how much load a spring actually creates is by measuring the spring in a load tester like this load machine. While this tool is expensive, you should be able to find a shop with one where you can test your springs. Always compress each new spring in a vise at least five to eight times before measuring spring load.

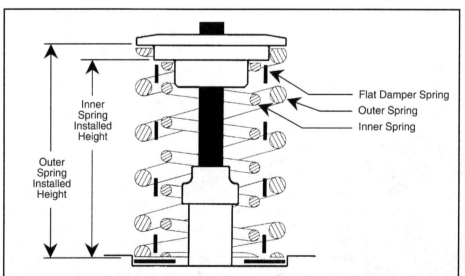

This drawing reveals how installed height is dictated by the distance between the spring seat in the head and the bottom of the retainer. The minimal retainer-to-seal clearance is a 0.050-inch clearance between the bottom of the retainer and the top of the valve guide seal at max valve lift. (Illustration courtesy of Crane)

It's always a good idea to chamfer the top of the spring where it contacts the retainer. This prevents sharp edges from creating a stress riser that could cause a retainer failure. This is especially important with dual or triple springs.

Always measure your spring's actual coil bind height by compressing a spring in a vise. Often, cam manufacturers are conservative with this spec and you can gain perhaps a 0.030– to 0.050-inch shorter coil bind spec that can help when packaging a high-lift cam.

cylinder head, but installed height, coil bind height, and retainer-to-seal clearance are all critical dimensions in the valvetrain game.

The trick in selecting the right valvespring for your application has much to do with the rest of the valvetrain. It makes little sense to choose a monster 1.560-inch diameter dual spring with over 700 pounds of load at max lift for a mild flat tappet hydraulic camshaft application since the spring pressure pushes all the oil out of the lifter before the engine can achieve a respectable engine speed. Conversely, you need some serious spring pressure if you plan on running an aggressive mechanical roller cam and spin the engine past 7,000 rpm in search of power.

If it sounds like literally thousands, if not hundreds of thousands, of combinations of lobe-pushrod-rocker-arm-spring-retainer-valve combinations for the small-block Chevy are available, you're probably right. Given this impossible combination of parts, you begin to see how difficult it is to come up with valvespring recommendations

for most engines. To introduce some sanity into this situation, the cam companies offer spring recommendations for each of their lobe designs. This is especially helpful in street-engine applications. At the time of this writing, Crane is planning on introducing a plan where you can call their tech department and get a spring recommendation based on the other Crane components in the valvetrain. This new Crane system is based on extensive test data combined with an impressive computer modeling program that puts a little more science into the black art of creating durable valvetrains.

Where this gets complicated is when the engine builder buys a cam from one manufacturer, an assembled cylinder head from another, combines the two components, and gives little thought to whether the springs are actually properly matched to the camshaft. Cylinder head companies address this situation by rating complete heads based on flat tappet or roller cam applications. The roller cam head applications generally use a larger-diameter spring with increased

seat and open load ratings, but that does not take into account the actual cam lobe's specific requirements.

This brings us to the concept that basic spring ratings such as seat and open load pressures really don't address all the information an engine builder needs to accurately choose a given valvespring. The easy route is to contact the specific cam designer and talk with the tech department to get specific recommendations for a given spring. This is perhaps the quickest way to obtain the specific spring information you need, but we can go over at least some of the aspects of spring choice that go into these recommendations. This also helps you understand some of the nomenclature and technical information that the cam companies deliver.

One of the more intriguing aspects of spring performance is a spring's own given inertia as it goes through a complete lift cycle. Like any other reciprocating component, the valvespring is accelerated to max lift where it stops, and then (assuming all things are right in the valvetrain) follows the closing flank of the cam as the spring then accelerates toward the seat. Basically, the opening flank of the cam lobe dictates the opening rate, but the spring is responsible for closing-side accuracy, since the spring is charged with the responsibility of following the lobe's closing rate. The spring must control the entire valvetrain, including its own inertial mass; therefore, the heavier the spring, the more of its own mass it must also control at higher engine speeds. Here is where things become challenging for the spring

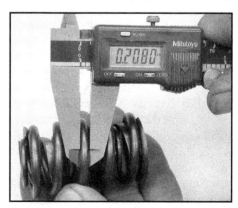

Wire diameter is the main factor in determining spring load. Larger wire diameters combined with shorter overall length create much higher spring loads.

One trick that shows up in both OE performance applications and aftermarket springs is the use of ovate wire flattened on the top and bottom to make it wider than it is tall. This allows the engine builder to squeeze more lift out of the spring before it hits coil bind.

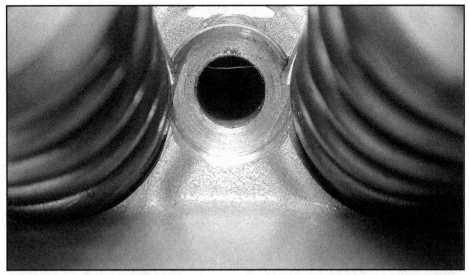

Packaging becomes a big problem with a small-block Chevy when adding larger-diameter springs. Aftermarket heads can incorporate larger spring seats, but you still have to squeeze that head bolt in between the springs. This often requires grinding flats on the washer to fit it between the springs.

design engineer. How do you design a spring with reduced weight when larger wire diameter and larger outside diameters are essential to increasing spring rate?

The latest GEN III and GEN IV GM engines offer an intriguing clue for this solution with the use of conical or beehive-shaped valvesprings. These springs taper the shape of the spring at the top, reducing both the diameter of the spring and the retainer. Obviously, the smaller the retainer, the lighter it can be. Add in a titanium version of this tiny retainer, and you have a formula for dramatic weight savings. But the conical spring has more advantages than just reduced mass.

The typical valvespring uses a consistent body diameter top to bottom. And if you remember our earlier definition of a spring, outside diameter is a variable in determining spring rate. By reducing the spring diameter at the top, the conical spring also changes the spring rate, creating a variable rate spring. So as the spring compresses, it starts with a relatively soft rate and then increases as the spring compresses, stacking the smaller diameter coils at the top, effectively increasing the diameter of the spring. As an added plus, because of its variable rate, the conical spring does not require a damper. Overall, since the spring is smaller at the top, it also enjoys the benefits of having much less mass to control. This means that for a given rate at higher valve lift values, the spring can control more valvetrain mass with the same rate or

Retainers should always fit the spring snugly on the spring's inside diameter. When using dual or triple springs, ensure that the inner springs are properly matched to the retainer. If not, this could cause big problems.

allow the engine to spin a little higher RPM before experiencing uncontrolled valve motion (or valve float).

Valvespring design innovations and constantly updated metallurgy continue to drive the racing valvespring market. These advances eventually trickle down to the street-engine market to allow even more radical cam lobes and, eventually, more power.

Since most performance applications are working with aluminum cylinder heads, valvespring seats are a necessity. Original production small blocks merely used the small outside diameter ridge left by the machining operation of the spring

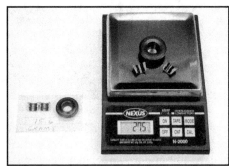

A distinct advantage for conical springs is the dramatically smaller beehive retainer and keepers (left) weighing a mere 15.6 grams compared to a typical dual spring steel retainer (right) at 27 grams. Less weight means the spring can apply more of its pressure to control the valve instead of the additional weight of the retainer.

seats to act as an outside diameter spring seat, so a machined steel spring seat was not required. But a performance engine, especially one that operates at high RPM, should be equipped with either an inside diameter or outside diameter style spring seat. While necessary to protect the soft aluminum cylinder head, the spring seat also serves as a solid base to accurately locate the spring to prevent it from dancing around under high-RPM operation. With proponents of both styles out there, we've found that the design of the spring seat is secondary to its use. If the spring is allowed to move on its base, this reduces its effectiveness and durability. This also means that the valvespring should be a snug fit into the spring seat in order to do its job effectively. Obviously, a spring seat also has an effect on installed height. Most spring seats measure around 0.060 inches thick.

Retainers and Keepers

Design for an engine component doesn't get much simpler than the valvespring retainer. And yet, we still have plenty to talk about when it comes to these highly loaded valvespring lids and their keepers. Frankly, all it takes is one retainer or keeper set to fail and allow a valve to pierce a piston for these pieces to illustrate their importance to the street-engine builder.

As spring pressures and engine speeds continue to climb, we ask the valvetrain to perform at increasingly aggressive levels. But before we get into all the trick parts, it's important to cover all the basic bases first. Perhaps the most important aspect of choosing a retainer is to emphasize that it must match the spring. Too often, enthusiasts get caught mixing and matching components that come not only from different manufacturers, but also from different parts of the world! Retainers must not only accommodate the proper valve stem diameter, but also the inside and outside diameters of the spring. Ideally, the retainer should fit snugly over the spring with the step in the retainer slightly interfering with the inside diameter of the spring. This helps locate the spring on the retainer so it doesn't move around.

Where it gets interesting is with dual and triple springs. The retainer still must locate each of the two or three springs to ensure that each spring is not allowed to migrate. Each locator appears as a step on the bottom side of the retainer. Of course, this also adds weight that must be controlled at speed. It's best to use the actual retainer with the spring when checking spring pressures, and to check each of the springs separately rather than all together.

The major misunderstanding when it comes to valve locks, or keepers, is that the interface of the groove on the top of the valve and the square edge

---

VALVE CURTAIN AREA

In discussion of valve lift and flow potential of any cylinder head and valve combination, you may run across the term "valve curtain area." This is simply the flow window created by the combination of valve diameter and its valve lift.

If you remember your high school geometry, we can calculate the actual valve curtain area by multiplying circumference times valve lift. To calculate circumference, multiply valve diameter times Pi. Let's use a typical 2.02-inch diameter intake valve and combine it with a valve lift of 0.500 inches. First, we calculate circumference:

Circumference = Valve Diameter x Pi
Circumference = 2.02 x 3.1417
Circumference = 6.34 inches

If you had a 1-inch valve lift, this would create a flow window of 6.34 square inches. With a 0.500-inch valve lift, the curtain area is half that figure:

Flow Area = Valve Circumference x
Valve Lift
Flow Area = 6.34 x 0.500
Flow Area = 3.17 square inches

If you really want to break down the critical details, the actual flow window should be calculated using the diameter of the valve at the point where the valve contacts the seat, which can be anywhere from 0.030 to 0.040 inches smaller in diameter than the overall size for an intake valve. Exhaust valves move the seat 0.050 inches inboard to protect the seat from the heat. The curtain area concept illustrates why it is important to place the valve seat contact point as high on the 45-degree valve seat as possible. Many machine shops place the intake seat right at the outer edge of the valve in order to increase the effective flow window area, but this is not practical for a street engine because the valve job is not durable. But let's look at how moving the seat outboard affects the flow curtain area. As an example, using 0.040 in from the outside diameter of the 2.02-inch valve gives us a flow curtain area of a much smaller 3.11 square inches, which is a loss of 2 percent flow curtain area compared to the 2.02-inch figure. This is one reason larger valves make such a difference.

Let's compare the 2.02 valve (actual seat diameter of 1.98 inches) with a 2.08-inch valve also with a seat diameter 0.040-inch inboard. The larger valve creates a flow window at 0.500-inch valve lift of 3.20 square inches, which represents roughly a 3 percent gain in flow area. Not huge, but certainly measurable on a flow bench.

Keep in mind that you can calculate flow window area for any valve lift. Take 0.200-inch valve lift as an example. With a 2.02-inch intake valve with a seat 0.040 inches inboard from the valve, O.D. equals a flow curtain area of 1.24 square inches. If we increase the valve size to 2.08 with the same 0.040 inboard seat position, this changes the flow window area to 1.28 square inches.

Flow curtain area isn't something you hear bantered about at cocktail parties (unless you hang out with tech-heavy gear heads), but it is another factor in determining power potential with regard to cylinder head flow. In an ideal world, air flow past an intake valve would be consistent around the valve's entire circumference. In reality, because of inertial flow effects, air tends to concentrate on the "back" side, or the long radius side of the valve as it enters the chamber. Improved port designs increase the height of the short-side radius in order to persuade the air to flow more uniformly around the valve, which improves power through better cylinder filling.

This steel retainer for a 1.437– to 1.500-inch diameter spring weighs in at a hefty 34 grams, while the titanium retainer for a conical 26918 COMP Cams spring (we know, that's an apples and oranges comparison, but life's rarely fair) measures at a flyweight 7 grams. That makes the steel retainer almost five times the mass of the smaller conical retainer. Most valvetrain experts estimate this weight difference could be worth 200 to 300 more RPM before encountering valve float.

Mild engines can get by just fine with stamped steel locks (far left), but applications with more aggressive spring pressures should invest in more durable machined locks (middle). Full-on race engines can benefit from larger 10-degree locks (right), but these also add weight.

locator in the lock are where the load is concentrated. This is not true. The groove in the valve merely locates the locks on the valve while the tapered outside edge of the locks fit into the retainer. It is this wedging action of the locks to the retainer that holds back all that spring pressure. With increasing spring pressures, this is why some manufacturers have moved from 7-degree to larger 10-degree locks that offer a greater surface area to distribute that load. Unfortunately, these larger locks are also heavier and are overkill for all but the most brutal mechanical cam for the street.

Seals

Like most seemingly unimportant components, valve stem seals make their own important contribution to overall engine power. The proper seal balances essential lubrication that keeps the valves sliding nicely within the guides while also limiting the amount of oil to prevent too much from entering the chamber. This is essential because if oil begins to contribute to the combustion process, the end result is a date with detonation that causes nothing but problems. Sealing the intake valve is especially important since vacuum on the port side of the valve can quite easily pull vast quantities of oil through the valve guide.

In the original days of the small-block, engineers relied on a big, tin shield that covered the top of the spring to act as a giant umbrella. This was combined with a tiny o-ring seal that occupied a second groove cut in the valve that allowed a measured amount of oil to run down the valve and into the guide. When racers began stuffing larger-diameter valvesprings into their heads, the tin shields went away, replaced by a small, hard plastic seal that fit directly over the valve guide, positively located on the guide rather than moving up and down with the valve stem. Generically referred to as "PC," or positive style seals, these pieces worked well for race engines that are often disassembled for maintenance. The disadvantage of PC seals is that their stiff constitution does not accommodate lateral movement in the valve, which quickly oblongs the seal allowing oil to leak into the guides.

This is most prevalent in street-driven performance engines where mileage quickly accumulates and lateral valve stem movement oblongs the hard plastic seals. It didn't take long before several manufacturers began offering more flexible rubber valve guide seals that have

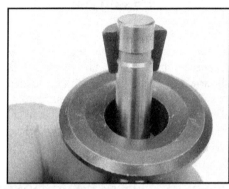

Retainer locks hold the valve in place by wedging the locks to the retainers on the outside taper, not on the inside diameter notches. The internal steps merely position the locks consistently on the valve stem.

experienced continual improvement over the years. Today, these seals are constructed of various materials such as Viton rubber and exotic synthetic mixtures intended to remain flexible in the face of ultra-high oil temperatures approaching 300 degrees F. The advantage of remaining flexible is to allow the seal to maintain properly on a valve stem that is not only moving up and down but also laterally.

Among the popular seals for the small-block Chevy, two different seal dimensions are based on both the outside diameter of

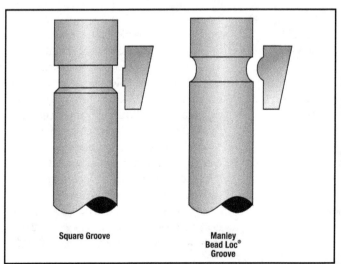

Square Groove

Manley Bead Loc® Groove

For ultimate valve retention, Manley sells rounded Bead-Loc keepers that employ a radius that must be matched with a similar radius on the Manley valve. The Bead-Loc is especially useful where the engine may encounter valve float that unloads the retainer from the spring.

ADJUSTABLE INSTALLED HEIGHT

One of the ways to customize your valvetrain is by establishing the proper valvespring installed height. The best way to approach this is to first discover which of your 16 valves has the shortest installed height, and then set the rest of the valves based on that height. Often, this may require adjusting the distance between the spring seat in the head and the bottom of the retainer. The easiest way to do this is with shims if shortening the distance is required. You can also try different retainers that modify that distance slightly up or down.

Crane has developed a slick little test kit designed to allow you to experiment with different machined steel 7-degree locks for 11/32- and 3/8-inch valve stem diameters to establish the proper installed height. For example, Crane's black locks are used as the standard or mid-point locks, while the yellow locks increase installed height by 0.050 inches, and the silver locks decrease the installed height by the same 0.050 inches compared to the standard black locks.

While you could add 0.050 inches worth of shims under the valvespring to decrease the installed height, using the silver locks is much simpler, especially if you determine that all 16 valves require this shorter height. This way, you don't have to invest in a ton of shims when you have to purchase locks either way. Of course, the taller yellow locks are useful when you run into situations where you need that extra 0.050 inches and you either don't want to or can't machine the valvespring seats for the additional depth.

The only down side to using the taller installed height locks is that this does move the retainer closer to the top of the valve tip and also to the rocker arm, which means you must check to ensure that at least 0.050 inches of clearance between the rocker arm and the retainer exists. You also need to ensure that the roller tip sufficiently clears the retainer. The best move if you don't have sufficient clearance is to find a rocker arm with additional under-arm clearance rather than machine the aluminum rocker arm body to create this clearance. Machining the rocker for more clearance can create a stress riser that leads to failure.

One trick to altering installed height is to use these different locks from Crane or COMP that can move the position of the retainer as much as 0.100 inches as either a + 0.050 or 0.050-inch retainer height change on the valve. When increasing installed height with locks, check to make sure there is sufficient clearance between the retainer and the top of the valve. If the two are very close to the same height, this could cause problems and you should consider other alternatives to increase the installed height.

Lash caps were originally used on titanium valves to prevent valve stem damage. These caps can also be used to alter valvetrain geometry and increase the stem diameter when using reduced stem valves. These caps require special locks to position the caps.

Aluminum heads require a steel spring seat. According to the cam manufacturers, there is no significant difference between outside diameter (left) or inside diameter (right) spring seat locators.

Conclusion

The idea with each of the chapters in this book is to expose you to the basic concepts of how each component operates and also to introduce you to new ideas and ways to apply these concepts in new and innovative fashions. Any performance engine benefits from a properly integrated valve component system that allows the engine to make all the power it can without limitations from the valvetrain. Combine this with excellent durability, which is essential with a street engine where high mileage is a requirement, and you have the makings of a first-class street engine.

the valve guide—either 0.530 or 0.550 inches, and the common small-block Chevy valve stem diameter of 11/32 (0.343 inches). The key to making a valve stem seal work in a performance engine is to ensure that the seal is compatible with the spring, retainer, and valve lift chosen for the engine. First, the seal's outside diameter must clear the spring's inside diameter. Then, it makes sense that the bottom of the retainer needs 0.050 inches or more clearance from maximum lift of the valve before meeting the top of the valve stem seal. If this clearance is not present, it takes the engine about six or eight revolutions before every seal in the engine is munched and no longer doing their job. Conversely, choose the proper seal, install it properly, and give it plenty of clearance, and these simple devices deliver a solid performance. It's details like these that make a well-thought-out performance engine such a rewarding experience.

Ever wondered why some small-block valves offer two grooves near the top of the stem? In the early days, Chevy used a very small O-ring that fit into the lower groove and sealed the space between the retainer and the stem to prevent oil from running down the stem and into the guide.

The best seals for a street-performance engine are the Viton rubber or new generation of silicon seals. They remain flexible and really dry up the intake valve guides to minimize oil use. The small spring holds the seal in place on the valve guide.

If you are serious about engine building, then it might be worth it to also have a selection of seal installer tools like these from Proform. The tool precisely installs the seal over the valve guide to prevent damage to the seal during installation.

The PC seal is still around even, though much more flexible seals do a better job. These PC seals offer the smallest outside diameter and are often the only seals that work in a small-block with dual springs.

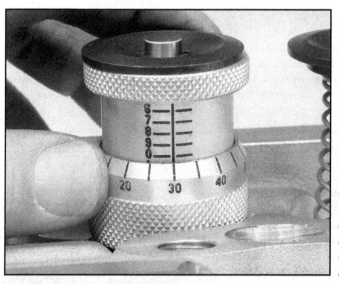

Many companies sell this handy tool called a height mic. Assemble each individual valve, retainer, keepers, and spring seat in the actual valve guide and then use the height mic to measure the actual installed height. The whole process takes less than a minute per valve and delivers accurate information to help you establish a common installed height for all 16 valves.

CARE, FEEDING, AND INSTALLING VALVESPRINGS

When installing a new set of springs, you have several options to enhance and increase the lifespan of these springs. The good news is that this has to do more with spending a little quality time with your springs rather than just spending more money. This means spending perhaps two to three hours of hand work.

To begin with, use 240-grit sandpaper to radius all the sharp edges of both ends of all 16 springs. Manley sells a cone-shaped valvespring-chamfering tool that chucks up into a die grinder using abrasive cones, but you can also do this by hand. The idea is to sand the inside and outside radius of the springs to prevent these sharp edges from eating into a steel or titanium retainer, and also to eliminate stress risers from contributing to a broken spring. Chamfering the inside diameter also prevents a stress concentration near the inside diameter of the retainer, distributing the load across the entire flat surface of the retainer where it belongs.

A new valvespring also delivers a slightly higher load value when it is brand new than it does even just 15 minutes after engine startup. A good spring loses between 5 to 15 pounds in this short time. If you want to get closer to the actual spring seat pressure, it's not a bad idea to cycle a spring 20 times all the way to coil bind before you check the pressure. This may not bring the spring down to its final seat pressure, but you are much closer than you are with a brand new spring.

ROCKER ARMS, STUDS, PUSHRODS, AND LIFTERS

Splitting the valvetrain into two sections allows us to go into more detail for each of the individual components. This chapter deals with the cam side of the valvetrain, including the rocker arm. Since this is perhaps the most important component on this side of the system, we start with the rocker.

Rocker Arms

All cam-in-block pushrod engines use a rocker arm to convert the reciprocating motion of the lifter and pushrod into motion that controls the valve. In simplest terms, the rocker arm operates like a child's teeter-totter in which the upward motion of the lifter is converted to downward motion of the valve. Along the way, simple leverage is employed to multiply the characteristics of the lobe by a ratio. In the case of the original small-block Chevy, the stock rocker-arm ratio is 1.5:1. This means that the lift generated by the cam lobe is multiplied by 1.5 times when delivered to the valve. Therefore, a cam with a 0.400-inch lobe lift would theoretically create 0.600 inches of lift at the valve. We emphasize the word "theoretical" because most rocker systems are less than 100 percent efficient, meaning that ratios are not always what they are published and deflection in the valvetrain also costs a certain amount of valve lift, especially when using high-rate valvesprings.

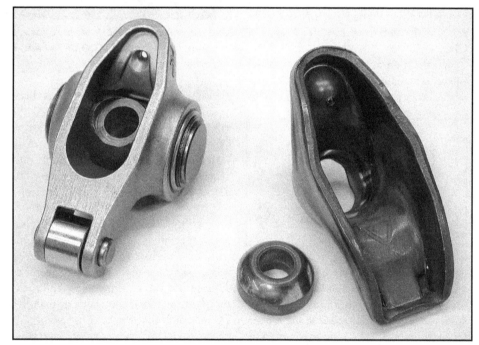

The original 265 ci small-block Chevy generated a tremendous amount of controversy around its "spindly" stamped steel rocker arms with their individual rocker studs. Eventually, the stamped piece has given way to full roller rockers to take advantage of higher valvespring pressures for higher-RPM use.

It's important to understand how rocker arms work in order to fully appreciate their abilities and limitations. If you look at a straight-side view of a rocker arm, whether it's a stud mount or rocker shaft version, rocker arms pivot around a central axis and the rocker tip that contacts the valve travels through an arc. The greater the valve lift motion, the greater distance the rocker tip must travel and therefore the wider the arc it transcribes. Since this is an arc, or radius, the rocker arm tip traverses a given distance. If the distance from the rocker pivot point to the valve tip is the same, the ratio remains constant throughout its travel. But because rocker tip creates an arc, the rocker ratio changes as it traverses this arc. When setting up a valvetrain, the ideal plan is to minimize the

As you can imagine, the rocker ball generates a tremendous amount of friction and heat. One way to improve lubrication is with these small oil grooves cut into the balls. Another good tip to improve rocker durability is to remove flash from the oil hole on the top of pushrod oil feed hole. Polishing removes a potential stress riser that can crack the pushrod hole.

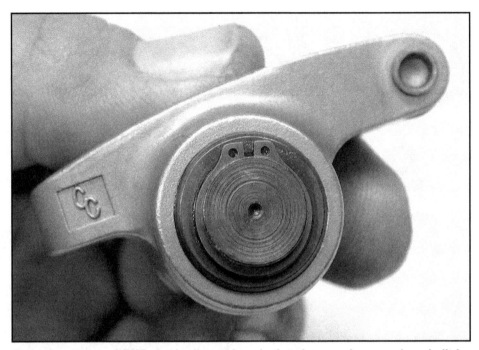

One advantage to COMP steel roller rockers is that these rockers can be rebuilt by sending them back to COMP where they are disassembled, inspected, and the required parts are replaced.

distance the rocker travels across the valve tip. This limits the change in ratio, and generally enhances performance. We get into the details of how to do that in Chapter 9.

The rocker arm contact point on the valve tip actually travels a significant distance across the top of the valve tip. With

Roller rockers are constructed of both aluminum and steel. While steel roller rockers may weigh more than aluminum, steel rockers use less mass at the rocker tip, so therefore require no more force to move than aluminum rockers. The aluminum rocker on the left is a Crane Gold Race while the steel rocker on the right is a COMP Cams Hi-Tech Stainless.

a properly designed valvetrain system, the rocker tip begins at a point just inboard of the valve tip center. As the rocker creates valve lift, the contact point moves outboard (toward the exhaust side of the engine). At roughly half of total valve lift, the contact point has now moved to the outboard of the valve tip centerline. At maximum valve lift, the rocker contact point moves back to its starting point. As

the valve lift curve begins its way back down, this reverses the pattern until the valve returns back to the inboard side of the valve tip centerline. If you were to label these points A (inboard) and B (outboard), the rocker tip travel could be described as A-B-A-B-A (see illustration).

A considerable body of evidence suggests an alternative to this configuration, especially when building an engine with extremely high valve lift curves. Some drag-race engine builders prefer to design their valvetrain to place the rocker tip on the valve centerline at max lift. Their idea is that they do not want side loads placed on the valve at maximum lift, which could create excessive valve guide wear. This is achieved by placing the rocker arm tip at the valve centerline just as the valve begins to open. At mid-valve lift, the rocker has moved toward the outboard or exhaust side of the valve stem tip. Then at maximum valve lift, the rocker tip actually travels back toward the intake side of the engine, arriving at the valve centerline at maximum valve lift.

With street or endurance engines, the key is to minimize the total travel of the rocker arm across the tip of the valve. The main reason for this is to min-

imize valve guide wear by minimizing the side-load thrust created by the rocker being off center of the valve tip. Generally, 0.040 inches is considered a decent number. Values exceeding 0.050 inches should be addressed with pushrod length to reduce the distance and improve the geometry. As we've noted, the greater the distance the rocker tip travels away from the rocker pivot point, the more this reduces the rocker arm ratio, resulting in reduced total valve lift.

One of the distinct disadvantages inherent with stamped-steel rocker arms is the friction created by the ball-stud design. With increased valvespring pressures, the load and heat created is almost

Increasing rocker ratio is accomplished by moving the pushrod cup closer to the rocker fulcrum. On the right is a 1.5:1 ratio rocker; on the left is a 1.6:1 rocker.

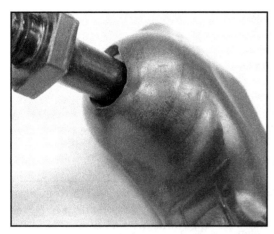

Stamped rockers use a slot cut in the base of the rocker that allows the rocker to move relative to the stud. With higher lift cams, make sure there is a minimum of 0.050 inches clearance between the end of the rocker slot and the rocker stud at max lift.

impossible to control, especially for the exhaust rockers that are also subject to increased heat transmitted through the valve stem. High-performance stamped-rockers often come with balls machined with grooves to retain oil to improve lubrication in the ball contact area. Stamped rockers also do not operate exactly like roller rockers. This is because the stamped rockers offer a slot through which the stud protrudes to locate the rocker. The higher the valve lift, the longer this slot needs to be in order to accommodate the increased lift. Because the rocker centerline is constantly changing, this limits the amount of movement of the stamped rocker tip across the valve tip face. In addition, stamped rockers offer an exceptionally wide tip contact area.

CRANE QUICK LIFT ROCKERS

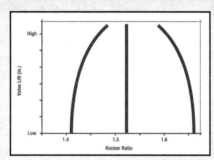

Geometry was never our best subject in school—too many angles. But someone at Crane has obviously spent some time working on a new angle for its rocker arm geometry. Recently Crane has developed what they call the Quick-Lift line of rocker arms designed to deliver a little more than the stated rocker ratio.

The key to how this works is the placement of the pushrod seat on the rocker body. Since the distance from the rocker centerline to the valve centerline is fixed, the easiest way to change rocker arm ratio is to move the pushrod seat in the rocker closer to the rocker centerline. For the Quick-Lift rocker, the pushrod seat is also relocated lower relative to the rocker centerline. As the pushrod moves the rocker arm from closed to full valve lift, the Quick-Lift rocker pushrod seat moves outboard from the rocker centerline, as well as upward. This reduces the ratio as lift increases.

As an example, let's say we have a standard 1.6:1 ratio rocker on an intake valve in a small-block. At 0.100-inch lobe lift with a theoretical 1.6:1 ratio, that would give us 0.160-inch lift at the valve. The 1.6:1 Crane Quick-Lift rocker actually delivers a 1.72:1 ratio at 0.100-inch lobe lift, delivering an additional 0.012-inch valve lift for the same lobe lift. By the time the valve reaches roughly 0.300-inch lift, the ratio has migrated to

its rated 1.6:1 ratio. The Quick-Lift design also works on the closing side of the lift curve, creating the 1.72:1 ratio as the valve approaches its seat.

The accompanying graph may help you understand how Crane's geometry works. A typical production small-block stamped rocker rarely achieves a true 1.5:1 rocker ratio. Because the rockers travel in an arc, at best these rockers deliver a ratio that starts around 1.42:1 or so and may achieve a ratio of roughly 1.46:1 to perhaps 1.48:1. This is illustrated by the curve on the left. Crane's standard roller rocker arms are designed to deliver as close to a consistent ratio throughout its lift curve as possible, as shown by the middle vertical line. With the Quick-Lift design, the ratio begins at a much greater ratio and then moves toward its rated ratio as lift increases as shown with the curve on the far right.

What this Quick-Lift design accomplishes is effectively increasing the area under the curve created by the lobe. In essence, this is similar to adding duration if you were to rate the duration at 0.100-inch or 0.200-inch valve lift figures. This may be especially useful with production-style engines sensitive to increased seat timing duration that can compromise idle quality. The Quick-Lift concept makes the cam appear slightly bigger to the engine by generating more valve lift earlier in the curve than would otherwise be accomplished with only a longer duration camshaft or a higher ratio rocker that could put the engine into valve float or cause piston-to-valve problems.

Of course, it could be said that this rocker was designed to enhance an otherwise conservative acceleration ramp lobe by pumping up the rocker ratio, and that may be true. Another limitation to this concept is that if the Quick-Lift rocker design creates a faster acceleration rate at low lift on the opening side, it must also perform the same on the closing side. This means that the valve accelerates toward the seat at a much greater rate due to the higher rocker ratio. For a typical street engine with mild acceleration rates, this is probably not a problem, but it taxes the valvespring more on the closing side. Crane has also matched the Quick-Lift rocker arm concept with a new line of Z-Cam lobes designed to take advantage of the Quick-Lift concept.

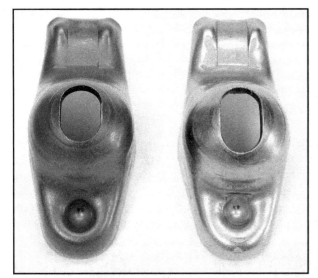

Crane's Nitro Carb stamped 1.6:1 rockers are built to actually offer closer to a 1.7:1 ratio at the lower valve lifts, eventually creating a 1.6:1 ratio at max valve lifts. You can check this by comparing pushrod movement to the amount the valve moves by using two dial indicators. If the pushrod moves 0.100 inches and the valve moves 0.170 inches, then the ratio at that point is 1.7:1.

All roller rocker arms with a fixed pivot point create an arc as the rocker moves the valve through its lift curve. The wider the arc, the more the ratio changes through the lift curve.

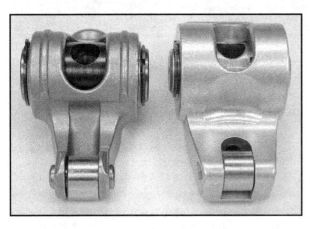

One advantage to steel roller rockers is that the smaller rocker arm tip offers more room to clear larger diameter valvesprings in that critical area just above the retainer. Minimum clearance is 0.050 inches.

These hydraulic lifters are fine for mild street engines, but the small U-shaped clip can pop out if it hits the valve float and could end up in the oil pump.

Roller rockers use a shaft with roller bearings to reduce the friction, which also reduces oil temperature. The cam companies also build a roller-tipped rocker that still uses the stock ball-stud arrangement. While these rockers offer an increased ratio, the fallacy is that the area between the roller tip and the valve tip face experiences some friction reduction. In reality, with a hydraulic tappet camshaft that employs a preload instead of a clearance value, the roller tip slides across the valve stem tip and does not roll. Mechanical cams with lash allow the tip to rotate, but only until the lash has been taken up, then the roller tip also slides across the valve stem tip. So purchasing a set of roller-tipped rockers in search of reduced friction does not deliver value based on that assumption. You're far better off investing in a set of true roller rocker arms.

The two basic types of true roller rockers are made of either aluminum or steel. Originally, all roller rockers were made of aluminum in search of reduced weight. Unfortunately, since aluminum is not nearly as strong as steel, aluminum rockers must employ a larger body to prevent deflection. Steel roller rockers are heavier, but the portion of the rocker that actually moves the greatest distance is still roughly the same weight as an aluminum rocker arm, so there is minimal loss of performance. Plus, many steel rocker arms, such as the COMP Cams Hi-Tech stainless rockers, are rebuildable—something that few aluminum roller rockers can offer.

It's All in the Ratio

After you've decided on the basic rocker arm design, the most important feature you need to decide on is the

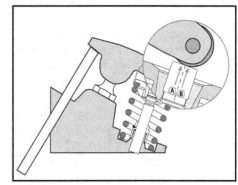

With an ideal pushrod length, the rocker tip travels from slightly inboard of the valve centerline, position A, to slightly outboard of center, position B, at half lift and then back to A at max lift. Then the whole process reverses on the return trip back to its seated position. The pattern ends up looking like A-B-A-B-A

Once the rocker arm contacts the valve tip and lift is created, the unit loading pressure created between the roller and the valve is so great that the "roller" actually slides across the valve tip rather than rolling.

rocker ratio. From 1955 until the GEN III engine came on the scene, the stock rocker ratio for a small-block Chevy has always been 1.5:1. The GEN III engine pushed this ratio up to 1.7:1 and just recently, the GEN IV LS7 bumps this to 1.8:1! This ratio is achieved by simply moving the rocker's pushrod cup closer to the rocker's pivot point. Increasing the ratio requires moving the pushrod cup closer to the pivot point since the distance from the rocker fulcrum to the valve tip must remain constant. Calculating the ratio is relatively easy by simply dividing the two distances into each other.

From this description, increasing rocker ratio also increases the lift. For example, let's say we have a camshaft offering 0.333 inches of lobe lift working with a 1.5:1 rocker ratio. Multiplying lobe lift time by 1.5 gives us a theoretical valve lift of 0.500. By increasing the ratio to 1.6:1, this bumps the valve lift up to 0.533 inches. Generally speaking, a 0.1:1 ratio jump kicks the valve lift up by around 0.030 inches. Especially if the camshaft is already installed in the engine, increasing rocker ratio is a quick and easy way to add additional valve lift. Several

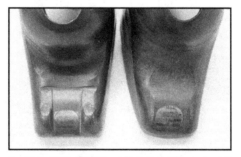

In the mid 1980s, all production small blocks began using "guided" rocker arms that use two small guides that straddle the valve tip to locate the rocker arm tip. Guided or "rail" rockers should not be used with guideplates since this could create a binding situation that would break parts.

other things worth investigating also occur when you increase rocker ratio.

Increasing the rocker ratio does not change the opening and closing point of the cam lobe. However, once the rocker arm begins its valve lift curve, the increased ratio opens the valve sooner in relationship to piston position. If you remember our discussion in Chapter 2 on cam basics, a more aggressive cam lobe (like a big roller cam versus a mild flat tappet for example) creates more

duration. This is evidenced by an increase in duration at 0.200-inch valve lift. An increased rocker ratio also creates a smaller version of this same effect with its more aggressive lift curve. Again, the opening and closing points don't change, but the valve lift curve does change.

Common sense also dictates that the valve must be subjected to a much quicker opening (and closing) rate any time the rocker ratio is increased. In our previous chapter discussion on valvesprings, it's obvious that notching up the rocker ratio means that the entire valve assembly accelerates up and back down from maximum lift much more quickly than it did with its lower rocker ratio. This means that the valvespring must be able to now control these additional acceleration rates. This is especially important on the closing side, since the idea is to prevent the valve from bouncing off the seat. As we mentioned before, this is often where the onset of valve "float" occurs.

Increasing rocker ratio means you have more to pay attention to than just measuring for coil bind, retainer-to-seal, and valve-to-piston clearance. All of these checks are important, but changing ratio also means that a valvespring fully capable of controlling the valve at 6,500 rpm with a 1.5:1 rocker ratio may succumb to valve float with a 1.6:1 ratio long before 6,500 rpm. This depends upon the

Budget rocker studs may look attractive, but our testing has shown that the upper portion can exhibit as much as 0.020 to 0.030 inches of lateral runout! Testing of ARP's centerless-ground studs reveals a total indicated runout of around 0.003 inches. Which rocker stud would you use?

Stock small-block studs are 3/8-inch (right), but if you are planning on using a mechanical roller cam with high spring pressures, a 7/16-inch stud (left) is probably a better idea.

Guideplates are used not only to maintain the pushrod position, but also to accurately locate the rocker tip over the valve stem tip. Ensure proper rocker arm tip location over the valve before torquing the rocker stud in place. This may require slight mods to the guideplate stud hole.

quality of the valvespring, as we discussed in Chapter 5. The final word here is that bumping the rocker ratio may not require any significant changes, or in cases where you're jumping to a much larger ratio like 1.7:1, the valvetrain may need a dramatic overhaul.

Studs and Guideplates

For the first 25 or 30 years, stock small-block Chevy heads used simple, 3/8-inch pressed-in studs that did an adequate job of offering a rigid pivot point for the rocker arm. But as performance applications, engine speed, and valvespring pressures continued to

increase, the aftermarket, and later the factory, converted to screw-in studs. If you really wanted to increase stud strength, many opted to go to 7/16-inch studs, which automatically required a different rocker arm to accommodate the larger stud. For many enthusiasts, this is as far as they've ever taken the thought process concerning rocker studs. But it turns out that the story goes far deeper.

real estate, which makes paying attention to details like the clearance between the valvespring retainer and the rocker arm a critical dimension. In one particular case, we noticed that we had a clearance problem between two rocker arms and their respective valvespring retainers.

It seemed odd that only two valves would have this problem. Subsequent investigation revealed that several rocker

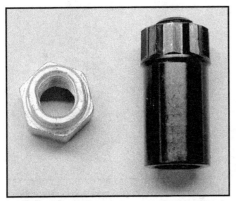

Poly locks (right) are included with all roller rocker kits, but if you are still using stamped rockers, go ahead and invest in a set of poly locks as well. The stock pinch-type locking nuts (left) really tear up studs, yet still loosen up over time.

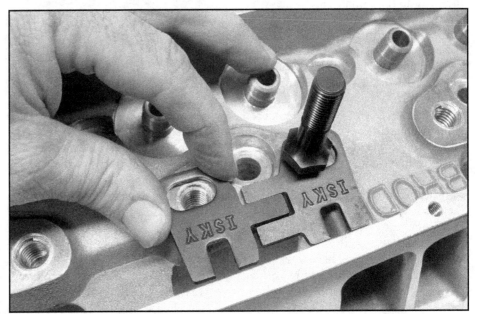

Isky makes adjustable guideplates that allow the engine builder to precisely locate the rocker tip over the valve. Then the guideplates can be marked and welded together to make the job permanent.

As engine builders continue to push the small-block Chevy envelope, larger valvesprings and heavy-duty roller rockers have begun to squeeze the available

studs, including the two with the clearance problem, exhibited significant lateral runout, what machinists call total indicated runout (TIR). When we measured these two particular studs, we discovered a total TIR of more than 0.025 inches! At first, we suspected the studs were bent, but when almost all studs showed significant runout, we realized that even new studs from this budget source were machined that way from the factory! We next measured a set of ARP small-block studs and found all were within 0.003 inches.

What we learned is that ARP machines their studs using a centerless grinding technique in which the studs are machined between two counterrotating grinding wheels. This ensures a much more accurate stud as opposed to lathe cutting, which is based on an assumed centerline with a tolerance stack-up that can create eccentricity. In our case, the two rocker studs that had a clearance problem just happened to place their eccentricity directly in line with the valve, reducing the distance between the valve and stud. If you think about this, any eccentricity causes all kinds of problems for accurate valvetrain operation. This can move the rocker arm tip so that it is no longer directly in line with the valve, or move the rocker tip in or out relative to the valve. This changes the effective rocker ratio. So with a cheap rocker stud, you could easily end up with an engine running with multiple rocker ratios! This is hardly conducive to making power!

This is not necessarily an exclusive endorsement of ARP products, although we've found very few examples of problems with any fasteners from that company. While other reputable fastener companies are certainly out there, we've found that we don't have to worry about the quality of ARP's products. In addition, ARP backs their pieces with significant engineering, sometimes difficult to obtain from other fastener companies.

Along with using a quality stud, we're also big proponents of using some type of poly-lock type stud-nut as opposed to a factory-style lockingnut. This is a requirement with roller rockers, but this discussion is aimed more at stock-stamped rocker use. All new stamped rockers come with those factory-type pinch nuts. Take our advice and throw them away

The iron Vortec head is a very popular budget-based cylinder head for street engines. When using 1.6:1 rocker arms with the Vortec head, the pushrod hole must be elongated to prevent binding the pushrod against the head. This photo is of a COMP Cams tool used on an earlier small-block head, but the idea is the same.

There are two basic types of pushrod guideplates—the more common flat style (right) and the stepped version (left).

and invest in a set of poly locks. If you know an engine builder, he probably has a pile of poly locks in his valvetrain bin. The problem with pinch nuts is that they

tear up the threads on the stud very quickly and also only work the best if you never adjust them once installed. Every time you move them, they lose a

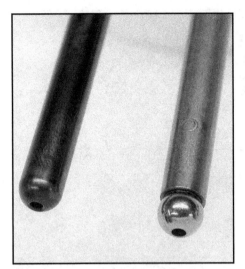

Stock pushrods generally employ welded ball-ends that can fail. For virtually any performance application in which you are running good springs and roller rockers, the smart move is to invest in a proper-length performance pushrod.

little of their locking force. Have you ever wondered why the older 1960s mechanical cams seemed like they needed constant adjustment? It's our opinion that these cheap locking nuts are the main reason for the necessity of constant valve lash maintenance.

Guideplates were a performance aftermarket invention designed to accurately locate the pushrod in high-RPM applications. Originally, stock small-block iron heads employed slots cut into the head to guide the pushrod. This is important because the stamped rocker/ball stud arrangement would allow the rocker to slide sideways unless the designers employed some type of guide system. With the advent of aluminum cylinder heads, the soft alloy could be easily eroded by a steel pushrod, so guideplates became required.

The most important point to drive home about aftermarket pushrod guideplates is that these are hardened steel plates to prevent them from undue wear when performing their intended function. This demands that the pushrods also be hardened. We get into pushrods later in this chapter, but do not make the mistake of using stock, non-hardened pushrods with hardened guideplates, or you will end up with a pile of metals shavings that will find

its way throughout your engine and into the bearings. That can ruin your whole day!

But just adding hardened pushrods and guideplates is not the end of the story. Unfortunately, not all guideplates position the pushrod where you want it. Most guideplates offer slightly larger holes that allow the engine builder to adjust their position relative to the valves, but often the engine builder may need more. In the past, builders often resorted to cutting these hardened plates and then re-welding them in the proper position. Isky took notice of this practice and now sells adjustable pushrod guideplates for the small-block Chevy that allow you to accurately position the rocker tip over the valve stem tip with the guideplate. Once the position is set, then you can permanently weld the two halves of the guideplate together.

Pushrods

On the surface, it appears that as an internal combustion engine component, life doesn't get much simpler for pushrods. The part itself moves, but it has no moving parts. It merely connects the lifter to the rocker arm while also transporting oil to the rocker through its hollow center. But when it comes to performance small-block Chevys, it seems that nothing is very simple. As it turns out, the pushrod is a critical component in the small-block valvetrain. It all comes down to durability and strength.

If you've ever watched a track and field event like at the Olympics, the pole vault is an interesting event from an engineering perspective. The vaulter uses a fiberglass pole designed to bend in the center, which lofts the athlete over the horizontal bar. While this works well for Olympic decathlon contestants, that same situation with a pushrod engine can be counter-productive to performance. As the small-block has continued to increase in engine speed in search of greater horsepower levels, the loads on pushrods have steadily risen with higher spring loads and more aggressive rocker ratios. Add in more RPM, and that stock 5/16-inch pushrod is stressed beyond its limits.

When that happens, the pushrod bends. More often, this is a temporary bending effort. Acceleration rates decrease as the lifter approaches the nose of the lobe, and the pushrod then straightens, just like a vaulter's pole. This imparts additional acceleration and lift on the rocker arm and valve at a position where acceleration is not desirable. This can result in coil bind, or possibly valve-to-piston contact, which can often result in a grenaded engine—not good.

This is especially prevalent in engines that spin well in excess of 7,000 or 8,000 rpm, but in certain situations this can occur even in engines around 6,000 rpm. The best way to counteract this situation is to employ much stronger pushrods that minimize this deflection. All the major cam companies offer high-strength pushrods, generally

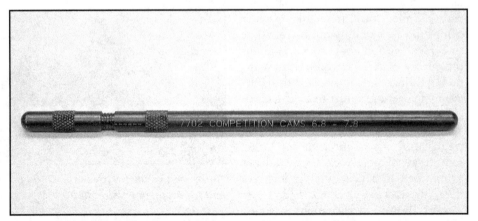

In our experience, COMP Cams makes the best pushrod-length checking tool because it uses a vernier caliper-like scale that helps you determine the pushrod length. COMP and Crane both offer performance pushrods in 0.050-inch lengths, which make ordering custom pushrods easy.

made of seamless, 0.080-inch wall thickness tubing with pressed-in ends. While these stronger pushrods do weigh more than stock units, this is one place where the additional weight is considered acceptable because of the positive effects of reduced bending. Several cam companies make adjustable-length checking pushrods to allow you to properly set the pushrod length. This procedure is covered in Chapter 9.

Lifters

As we've reviewed in the cam basics chapter, four types of lifters are used in a small-block Chevy. For flat tappet lifters, both hydraulic and mechanical styles are used. For roller lifters, the same hydraulic and mechanical styles are also used. Let's begin with the flat tappet design.

The small-block Chevy has retained the stock 0.842-inch tappet diameter since the very first small-block Chevy engine made noise in 1955. Amazingly, you could take a stock small-block lifter out of an original 265-ci small-block and use it in a late-model small-block even today. While referred to as a flat tappet, the name belies its actual construction. Each flat tappet lifter is actually ground with a slight crown to its face. This gives the lifter face a curvature that helps create a spin motion required of all lifters. This spin motion helps the lifter survive its first few minutes of life in a new engine while it establishes its wear pattern. Once properly broken in, the lifter continues to spin slightly during engine operation to help maintain a uniform contact area with the cam lobe.

A "flat" cam lobe is most often blamed on poor material quality or heat treat, but usually a flat cam lobe occurs due to improper cam break-in procedures. The details of this procedure are covered in Chapter 9. It's also worth mentioning here that flat tappets should always be kept paired with their respective cam lobes if the cam is removed from the engine, and used lifters should never be used on a new cam.

Mechanical flat tappets are the simplest of all the lifter designs. The lifter is literally solid with machining accomplished to transfer oil from the

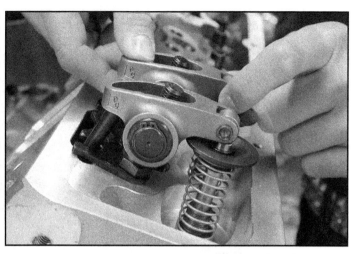

The best way to check pushrod length is to set up the specific valve with a lightweight checking spring and use an adjustable-length pushrod to establish the proper length. Using these checking-pushrods with big springs quickly bends the checking tool.

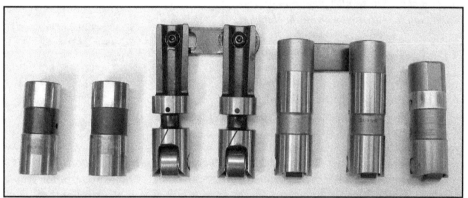

Lifters come in several variations. On the far left is a mechanical flat tappet, next is a flat tappet hydraulic lifter, next is an aftermarket mechanical roller tappet, followed by an aftermarket hydraulic roller, and finally on the far right is a factory hydraulic roller follower.

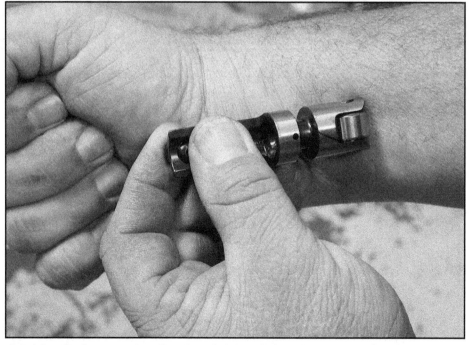

A quick test of a tappet's rollers is to lightly pull the roller across your inner forearm, where the skin is very sensitive. If you feel any resistance to movement, there could be problems with the roller bearings.

Most late-model performance pushrods are made of heat-treated 4130 chromemoy steel with a wall thickness of either 0.065 or 0.080 inches. These stiff pushrods prevent deflection and improve valvetrain stability.

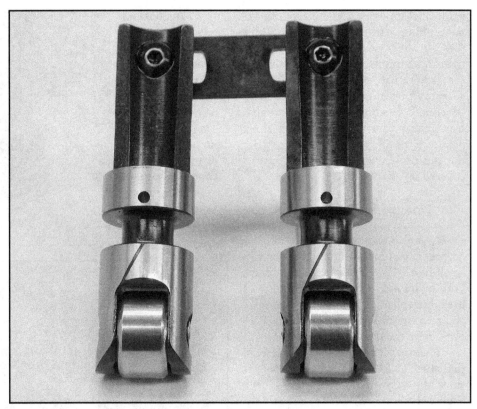

lifter galley up through the pushrod. The solid lifter requires a certain amount of clearance, or lash, in the entire valvetrain system for each lifter in order to compensate for physical growth in the engine as it transitions from cold to normal engine operating temperature. This lash is generally between 0.010 and 0.030 inches and specified by the cam manufacturer. Lash is most often spec'd as "hot," meaning that it should be

The big concern with roller tappets is ensuring adequate lubrication to the rollers. COMP Cams' Xtreme roller lifter employs a groove that directs lube to the rollers. Crane claims that all its roller rockers employ a similar internal lube channel which is just as effective but just not visible.

LIFTER PUMP-UP

Hydraulic lifters use a certain amount of preload employed to accommodate changes in valvetrain expansion due to heat. The most commonly used factory specification calls for 1-1/2 turns down on the rocker arm adjusting nut once all clearance has been removed. This equates to depressing the piston in the lifter roughly 0.060 inches, which is quite a bit of preload.

The problem with this specification is that in a high-RPM situation the valvespring may lose control of the valve, especially as it approaches its seat, where the valve bounces. This creates a clearance in the valvetrain on that particular lobe. When this occurs, engine oil pressure pushes the hydraulic piston

upward to compensate for this clearance. Once this occurs, the valve is now held off its seat, not sealing, which kills power, creates a rough-running engine, and creates what's been termed lifter pump-up.

Several versions of anti-pump-up lifters are sold through various cam companies, but the real key to help prevent lifter pump-up is both simple and effective. Ideally, properly applied valvesprings with more pressure or a lighter valvetrain help reduce valve bounce and the onset of valve float. But short of that, a much tighter tolerance on lifter pre-load also helps delay lifter pump-up.

The generally accepted performance preload figure is closer to a 1/2

turn of preload on the lifter, which on a 3/8-inch rocker stud with 24 threads per inch equals roughly 0.020 inches of piston preload. Some aftermarket cam companies, like COMP Cams, offer a Pro Magnum lifter designed to operate at a much tighter 0.002- to 0.004-inch preload that virtually eliminates the possibility of lifter pump-up. Part of the reason for this tight tolerance is a much stronger and heavier retainer clip used at the top of the lifter to retain the internal piston. With a much tighter preload, it's probable for the lifter piston to contact the clip, and this heavier piece prevents the lifter from coming apart. This happens with more standard lifters with a very tight preload.

All small-block Chevys use a stock lifter diameter of 0.842 inches (left). Since flat tappet lifters are velocity-limited by the lifter diameter, some enterprising engine builders step up to larger Ford 0.875-inch or Mopar 0.904-inch lifters (right). A larger tappet diameter is only worthwhile when combined with a lobe designed to take advantage of the larger lifter diameter.

The factory hydraulic roller cam system uses eight cast tie-bars that slip over a pair of lifters and are then retained by the eight-legged spring steel "spider" bolted to the lifter valley in the block. Aftermarket roller tappets use a simple, free-standing tie-bar system that works well.

checked only after the engine has achieved normal operating temperature. Generally, this lash should be checked periodically. The last production small-block Chevy to use solid lifters was the 1970 Z/28 LT1 engine. A quick and easy way to set lash is covered in Chapter 9.

Hydraulic flat tappets are designed to eliminate the need for periodic lash adjustment by using a small piston inside the lifter body supported by a small volume of oil in a chamber underneath the piston. Engine oil under pressure is supplied in this chamber and automatically compensates for growth in the valvetrain due to temperature changes. This is accomplished by depressing (or preloading) the piston in the lifter chamber a specified amount.

Hydraulic flat tappets are by far the most popular for street performance applications because of their inexpensive price and low maintenance requirements. The only limitation to the hydraulic flat tappet design is that the engine builder can only increase valvespring pressure up to the point at which the spring pressure eventually pushes the oil out of the lifter, eliminating much of the cam lift and killing power. Increasing engine oil pressure can compensate slightly for this situation, but the best fix at that point is to swap to a mechanical cam instead. High spring pressures are intended for high

engine speeds, which means little need for the low-maintenance advantages of a hydraulic tappet anyway.

Mechanical roller tappets were first designed for diesel engines used in the

very early 1900s. Later, they were used mainly in ultra-high-end race engines and were very expensive. Like many race-only parts, these roller tappets eventually found their way to the street,

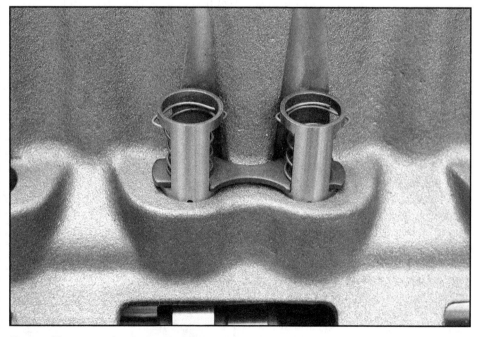

Crane offers a mechanical roller tappet design that employs a spring-loaded horizontal tie-bar. When swapping cams, first unload the load from the valvesprings. The springs push the lifter up, allowing the cam to be changed without removing the intake manifold.

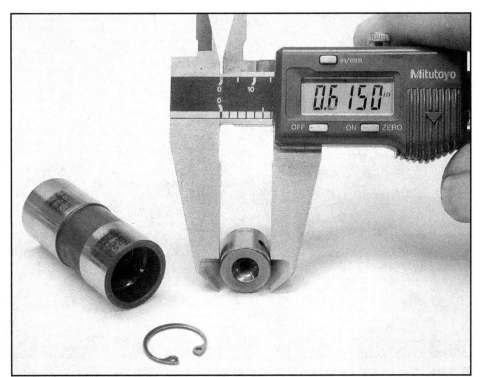

When searching for a high-quality performance hydraulic flat tappet, look for a lifter with the snap ring style retainer, as opposed to the thinner square-style clips used in standard lifters.

Stock flat-tappet hydraulic lifters employ a 0.615-inch internal piston that "floats" on an internal cushion of oil that automatically compensates for dimensional changes in the engine based on temperature.

but they were still very pricey. It wasn't until Chevrolet began to use hydraulic roller tappets in production engines that the trickle-down effect became more of a torrent. By the mid 1990s, performance hydraulic roller cams had become commonplace and accepted by an increasing number of enthusiasts. While the lifter diameters remained the same at 0.842 inches, production hydraulic roller engines use a specific lifter retaining system that was difficult to retrofit back to earlier non-hydraulic roller tappet small-blocks.

This created a demand for retrofit hydraulic roller tappets that now all the major cam companies offer. These lifters use the more traditional aftermarket tie-bar design to connect two roller tappets together so that the roller remains aligned with the cam lobe. The factory design uses cast bars that slip over the taller lifter body. These tie bars are retained by a large, spring-loaded device referred to as a spider because of its eight legs bolted to the lifter valley with three bolts. This means that factory hydraulic roller tappets cannot be used in an earlier, non-roller cam block. Most cam com-

panies offer a complete retrofit kit to accompany an aftermarket roller cam for these earlier engine blocks.

The top of the line for roller lifters has to be the mechanical roller lifter. While completely streetable, these applications do become expensive, although the price difference between a complete mechanical roller lifter cam and valvetrain and a hydraulic roller cam assembly is not that great. The

biggest hurdle for mechanical roller cams seems to be that they have a reputation for requiring almost constant lash adjustment. This couldn't be further from the truth. The reality is that if the valvetrain is set up properly and the components experience minimal wear, the lash really shouldn't change unless problems arise.

Where there have been cases of failures, this most often occurs in those cases where overly-enthusiastic street engine builders spec a race-only mechanical roller cam for a street engine in search of ultimate power. Generally, drag-race-ori-

Small-block Chevy intake ports are often limited by the pushrod placement. By using offset lifters, like the lifter on the left, this allows more room for the pushrod to clear the wider intake port.

VARIABLE DURATION LIFTERS

Rhoades Lifters are generally given credit for building the first commercially available variable duration lifters. The idea was to create a "lost motion device" where at low engine speed, the lifter uses a wider clearance between the hydraulic lifter's internal piston and its cylinder. This creates an increased bleed rate–the rate at which the lifter exchanges the oil in the chamber below the hydraulic tappet's piston. This increased bleed rate creates a certain situation. When the lobe begins to push up on the lifter, oil is squeezed out from below the lifter piston so that the lifter body begins its upward movement with lobe lift, but the lifter piston (connected to the pushrod) does not initially move. Eventually, as the lobe increases velocity, the lifter creates lift.

At first, this would seem to be hardly desirable. But this increased bleed rate relies on low engine speed to accomplish this task. So, for an engine with long duration specs and considerable overlap, using a bleed-down lifter generally increases idle quality and low-speed torque while, at least theoretically, not sacrificing any top-end power. This occurs because as engine speed increases, oil has less time to bleed out of the lifter. The idea is that at peak engine speeds, the lifter follows the lobe exactly and the engine can make maximum power. This concept operates on the principle of bleed rate, which can't be changed once the lifter is machined. But bleed rate can be affected by both oil temperature and viscosity. Hot or thinner oil bleeds more quickly, while cold, thicker oil bleeds more slowly.

Overall, this concept does work, and it is possible to improve idle quality

by 1 to 3 inches of manifold vacuum depending upon the lifter's bleed rate. In addition, these so-called "variable duration" lifters do tend to increase mid-range torque. However, there is also the potential for lost peak power as well since the bleed down rate is rarely exact or consistent. While these bleed-down rate lifters do improve low-speed torque, they generally are more of a crutch applied to street engines that suffer from excessive-duration camshafts for the application. In these situations, bleed-down lifters can be used to band-aid the problem, but in almost all cases, a smaller cam with shorter duration specs is the best solution.

In the world of racing flat tappet lifters faced with high spring pressure loads, COMP has come up with a 0.875-inch diameter lifter with a special 0.012-inch hole drilled in the center of the face to apply direct lubrication to the lifter-lobe interface. Plus, evidence suggests that this oil contributes to a slight smoothing of the lifter acceleration profile.

ented camshafts are designed with ultra-aggressive profiles that tend to be extremely hard on the valvetrain. This requires the racer to perform lash adjustments much more often. Eventually, these race cams, if used on the street, cause valvetrain problems (usually spring failures) because of the aggressive nature of the lobe profiles. This may be part of the reason for the street set believing that all mechanical cams require constant lash adjustment.

We've now covered most of the cam and valvetrain components on an individual basis to give you an overview of how these components inter-relate. While each piece should be taken on its own merits, hopefully, you can begin to see how all these parts rely on the rest of the system to operate properly. Like the links of the proverbial chain, the valvetrain is only as effective as its weakest component. But before we wrap up this discussion, let's move on to the next chapter, which deals with cam drives.

CAM DRIVES

Stock cam drive systems (right) most often use a link belt type chain, which is great for durability, but creates more heat at high engine speeds compared to a true roller type chain design (left).

The task is simple enough. The camshaft is designed to spin at exactly half of engine speed. Connect the crankshaft to the camshaft with an accurate mechanism that reliably spins the cam and you have the cam drive. Engineers of the original small-block Chevy decided on a chain drive for the Mouse motor, and in multiple versions it has performed admirably. Of course, hot rodders can never leave anything alone, and over the years have devised several variations on the cam drive theme. This chapter looks at most of these ideas and investigates the advantages and disadvantages of each.

As we mentioned, the original small-block used a pair of cogged wheels and a chain to drive the cam. The small-block relies on a crank gear with exactly half the number of teeth on the crank as on the cam. This spins the crankshaft at exactly half engine speed. The stock Chevy crank gear counted a mere 18 teeth on the crank gear with 36 teeth on the cam gear using a link belt type chain to connect the two. The Achilles heel of this system focused on the aluminum cam gear that employed a nylon covering over the teeth to prevent wear and reduce noise. The problem was that eventually, the nylon succumbed to heat

and wear, which caused the plastic teeth to crack, allowing the cam to easily slip a tooth or two.

Chevy redesigned the cam drive in 1967, going to a steel gear with excellent durability. But this also spurred the aftermarket to create its own versions. Hot rodders like Pete Jackson decided to eliminate the chain drive altogether, opting for a gear-drive system using an idler gear to spin the cam in the proper direction. The spur gear system, while accurate, created its own distinctive

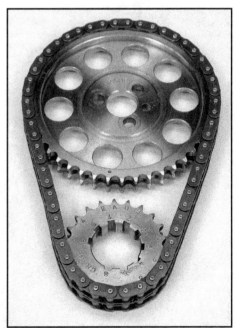

This Crane billet gears and double roller chain are both incredibly strong and very accurate. This would be a great choice for a hot street engine or even a mild race engine for good performance and durability for the price.

whine, much like a Gilmer cogged belt drive on a 6–71 supercharger. While some enthusiasts still think this is cool, the constant whine for a street engine never caught on and few of them exist on the street or the drag strip. Another negative consideration was that many racers believe that a direct connection between the firing pulses absorbed by the crankshaft and the camshaft is detrimental to smooth camshaft operation, while a chain promised to isolate these firing pulses somewhat.

Along with much stronger single-roller and double-roller chain designs, racers also wanted an adjustable drive mechanism that would allow the builder to easily change cam phasing relative to cylinder Number One and top dead center (TDC). This phasing requires precise location of the cam since a mere 0.005-inch movement of the camshaft changes the cam phasing one degree. In the early days, machinists created offset bushings that could advance or retard the camshaft between 1 and 8 degrees. You didn't need to create more than 8 degrees of freedom since on the original small-block camshaft gear each tooth represented 10 degrees of camshaft movement since the stock wheel had 36 teeth. Since then, manufacturers have added more teeth for more strength, reducing the degree spread even further. For example, a 44–tooth cam gear offers a mere 8.18 degrees between teeth. This is another reason why missing the prop-

This Cloyes Hex-Adjust system uses a small bushing as an eccentric – loosen the cam gear bolts and move the cam drive to advance or retard the cam.

er location by even one tooth on the cam gear makes such a drastic difference in cam phasing.

Cloyes is probably the most well-known of the companies offering adjustable street cam drive sets. Cloyes' most recent innovation is an adjustable upper gear that locks in place with a six-bolt retaining system. The gear allows the engine builder to quickly loosen these six bolts and advance or retard the cam-timing indicator. This allows rapid and accurate changes to the cam timing without

Most quality cam drive systems now employ a multi-key crank gear. This Crane Pro-Series steel billet CNC-machined piece allows nine different keyways with up to 8 degrees of advance or retard in 2-degree increments.

having to remove the cam gear from the engine. This still requires the engine builder to properly degree the cam the first time to ensure that cam phasing is correct, but subsequent changes can be made without having to degree the cam again. Chapter 9 includes the step-by-step procedure for degreeing a cam.

While dual-row, full roller cam drives have become the drive mechanism of choice for most street performance engines, the search continued for a more accurate means of spinning the cam. Dan Jesel is generally credited with creating

THE DELAY

Belt drives are the hot ticket for the stronger engine buildups, especially for high-RPM engines. According to engine builders we've spoken to, while belt drives do work well, it seems they tend to retard under load. If you merely free-rev the engine with a timing light connected to the engine, the timing is where it's set. However, a couple of enterprising engine builders rigged a self-powered timing light to their engine while it was under a

wide-open-throttle load and simultaneously videotaped the numbers created by the light on the damper. Under load, they learned that the belt drive retarded the timing by two degrees.

This is really not a huge issue since A-B testing of a timing curve merely means that the timing the engine requires is static set slightly higher than what the engine really needs. Therefore, the engine tuner sets the timing at 34

degrees BTDC while the engine actually creates best power with 32 degrees. We take the time to point this out only to show that not everything happens the way we think it does, even with race-quality, high-end parts. It's more about maintaining a healthy dose of skepticism around all high-RPM engine functions while searching for that elusive extra power.

This is Crane's billet steel cam drive. Note the brass thrust washer used to prevent block wear from the harder steel gear. The Crane uses a three-position crank gear to select "straight up" timing, 4-degree advance, or 4-degree retard.

This is a gear drive system that uses gears instead of a chain. The two idler gears reverse the direction of rotation so the cam spins in the proper direction. Otherwise, you would need a reverse-rotation camshaft.

the first belt drive system for the small-block Chevy. The idea was to further isolate crankshaft pulsations by using a cogged rubber belt that could maintain timing accuracy even at ultra-high engine speeds. While some race-engine builders were skeptical at first, it didn't take long before the belt drive system became a staple on virtually every drag and road race small-block built today.

One beauty of the belt drive system is that it does not require oil lubrication, which means it can operate without a timing cover. This places the system out where it can be quickly accessed for maintenance or cam phasing changes. The down side to the belt drive system is that most systems are much more expensive, roughly $800 compared to around $100 to $150 for their chain drive cousins. For a street engine, debris finding its way in between the timing belt and gears on those open-front systems is also a concern, although the chance of this is rare. It appears that those who are willing to spend the money also want to display their high-tech hardware rather than keep it shrouded under some type of cover.

Practical Applications

While trick parts are always in the limelight of any camshaft and valvetrain selection process, the key to a durable and successful valvetrain depends more on the proper application, usage, and installation of the parts than whether these pieces fall into the category of Most Romantic. For example, the most expensive Jesel belt drive system bolted in place does little to enhance performance if the cam is retarded 6 degrees because of an installation error. So before you get all caught up in the romance of exotic parts, it's worth the effort to go over some practical application notes that help the engine builder avoid some common pitfalls.

One of the first things you can check to avoid problems is to ensure that the camshaft actually slides completely in the new cam bearings you just installed. Often, entry-level engine builders wait to install the camshaft until after the entire rotating assembly is in place. Often, a new set of cam bearings can be slightly

The inherent problem with gears is that the crank does not spin smoothly when the engine is running. The crank is constantly accelerating and decelerating, and these pulses are directly input into the cam from the crank. That's why the belt drives have become so popular with race engine builders— the elastic belt insulates the cam from these pulsations.

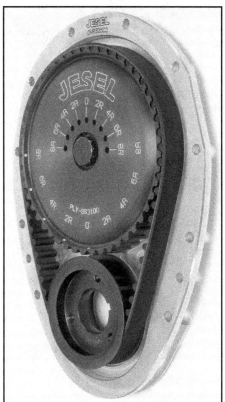

This is COMP Cams' belt drive. They actually offer two versions, one with the idler pulley and another without. According to the engine builders we talked to, the only problem with the idle is the speed required to spin because of the small pulley size.

Jesel was the originator of the belt drive almost 20 years ago. This company has probably generated more research on this component than any other company.

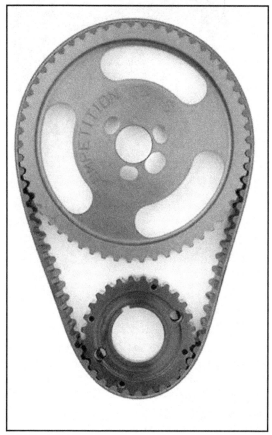

undersized after installation, which prevents you from slipping the camshaft into the block. By checking camshaft fit before final assembly, you can easily avoid this pitfall by installing one or two new cam bearings.

It's always a good idea to pre-assemble your engine at least once to check clearances and gauge how well the systems fit in the engine.

This is also an opportune time to check the cam drive system alignment. First off, ensure that the crank gear is fully seated on the crank nose with the tapered end of the crank gear toward the rear of the engine. Assuming we're using a chain drive system, once the crank gear is in place, slip the cam gear and chain in place over the cam's drive pin. Bolt the cam drive gear onto the cam and then use a straightedge to ensure that both gears are aligned. This does not have to be a perfect marriage, but it does happen that the cam gear can be slightly offset to the rear of the engine. If this occurs, you may want to employ a bronze thrust washer behind the cam gear to protect the block from wear. This is a virtual necessity if you are using a billet steel gear that could easily generate significant wear on the face of the soft cast-iron or aluminum block.

Flat tappet camshafts are machined so that alternating cam lobes force the cam both fore and aft. This negates the typical rearward thrust created by the camshaft. Keep in mind, however, that the helical cut on the distributor drive gear tends to impart forward thrust on the camshaft. Chevrolet addressed this dilemma with its hydraulic roller cammed engines by creating a step on the front of the cam nose that is nested inside a thrust plate that bolts to the front of the block. This became standard on most small-blocks built after 1988. To use a roller cam in an earlier small-block, the best solution is to employ a cam button.

Several styles of cam buttons including aluminum, nylon, and a rollerized bearing style are available. Simplicity is the key to the nylon or aluminum styles,

but they suffer from significant wear that gradually allows the cam to move forward, retarding ignition timing by as much as 15 degrees. The best solution is the roller style cam button. Not only does it not suffer from wear, but it also allows the engine builder to easily establish the proper camshaft endplay (0.005 to 0.010 inches).

If you are using either a hydraulic or mechanical roller camshaft and combining that with an engine-driven fuel pump, you also need a custom fuel pump pushrod compatible with the steel lobes on the roller cam. COMP Cams, for example, offers two different styles of fuel pump pushrods—bronze-tipped and composite tip rods. Either work well, but you need to check for wear after a few thousand miles to ensure durability.

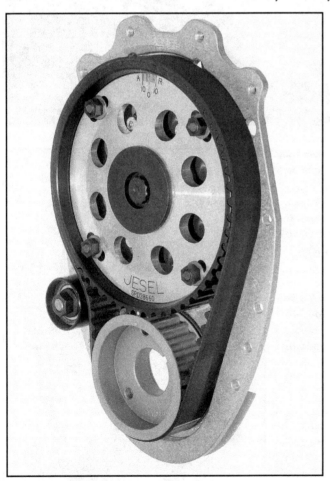

Tension is critical with belt-drive systems. The problem is that designing a drive without a tensioner means building a custom-length belt that adds cost. Some versions offer an idler pulley to use existing length belts. The downside is that the small diameter tensioner must spin very fast to keep up with the cam speed. This means the bearings have a limited life span.

If you are looking for the ultimate in how to drive the cam, you can't go wrong with a Jesel belt drive. The price is much steeper than chain drives, but the payoff is cam accuracy.

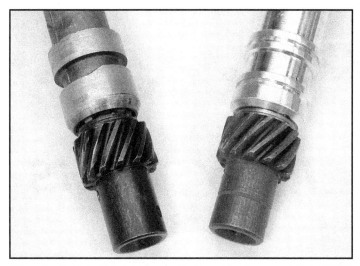

The stock GM distributor shaft diameter is an oddball 0.491 inches. When MSD began building distributors, they upped the dimension to a more standard 0.500 inches. This means that stock GM gears won't interchange on an MSD distributor, and vice versa. This is important when swapping distributors on engines with specialty camshafts.

High-volume and high-pressure oil pumps increase the load required to run through the distributor drive gear on the cam and through the distributor gear itself. As these loads go up, the lifespan of these components decreases. It's almost becoming common knowledge now that excessive oil pressures are usually not necessary.

Oil pressure is an issue that many engine builders overlook when building a stout street engine. Often, the "more is better" routine points them in the direction of a high-volume/high-pressure oil pump when detailing their engine. Since the oil pump is driven off the bottom of the distributor, this means that every ounce of power required to drive the oil pump must come through the distributor gear. These high-volume/high-pressure pumps place an increased load on the cam and distributor gears that can cause accelerated wear. This is especially true if you are using a bronze distributor gear on a steel billet roller camshaft.

Today, most street cam manufacturers are adding a pressed-on iron gear and rear journal to their street roller camshafts that do not require a soft bronze gear. However, it is still possible to create increased wear on even sintered iron gears with a high-volume/high-pressure oil pump. Most, if not all, street-driven small-blocks do not need a high-volume pump nor do they require high pressure. Even the old tried-and-true 10-psi-per-1,000-rpm rule of thumb is slightly higher than it needs to be since we've seen engines that have run with as little as 50 psi of oil pressure on a 500 hp small-block at 6,000 rpm WOT for more than 30 minutes with no appreciable wear problems. Even 60 psi at 6,000 rpm is

COMP Cams now makes a composite distributor drive gear that, while expensive, is compatible with either iron or steel cam gears and is much more durable than any other gear out there.

more than safe and does not create distributor gear wear problems.

Another trick you can employ to improve lubrication on the distributor and cam gears is to file a 0.030-inch slot in the top groove of the distributor body. With the slot located here and the distributor properly timed in the engine, the cam-distributor gear interface gets a direct spray of oil. This oil spray reduces gear temperature while also reducing wear by adding a greater volume of oil between the two gears. The key to this trick is accurately positioning the slot so that it sprays directly on the cam gears. Keep in mind that adjusting ignition timing directly affects the placement of this slot.

The problem with running a soft-bronze gear on a hard billet-steel cam blank, like for a mechanical roller cam, is that the distributor gear is very soft and wears quickly, increasing the potential error in ignition timing.

Conclusion

The mere act of connecting the camshaft to the crank is a pretty straightforward proposition. Whether you subscribe to the latest in small-block art with a Jesel belt drive system, or rely more on the performance-proven roller timing chain system, establishing the optimal relationship between the crank and the cam is nevertheless essential. Put a little thought and effort into this connection and it pays off with a durable engine that makes great power for years to come.

SHAFT ROCKER SYSTEMS

One of the things that made the small-block Chevy so revolutionary in 1955 was its valvetrain. Up until this point, shaft rocker systems were the accepted standard for most production engines of the day. This design was cumbersome, and the small-block dumped that idea in favor of individual rocker studs and an innovative stamped-steel rocker arm that was lighter and much cheaper to build. The idea soon became a production standard for production V8 engines. For performance engines, the stamped rocker soon gave way to the roller rocker while still retaining the stud mount concept.

While individual rockers have many advantages, they also harbor many negative traits that become increasingly apparent as engine speed and valvespring pressures increase as part of the search for more horsepower and torque. Racers and manufacturers have developed several band-aids to cover up these stud-mounted rocker limitations such as rev kits and stud girdles, but the real fix for a solid, reliable, high output, high-RPM performance engine is, ironically, to take a giant leap back with a shaft rocker system.

A shaft rocker system is inherently superior to a rocker stud design, and only a couple major items make that decision difficult. The biggest hurdle to overcome is the price. Shaft rocker systems always cost more than stud-mounted rocker arms. The price differential has softened in the past several years with budget-based "street" rocker shaft systems introduced by Jesel

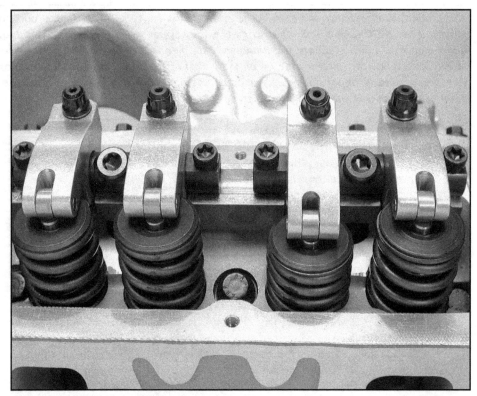

This is the Jesel SS or Street Series shaft rocker system for a 23-degree small-block Chevy outfitted with AirFlow Research aluminum cylinder heads. The Jesel system employs billet steel stands and centerless ground steel alloy rocker shafts bolted to the cylinder head with Torx bolts. This offers much more rigidity than a stand-alone 3/8- or 7/16-inch rocker stud.

that now cost around $800 for a small-block Chevy. Other systems can run $1,000 or more depending upon several variables. The other minor factor has more to do with a slightly more complex installation procedure, but that's a small point when compared to the many advantages that shaft rocker systems offer. In order to understand why shaft rockers are superior, we first have to

look at the basic design limitations of the stud-mounted rocker arm.

Fulcrum Length

The small-block Chevy stud-mounted rocker system employs a set distance between the centerline of the stock rocker stud and the valves. Since the small-block valves are in line, this is a spec for both the intake and exhaust valves. On a given roller rocker, for example, this spec also dictates the distance from the centerline of the roller fulcrum to the centerline of the roller tip. Jesel calls this distance 1.425 inches while T&D references 1.450. As we've seen on rocker arms in Chapter 6, this distance establishes an arc created by the rocker arm tip as it traverses through its lift curve. If you could establish a longer fulcrum arm, either by moving the rocker stud away from the valves or moving the valves to increase the distance to the rocker stud, this would increase the distance of the fulcrum arm and therefore reduce the radius of the arc. Increasing

The key to any shaft rocker system is the increased fulcrum length of a shaft rocker versus a stud-mounted rocker of the same ratio. This is because the shaft-mounted system can be relocated away from the valve to increase this distance. The difference can be as much as 0.070 to 0.150 of an inch increase in fulcrum length and is seen in the longer fulcrum shaft rocker on the left.

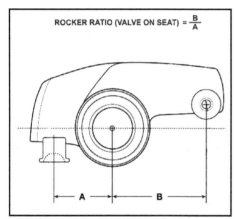

ROCKER RATIO (VALVE ON SEAT) $= \dfrac{B}{A}$

This photo illustrates not only how a rocker arm works by multiplying the distance from the pushrod cup to the centerline of the rocker (A), but also the length of the fulcrum arm (B). For a 1.5:1 rocker arm, B is one and a half times longer than A. (Illustration courtesy of Crane)

this length reduces the distance the rocker arm tip travels across the face of the valve tip. While this may not seem like much, when we get into extremely high valvespring pressures and tall valve lifts, this distance becomes important.

The original small-block Chevy engineers probably never envisioned that racers would take their basic design and cram valve lifts approaching 0.800 inches into their original design. These stratospheric valve lifts create increased rocker arm tip travel across the face of the valve tip. In the days before rocker shafts, or if class rules did not allow shaft systems, racers resorted to moving the rocker stud away from the valve center-

line and using big-block Chevy rocker arms that employed a longer 1.650 inches of fulcrum length. The increased length is the real key to understanding why rocker shaft systems are inherently superior to stud-mounted rockers for the small-block Chevy.

Relocating the rocker stud on any engine is a tremendous amount of work, which only dedicated racers would undertake in search of more power and durability. Back in 1979, Dan and his brother Wayne Jesel realized the disadvantage of the rather short small-block Chevy fulcrum length. They decided the easiest way to overcome this limitation was to increase the length by creating a rocker shaft system. By first building a base that bolts into the stock rocker stud holes and using that base to move the

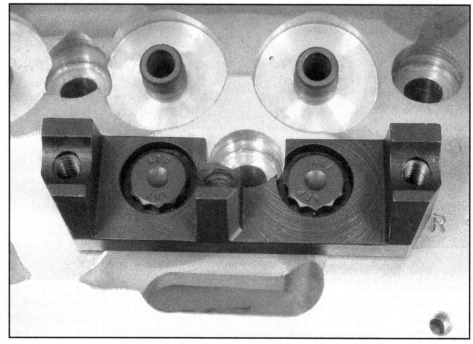

Shaft rocker systems use a pedestal to establish the position of the shafts to the head. Most aftermarket systems use a steel base to act as a solid foundation for the valvetrain.

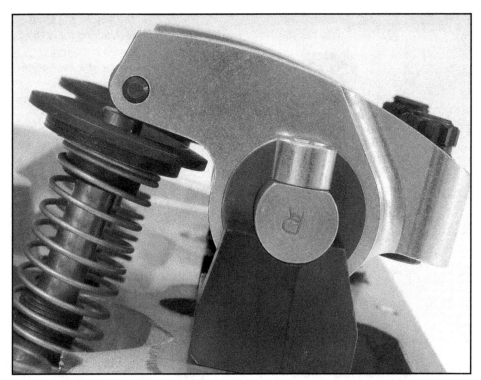

Then the paired rockers and shafts are bolted to the pedestal. One key to a proper installation is to establish the ideal height for the shaft and the rockers. Each company accomplishes this differently, but it relates to the valve stem height. Be careful that you read the directions thoroughly since this is a critical point in the installation.

crum length of 1.515 compared to higher ratios of 1.6 to 1.7:1 ratios using a 1.545-inch fulcrum. For T&D shaft rockers, the relationships are the same, but with fulcrum lengths of 1.53, 1.60, and 1.650. So far, this discussion has been limited to stock type 23-degree valve angle heads. When you get into the 18-degree, 15-degree, and SB2.2 heads, these relationships also change since both the valve angle and the distance between the rocker stud and the valve centerline also change—for the better. Since this book it targeted at the performance street market, we stick with the 23-degree cylinder heads and leave the race head valvetrain discussion for another time.

But shaft rockers are about much more than just fulcrum length. It should be apparent that placing a pair of rocker arms on a large-diameter, common shaft would also create a much more stable platform from which to operate a pair of valves at high RPM. When a rocker arm begins to open the valve, it multiplies the lift from the pushrod by the rocker ratio, which also multiplies the force

centerline of a set of paired rockers on shafts, they could increase the fulcrum length and gain an advantage over the stock stud-mounted rocker system. For example, increasing the stock fulcrum length from 1.425 to 1.545 inches is only 0.120 inches, but this small increase is worth a significant reduction in roller tip movement across the face of the valve tip. While only incremental improvements, multiplied by 16 valves and working against valvespring pressures upwards of 800 pounds at maximum lift, the improvements become readily apparent. Jesel's technical information claims a 1.545 fulcrum length shaft rocker system creates 10 percent reduction in arc sweep.

Jesel, T&D, COMP Cams, Crane, Crower, and others all build shaft rocker systems that would make an excellent high-end street valvetrain, but not all of them build their systems the same way. Jesel and T&D change the fulcrum length, depending on the rocker ratio. For a stock 23-degree small-block Chevy head using stock a 1.5:1 rocker ratio, Jesel, for example, creates a shorter ful-

The next step is to measure for proper pushrod length. This can only be done after the rocker stands are properly positioned. Generally, pushrods should not be ordered until you can at least pre-assemble the engine with all the exact parts you are using. Due to limited pushrod cup adjuster range, the pushrods need to be within 0.050 inches of the ideal length.

from the valvespring that works against the fulcrum point. By design, an individual rocker pinpoints this force on the stud, which creates a bending force. This is why rocker studs have become so important to a performance engine. With a shaft rocker system, the bending force from the valve is distributed over a much broader area of the entire shaft with the result being far less valvetrain deflection with a given valvespring pressure.

Offset Rockers

As horsepower levels continue to escalate, cylinder head ports continue to grow, especially in width. This encroaches on the area reserved for the pushrod, requiring the engine builder and valvetrain designer to come up with offset lifters and rocker arms. Crane, for example, offers both 0.150- and 0.225-inch left and right offset stud-mounted roller rockers, but these rockers virtually demand some kind of stud girdle to help control the additional bending moment created by the offset

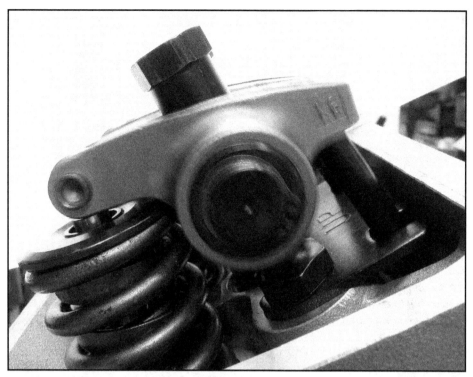

One disadvantage to a stud rocker design is that the rocker arm drops down on the stud when the cam hits the base circle on a mechanical lifter camshaft application. Then, on the opening flank, the lobe slams the entire lifter body up against the poly lock. Besides creating noise, this also sends a shockwave through the valve and spring, especially at higher engine speeds.

ROCKER SWEEPS

It can't be stated enough times how critical valvetrain geometry is to both improved performance and durability. We've mentioned proper pushrod length in the rocker arm chapter, but because of different variables with shaft rocker systems, it bears repeating.

Stencil this statement somewhere around the workbench area where you do your engine assembly. The ideal rocker shaft centerline is established when the contact point of the rocker tip to the valve is in the same place at valve closed as it is at maximum valve lift. This means that the roller tip is located somewhere inboard of the valve centerline with the valve closed. It then sweeps across valve centerline to a position just outboard of centerline at half lift. Then, the rocker tip travels back across the valve

centerline to its starting point inboard of centerline at max valve lift. Then, as the valve goes through the closing side of the lift curve, the rocker tip repeats its motion back across the valve centerline at half lift and then returns to its valve-closed position on the inboard side of the valve centerline.

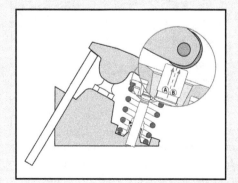

This may sound confusing, but look at the drawing and imagine the roller tip traveling from its valve-closed A position with position B as the point of farthest travel across the face of the valve tip at half lift. The entire rocker arm tip journey could be condensed down to these essential movements: A-B-A-B-A.

In addition to this travelogue, the distance across the face of the valve tip represented by A to B should be the shortest distance possible. This not only reduces travel distance for each of the 16 rocker arms, but also reduces the amount of side loading on the valve, which improves valve guide wear, and perhaps increases power. This also improves valve lift because this has minimized rocker arm ratio changes.

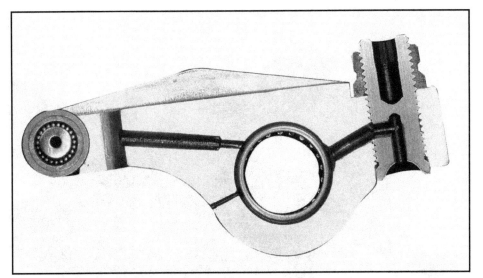

T&D's shaft rockers offer internal oil passages from the adjuster to the rocker shaft and on out to the roller-bearing-equipped rocker tip. T&D also offers an optional 0.040-inch valvespring-oiling hole that sprays oil directly on the valvespring.

pushrod cup in the rocker. This motion is also concentrated on the stud centerline, subjecting the stud to now two different forces.

The better solution is a rocker shaft system that, by design, can more easily accommodate these offset forces. With an offset pushrod cup, the bending force tends to be spread over a much larger area with increased bearing surface compared to the rocker stud design. Both Jesel and T&D offer various offsets for both left- and right-hand rockers. T&D,

for example offers eight offsets from 0.080 to a massive 0.700 inches. Often an offset rocker can be combined with an offset lifter to move the pushrod out of the way of a wide intake port. Many engine builders would rather include as much offset in the rocker as possible since they feel that the tradeoff of increased lifter bore loading from the offset lifter can be excessive, while others are willing to accept increased lifter bore wear in favor of less angle on the pushrod. Lifter offset also reduces the

amount of offset required from the rocker arm. It's always a good idea to operate a pushrod as close to vertical as possible, since pushrod angle also imparts a bending moment into the pushrod that is not an issue in pure vertical motion.

Another reason for offset rockers is to accommodate aftermarket cylinder heads with revised valve placement. The "60/40" arrangement for the small-block Chevy is becoming increasingly popular with cylinder head manufacturers where the intake and exhaust valves are relocated in relation to the cylinder. The intake valve is moved closer to the cylinder bore centerline to unshroud the valve, while the exhaust valve is moved away from the intake to leave room for larger valves. With stud-mounted rocker systems, these slight variations in valve placement can be easily accommodated with pushrod guideplate changes. But with shaft rocker systems, moving the valves in relation to the cylinder bore requires changes to the entire system since the rockers are fixed. This is the reason for the multiple part numbers required for shaft rocker systems and another reason for their added cost.

Practical Applications

Stud-mounted rockers have an additional disadvantage when used with mechanical lifter camshafts in regard to lash. With a stud-mounted rocker, when the cam reaches the base circle, the rocker arm immediately drops down on the stud by the amount of the lash divided by the rocker ratio. So if you have a roller cam using 0.020 inches of lash, the rocker slides down the stud by roughly 0.012 inches, assuming a 1.6:1 rocker ratio. While this isn't much, at high RPM when the cam comes up on the opening flank of the lobe, the entire rocker arm slams up against the poly lock until this clearance is eliminated. This imparts a vibration that Spintron studies have identified as a spike in the valvetrain. While this lash is still present in a rocker shaft system, that clearance does not accelerate the rocker arm vertically. It reduces mass moving to the length of the fulcrum of the rocker arm only as opposed to the mass of the entire rocker arm body.

A shaft rocker can more easily accommodate offset rockers needed to clear wide intake ports. The offset can be easily seen by looking straight down on the rocker to see if the pushrod cup lines up with the roller tip. If it doesn't, the rocker is offset either left or right.

Another small factor has to do with the clearance between the hole in the stud-mounted rocker and the size of the stud. The ideal situation is a snug fit between these two components, but production variables can make this somewhat sloppy. Any clearance here tends to allow the rocker to move around on the stud, which is also not desirable. This has more to do with lower-quality rocker studs than variations with rocker arms, but it's something else that should not be ignored.

As we've seen in the chapter on rocker arms, pushrod length is critical to improving valvetrain efficiency. With a rocker shaft system, pushrod length is especially critical for several reasons. Since the rocker arm pivot point is fixed on a shaft system, the lash adjuster location moves to the pushrod end of the rocker arm. Reducing mass in a rocker arm is especially important at high engine speeds, so adding an adjuster on this end must be done with an eye toward reducing weight. If you add a large adjuster with its required larger area in the rocker, this additional mass must be accelerated up and down with each valve motion curve. Every gram of mass the rocker shaft companies can trim from the rocker sys-

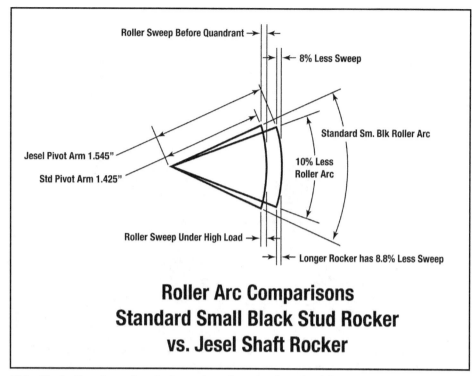

Roller Arc Comparisons Standard Small Black Stud Rocker vs. Jesel Shaft Rocker

This illustration from Jesel shows how lengthening the fulcrum arm decreases the amount of travel of the roller tip across the tip of the valve. The longer fulcrum rocker ends up scribing an 8.8 percent shorter sweep across the valve. That may not sound like much, but it's significant enough to improve valvetrain efficiency.

tem (especially that mass located farther from the pivot point) means less mass for the valvespring to control at high engine speeds

To reduce this mass, the shaft rocker companies limit the range of adjustment in the pushrod cup to around 0.050 to 0.080 inches. The reason for this is to ensure sufficient thread engagement with the adjuster to the rocker arm body. In addition, T&D creates internal oil passages in the rocker arm that direct oil from the pushrod. Oil is fed by an internal passage in the pushrod cup adjuster that flows directly to the bearings in the fulcrum and also out to the roller tip bearings as well. Plus, T&D offers an optional spring oiling passage that directs some of this oil to spray directly on the coil spring for cooling.

Because the rocker arm scribes an arc through its lift curve, several opportunities are available to establish what the true rocker ratio is. Most companies choose to establish the rocker ratio at the point of maximum valve lift, where most engine builders check it. With stud-mounted rocker systems, the cam may in fact be generating the proper valve lift, but because of significant rocker stud and rocker arm deflection, this may end up creating 0.010 to 0.020

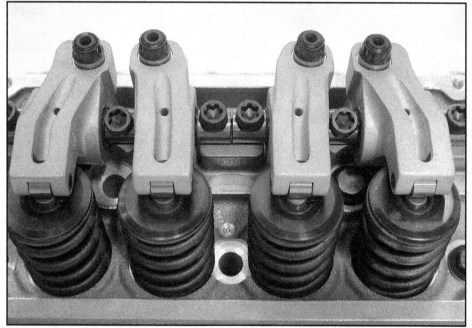

Crower also has a shaft system that employs 17–4PH stainless steel rocker arms with an 11/16-inch shaft for increased stability. Rocker ratios range from 1.5:1 to 1.8:1 for the small-block.

Crane's shaft system looks similar to most of the other systems, but offers a significant difference besides the usual increased fulcrum improvements.

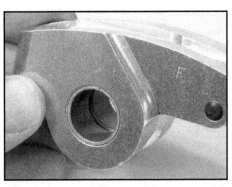

The Crane system uses a special, proprietary bushing material that, according to Crane, is worth some power at higher engine speeds over competitive shaft systems.

Setting lash with a rocker shaft system is accomplished with a simple feeler gauge and setting the clearance with the adjuster located on the pushrod side of the rocker.

inches less maximum valve lift, even with the proper rocker ratio. Shaft rocker systems are subject to much less valvetrain deflection and as a result can recoup much of this lost valve lift, like gaining valve lift without going to a bigger cam or more rocker ratio.

This longer fulcrum length also generates much more clearance for larger-diameter valvesprings. Packaging is already a tight issue with the small-block's rather cramped real estate under the valve cover, so anytime you can gain an advantage of more clearance along with better performance, this is an additional plus.

Crane has recently introduced a new shaft rocker system for the small-block Chevy they claim is worth an additional

20 hp over other shaft type systems. It's based on an innovative bushing design capable of withstanding extreme valvespring pressure abuse. Crane's point is that roller bearings require power to accelerate and decelerate with each valve lift curve. By using this new bushing material (actually, Crane prefers to call this a bearing), Crane claims that this power can be recouped as "lost" horsepower along with reduced heat with lower oil temperatures.

While we have not tested this valvetrain system as yet, discussions with Crane revealed that these horsepower improvements would only be seen on a high-RPM, competition engine where these gains can truly be measured. In other words, your 6,000-rpm street engine would probably not see much, if any, improvement over a competitive shaft system. This brings up an interesting question of how much power resides in a shaft rocker system over a quality stud-mounted roller rocker system. The answer to this question is always predicated with multiple layers of qualifying statements like the standard "it depends upon the application" response. However, it would be safe to say that engines spending more time above 6,000 rpm would be better served than engines that rarely achieve that higher speed. The engine's actual horsepower level also plays into this equation. Ten hp from a 500-hp engine is significant since it's a two percent gain, but 10 horsepower from a 750-hp engine represents barely more than one percent. But

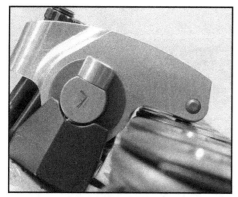

Another advantage to shaft rockers is the increased valvespring clearance gained with the longer fulcrum. Most shaft systems can accommodate springs as large as 1.640 inches.

to hazard a rule of thumb, most of the rocker shaft companies offer a rocker shaft system with the same rocker ratio that should be capable of roughly 10 hp on a 500-plus hp engine.

When you combine the obvious geometry advantages of a shaft rocker system over stud-mounted roller rockers, this alone is probably worth the investment, especially if you're building a stout small-block that plans on seeing some serious RPM. Add the increased durability and possible power increases that can come from these improvements and the only reason you shouldn't invest in a shaft rocker system is if your budget can't stand another hit. In that case, we'd suggest finding the money because these shaft systems are certainly the way to go.

ROLLER TIP TRAVELS

This chart, courtesy of T&D, illustrates the differences in roller tip travel for a valve lift curve of 0.650 inches along with the percentage of improvement for each improvement in fulcrum length. The Difference column expresses the improvement in percentage while the far right Cumulative Difference column indicates the additive affects of going from a stock fulcrum length to each progressively longer fulcrum length.

Rocker (fulcrum length)	Roller Travel 0.650-inch lift (inches)	Difference	Cumulative Difference
1.450 (stock SBC)	0.037	–	–
1.520	0.035	5%	5%
1.600	0.033	6%	10.8%
1.650 (stock BBC)	0.032	4%	13.5%

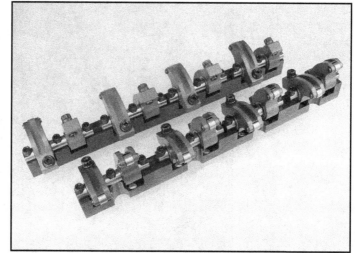

COMP Cams' shaft rocker system also employs an 8620 steel hardened shaft and a 2024 T351 billet aluminum rocker body with 0.040-inch internal oil passages from the pushrod cup, to the shaft and out to the rocker tip.

BASE CIRCLE CHRONICLES

While you might be thinking that we are obsessing over pushrod length in this book, it keeps coming up because it's important. For shaft rocker systems, the adjuster located in the pushrod cup of the rocker has a limited range of adjustability. In the case of T&D rockers, this range is limited also because moving the adjuster too far cuts off the flow of oil from the pushrod!

Since shaft rocker systems are most likely to be used more often on roller cam engines than flat tappet small blocks, it's imperative when measuring pushrod length to make sure to measure both an intake and an exhaust lobe. This is because cam companies often change the base circle radius for an exhaust lobe. If the base circle is smaller than the intake lobe, (which is common) this requires a longer exhaust pushrod than the intake side of the engine. This also requires you to pay close attention to details when assembling the engine since this difference may be minimal. As the cliché says, the devil is in the details.

HOW TO INSTALL AND DEGREE A CAM

The hands-on part of working on a car is always fun. This chapter consists of three parts – the first looks at installing a new performance camshaft, the second details accurately degreeing the camshaft in the engine, and the third part goes over some cylinder head and valvetrain assembly ideas.

It's always a good idea to test-fit the cam in the block long before the rotating assembly is installed. It's not unusual to find that a new cam does not fit in a block with new cam bearings, and with the rotating assembly in the way it's tough to work around those parts.

Bolt It In

We are detailing the installation of a brand new performance flat tappet hydraulic camshaft in an engine on an engine stand. Assembly in a car is exactly the same except that you have to deal with cramped quarters and perhaps have to remove some of the car's sheetmetal to squeeze the cam in through the front.

For our installation, we have a brand new engine that has just been fitted with new cam bearings. Small-block Chevys employ different cam bearings for different positions in the block. The rearmost bearing is installed first, pro-

Using a simple cam handle makes installing a cam much easier, especially when the cam is all lubed up and installed mostly into the engine. A good handle also saves nicks and bumps on the cam bearings.

gressing toward the front. The front bearing is the largest outside diameter with two oil holes instead of just one. Once the bearings are installed, take the time to install the cam before the final assembly procedure. Often, cam bearings get a little tight, which can require changing a bearing in order to make the cam fit. This is much easier when the engine is still apart, rather than discovering that the cam won't fit only after the rotating assembly is installed.

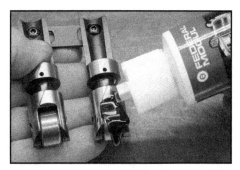

Do not put heavy moly lube on a roller cam lobe. This heavy paste can actually block oil to the lifter and cause a premature failure. Instead, just use that heavy green or red oil available from engine rebuilder sources.

Be careful to match up the mark on the crank gear key-way with its proper mark on the crank tooth to ensure the cam is actually in its correct position. With multi-keyway crank gears now, it's easier than ever to make a mistake.

Clean the new camshaft and lube all the cam lobes with the break-in lubricant supplied by the manufacturer. Use the lube sparingly, since this is only necessary for initial start-up. We like to use a cam installation tool to give us leverage on the cam, especially after it is more than halfway in the engine. Be careful to avoid nicking the cam bearings if at all possible—this is where the tool really helps. If you don't have a cam tool, you can use a length of 5/16-inch threaded rod. Short of that, use the j-hook shaped spare tire hold-down bolt from your 1960s Chevy muscle car.

With the cam in place, turn the crank until the crank gear mark is straight up. Then place the cam gear over the nose of the cam and turn the cam until the pip mark on the cam gear aligns with the crank gear. Now remove the cam gear and slide the chain over the gear and rein-stall the assembly over the cam nose. This may be somewhat tight with a new chain. Once the cam gear is located over the nose of the cam, install the three 5/16-inch cam bolts and snug them down. We can torque them later, after we ensure the cam is degreed properly.

Before we start with the cam degreeing, it's also a good idea to check that all the lifters fit their lifter bores without sticking and can rotate easily in their bores. Lifters must be able to spin in their bores in order to wear properly. If a lifter doesn't spin, check the bore for sharp edges that may cause the lifter to hang up. Sometimes this requires chamfering the lifter bores to ensure the lifters fit properly.

Another detail worth mentioning is that you do not need to soak new flat tappet hydraulic lifters in oil before installing them in the engine. This is just extra work that isn't necessary. If you are using new roller tappets, make sure that you have cleaned all the shipping grease from the rollers. After that you should soak the lifters to permeate the rollers. Soaking them overnight is a good idea. Once

Don't forget to lube the cam gear when installing a new cam. The heavy engine lube or moly paste helps prevent galling or damage to the gear during the break-in process.

Make sure all 16 lifters fit snugly in their bores without hanging up or sticking. Small blocks seem to be prone to slight burrs on the bottom of the lifter bores that can easily damage a lifter. If the lifter won't move up and down with your fingers, there's something wrong.

All the major cam companies sell a complete cam degree kit, such as this kit from COMP. You can build your own and can save some money, especially if you already have a dial indicator and a magnetic base.

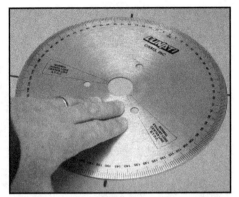

Here's a simple trick for checking degree wheel accuracy. Mark the four main 90-degree positions on the degree wheel (TDC, 90, 180, 270) on a large piece of cardboard. Then turn the wheel and see if the degree wheel reads the same number of degrees "off" the 90s at each of the four locations. Don't be surprised if the wheel is off by one degree or so. If it's off more than that, think about using a more accurate wheel.

you've installed the remaining lifters, pushrods, and rockers, you can set the lash or preload (see "Setting Lash" sidebar). Preload for hydraulic lifter engines is another frequently asked question. Factory specs often call for as much as one or 1-1/2 turns down from zero lash. This moves the hydraulic piston as much as 0.060 inches down in the lifter body. This much preload makes it far easier for the lifters to "pump up" and cause problems. A better idea is to merely preload the lifters between one-quarter and one-half turn.

By reducing the lifter preload to a 1/2 turn from zero lash, this places the internal piston closer to roughly 0.015 to 0.020

inches of preload. This is a much tighter preload and generally allows 100 to 200 more RPM of engine speed. This is also a good place to lobby for poly locks for all small-blocks, regardless of the style of rocker arm you're using. Those stock locking nuts that the factory uses are horrible and merely tear up the threads even on good studs. Invest in a set of poly locks and you'll be happier for it.

Tools to Get Your Degree

Now that our cam is installed, let's run through the procedure for degreeing in a camshaft. We assume that the engine

If you plan on building more than one engine, think about the major advantages of using one of the larger-diameter professional degree wheels. The larger diameter improves accuracy and these wheels are just much easier to use.

is on a stand and that the heads are not yet installed, although that changes very little from degreeing a cam with the heads on and the engine in the car.

Let's first take a look at the tools we need to accurately degree a cam. While some may think that this process requires a pile of expensive tools, you can do it very easily with a degree wheel, a crank nut, dial indicator and magnetic base, and a length of coat hanger wire—that's it. Add a couple of hand tools and some hardware and you're ready to go. Or, you can purchase a complete cam degree kit from any of the major cam companies like COMP, Crane, Isky, or Erson. The kits vary, so you might want to investigate each company's assortment list thoroughly before you make your choice, but they all work equally well. We've been degreeing cams for so long that we assembled our own kit from several sources and it works just fine. It ultimately comes down to what you are comfortable using.

One important point worth emphasizing is that as the degree wheel diameter becomes smaller, the accuracy also suffers. Perhaps you've seen those large professional degree wheels that Powerhouse sells for a bunch of money. The advantage of the larger wheel is more space in between each individual degree point. As the wheel diameter becomes smaller, space between timing marks becomes smaller. This is important to point out because engine builders might agonize over a 1-degree difference in where the cam is located, yet not realize that their degree wheel probably doesn't possess that level of accuracy. We've measured small degree wheels and found them to be off by as much as 2 degrees, but only in certain places on the wheel!

Let's look more closely at the tools. You have several options when mounting the degree wheel to the crank snout. The best degree wheel mount we've found is one sold by Powerhouse and COMP Cams. It is designed specifically for a small-block Chevy. This mount slides over the crank snout and locks in place with a setscrew. On the front of this tool is a large threaded nose with a locking collar. This tool requires the degree wheel to have a large center

Here's where it's easy to mess up. The Number One intake lobe on all small-block Chevys is the second lifter from the front. The first lifter is Number One exhaust.

The Pro adapter is the best way to go for turning the engine while degreeing. However, the old standard crank nut and a large adjustable wrench have also worked well for many years.

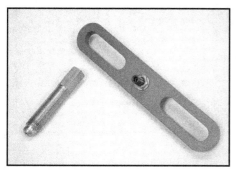

There are two types of piston stops, one for the cylinder head off the engine and the other for when the head is bolted on. The key to either is to ensure that it does not deflect when the piston contacts the stop.

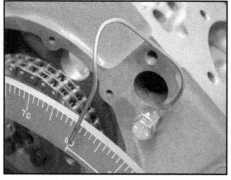

The degree wheel pointer can be as slick or as simple as you like. We merely use a length of coat hanger wire bolted to a water pump bolt hole and bend into place. It's simple and it works.

opening for the mount, which means you may have to buy a new degree wheel to match. This mount was originally designed for use with those large-diameter professional degree wheels, but smaller wheels that also accommodate this larger crank mount are available.

Before the days of these large diameter degree wheels and pro mounts, the next best thing was to use what is called a crank nut. This is a large hex nut with a round center broached with a keyway slot that it is splined to the crank. These crank nuts are inexpensive, but you quickly learn that the nut requires an expensive adjustable wrench in order to turn the engine over. The whole reason for these specialty tools is a quest for accuracy. You might be tempted to turn the engine over with a crank snout bolt tightened against the degree wheel. Unfortunately, the degreeing process requires you to turn the engine counterclockwise, which loosens the crank bolt and allows the degree wheel to turn, which only serves to cause frustration. So, step up to one of the better degree wheel mounting approaches. Ultimately, this saves time and limits your frustration.

You also need a dial indicator to measure lifter rise and combine that with a magnetic base. Some of the degree

wheel kits use custom mounts for the dial indicator, but the magnetic bases are inexpensive now and they're the easiest to use. You also need some kind of pointer for the degree wheel. We use a length of coat hanger wire and a bolt and nut arrangement, which works just fine. A piston stop is required in order to determine top dead center. The small-block has two different styles, depending upon whether the heads are on or off the engine. Powerhouse also makes an inexpensive piston stop for engines with the heads off that spans the cylinder with an adjustable stop bolt. Or you can make your own out of a piece of scrap steel or aluminum with a center-mounted bolt and nut as a stop. If the heads are on the engine, you can use a threaded piston stop that merely screws in through the spark plug hole. However, be aware that certain aluminum heads (like Air Flow Research castings, for example) place the spark plug hole pointing "uphill" so that with a flattop or dished piston, a screw-in piston stop won't work.

In this case, we have a tip for you that can do the job so you don't have to yank the head to degree the cam. If you have one of those on-the-head, over-center valvespring compressor tools that compresses the valvespring and holds the spring down when you over-center the lever arm, this can be used as an ad-hoc piston stop. Just be sure to rig up an adapter that contacts either just the valve or both the valve and retainer. Otherwise, the spring compresses and the valve might drop if separated from the retainer.

HOW TO READ A CAM CARD

All cam companies include a timing card with their camshaft. Each company designs its cam card with similar specs, intended not only to clue you in on the actual specs of the cam, but also to allow you to check the installed position of the cam against the card. By this point in the book, you should be familiar with all the terms, so this walk-through is easy. If not, then you should consider going back through Chapter 2 to ensure that you know what all these terms mean.

The accompanying printout is from a COMP Cams timing card. Other cam company cards are similar, some with more information and others with far less. To start, the top portion is pretty easy since this is the cam part number. Note the grind number, which actually tells you something about the cam. In this case, the "R" in the number indicates it is a roller cam while the 300 indicates its intake advertised duration while the 10 refers to the lobe separation angle. Next, we also have valve adjustments. We chose a mechanical roller cam for this exercise so that we'd have valve lash numbers. Note that both the intake and exhaust lobes should be lashed at 0.020 inches. Right underneath this is the gross valve lift numbers. Since this is a single-pattern cam, both the intake and exhaust lifts are the same. Note also the word "gross." You could substitute "theoretical" here based on the stock small-block's 1.5:1 rocker

ratio. If you measure the actual valve lift, it may be slightly less depending upon valvetrain deflection. Also remember that "net" or final valve lift is gross lift minus the lash. So the true valve lift is actually 0.555 inches.

Moving down another line on the card indicates duration at 0.015-inch tappet lift. These numbers also fall under the "intake" and "exhaust" columns. Note that this is advertised duration but the measuring point is 0.015 inches, which accounts for most of the cam's clearance ramps.

Now we get to the real meat of the cam card. The opening and closing points indicate valve timing at 0.015-inch tappet lift. For this cam, the intake lobe should open at 44 degrees BTDC and close at 76 degrees ABDC, while the exhaust should open at 84 degrees BBDC and close at 36 degrees ATDC. These numbers are fairly self-explanatory. For its hydraulic cams, COMP calls out 0.006 inches for opening and closing point information while Crane uses 0.050 inches for its opening and closing specs, so this means you really have to read these cam cards to make sure you check them where the cam companies spec them.

Next, the card states that these specs are for a cam installed with an intake centerline of 106 degrees. This is a process that we'll also go over in detail in a separate sidebar if you prefer to degree your cam using this procedure.

Next, this is Duration at 0.050-inch tappet lift for both the intake and exhaust lobes with a spec in this case of 255 degrees. The next line is maximum lobe lift, which is a useful number to compare to the actual lobe lift measured for each lobe. The final number in this listing is the lobe separation angle, which in this case if 110 degrees.

```
PART # 12-705-8
ENGINE CHEV SML BLK 265-400

GRIND NUMBER CS 300A-R10
  SERIAL NO 000000
                        INTAKE    EXHAUST
VALVE ADJUSTMENT        .020       .020
GROSS VALVE LIFT        .575       .575
DURATION AT
 .015 TAPPET LIFT       300        300
VALVE TIMING       OPEN      CLOSE
AT .015 INT        44 BTDC   76 ABDC
       EXH         84 BBDC   36 ATDC
THESE SPECS ARE FOR CAM INSTALLED
AT  106  INTAKE CENTER LINE
                        INTAKE    EXHAUST
DURATION AT .050        255        255
LOBE LIFT               .3834     .3834
LOBE SEPARATION         110

RECOMMENDED CC VALVE SPRG 977-16
VALVE SPRING SPECS FURNISHED
WITH SPRINGS
```

Finally, most cam companies also indicate the valvespring part number they recommend for this particular camshaft. A cam card contains a wealth of information, and you should make a habit of keeping all of your cam cards in a safe place where you can easily reference them at some point in the future. If you lose the card, don't freak out since the major cam companies now offer all their

Degree Program

Now that we have a handle on the tools needed for the job, let's get to it. This first procedure is the most important step in the entire degree process. If TDC is not set accurately, all subsequent values will be incorrect and all your effort is for nothing.

After you've mounted the degree wheel on the crank snout, turn the

engine over until Number One piston (driver side front) is at TDC. For this effort, just get the piston close. Now set the wheel to indicate TDC with the pointer. Now turn the engine counterclockwise about a quarter to half turn, and mount the piston stop securely in place. Now, turn the engine clockwise slowly until the piston contacts the piston stop. Record the number indicated on the degree wheel. This is in degrees

before top dead center or BTDC. Now, turn the engine counterclockwise again all the way around until the piston hits the piston stop. Now record this value, which is indicated on the degree wheel on the opposite side of TDC. Since we only roughly set TDC on the wheel, the two numbers are probably not the same. If they are, you're at TDC already. More than likely, the numbers do not agree.

HOW TO READ A CAM CARD (CONTINUED)

cam cards on their web site where you can easily print a duplicate.

Before we wrap this up, we've also included a couple of lines on a Crane timing card that you might find somewhat confusing. On some very short duration camshafts, Crane indicates the intake and exhaust opening and closing points at 0.050-inch tappet lift in parenthesis as shown here:

Cam Timing Duration		Opens	Closes	Max Lift	
@ 0.050	Intake	(4) ATDC	34 ABDC	109 ATDC	210
Tappet Lift	Exhaust	47 BBDC	(11) BTDC	119 BTDC	216

Since we have a short-duration cam with an intake duration at 0.050-inch tappet lift of only 210 degrees, the valve doesn't open BTDC—it opens after as the ATDC indicates. However, cam junkies know that a quick way to calculate total duration is to add the opening and closing numbers together along with 180 degrees (between TDC and BDC). But since this cam (at 0.050-inch tappet lift) actually opens the intake ATDC, you have to subtract the 4

degrees rather than add it. That's what the parentheses indicate. This means you have (-4) + 180 + 34 = 210. The same is true for the exhaust side. Instead of adding 11 degrees for the closing point, you would need to subtract, which means you have 47 + 180 + (-11) = 216.

If we were to list the numbers at 0.004 inches (Crane's choice for advertised duration), the intake opening point would now be expressed (in this case) as 20 degrees BTDC and the closing point is 66 degrees ABDC, so now you can do straight addition: 20 + 180 + 66 = 266 degrees of duration. The subtraction moves are only necessary with very short duration camshafts with the checking numbers at 0.050-inch tappet lift, but it is important to know why some of the numbers are given in parentheses.

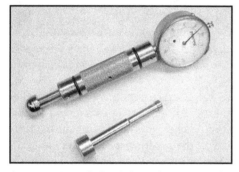

It may seem obvious, but always use the correct style of lifter when degreeing the cam. Don't use a roller lifer on a flat tappet cam or vice versa. The pro style tool allows you to easily change the lifter follower design.

Let's say that the numbers are 24 degrees BTDC and 20 degrees ATDC. This creates a spread of only 4 degrees, so we merely split the difference and move the degree wheel (or the pointer, your preference) so that the wheel reads 22 degrees on both sides of TDC. This is when you know that the position of TDC on your degree wheel is correct. Always double-check your reading after moving the degree wheel and if for any reason your degree wheel moves during

the degreeing process, you must go back and reset TDC. No shortcuts exist when it comes to establishing TDC.

Once we have TDC set, now use your fabricated lifter or cam follower along with the dial indicator and magnetic base to read lifter movement. Remember to place your lifter in the sec-

For a flat tappet or a roller cam, you can also gut a typical lifter, fill it full of washers and invert the pushrod cup on top—just make sure it's stable. If the bottom of the cup is flat, drill or hammer a small indentation to locate the dial indicator and you're ready to go.

ond lifter bore from the front, since this is the intake lobe for Number One cylinder on a small-block Chevy. If you place the lifter in the first lifter bore, you measure the opening and closing points for Number One exhaust lobe. Once you are properly set up, run the lifer through three or four complete lift

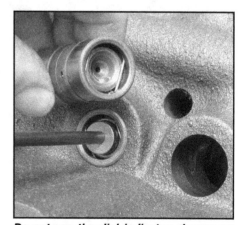

Do not use the dial indicator plunger on the radiused pushrod cup of a typical lifter. The small dial indicator plunger will not seat properly, producing inaccurate readings. Instead, create an accurate locating position or use the edge of the lifter.

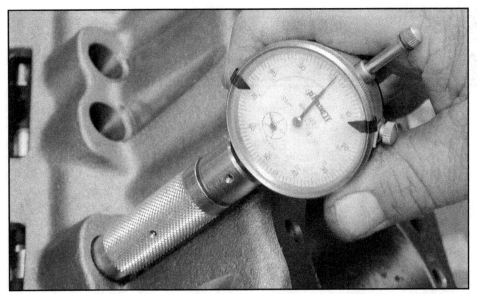

Always make sure to rotate the lifter through several cycles to double check that the lifter and dial indicator returns to zero on the cam's base circle. If not, find out why before you continue.

If using a magnetic base and dial indicator, make sure the dial indicator plunger is lined up with the lifter travel. Also make sure there is sufficient dial indicator travel to read at least 0.350 inches of lobe lift. This is why using this professional device is more accurate.

Mount the degree wheel and bring the engine up to TDC for Number One piston and roughly set the TDC.

Back off the engine turning counterclockwise and mount the piston stop over the bore.

cycles to ensure that the lifter and the dial indicator always return to zero. If not, determine what is causing the lifter to hang up before moving forward with the degree process. Usually, the dial indicator is placed incorrectly and runs out of travel. With your dial indicator set, we can now get to the actual degree process. What you discover is that it takes more time to set everything up than it does to actually determine where the cam is positioned.

With the lifter on the base circle of the cam, slowly turn the engine clockwise until the dial indicator reads 0.050 inches of lifter rise and jot down the position of the degree wheel. This is the position of the Number One intake at 0.050-inch lifter rise. Most cam cards indicate this position for the intake at BTDC. Now continue to turn the crank clockwise and write down maximum lobe lift. After making that notation, continue clockwise until you near lifter closing. This is easy

to see because the lifter's rate of change on the dial indicator slows down. Stop at 0.050 inches of lifter rise off the base circle on the closing side and again note the reading on the degree wheel. This is the intake closing point at 0.050 ABDC. Always note these positions when turning the crank clockwise.

It's relatively easy to turn the crank past the 0.050-inch closing point, so if you do, don't sweat it. Merely turn the crank counterclockwise roughly 50 to 60 degrees and then turn the crank clockwise again until you reach the 0.050-inch closing point. The reason you back the engine up that much past the 0.050-inch point is to compensate for any looseness or slack in the chain that creates an error if you merely move the crank backwards to achieve the 0.050-inch mark.

Comparing the opening and closing points of the intake valve against the manufacturer's cam card, you now know

INTAKE CENTERLINE METHOD

As with many things in life, there's more than one way to degree a camshaft. For years COMP Cams has suggested using the intake centerline method for degreeing a camshaft. This step requires a little simple math, and we will run through the process so you're familiar with the procedure.

Set up the degree wheel and dial indicator in the typical manner. Once you've established TDC, rotate the engine until you find maximum valve lift on the intake lobe. Now zero your dial indicator. Next, turn the engine counterclockwise until the dial indicator reads 0.100 inches or so. Now rotate the crank in a clockwise direction and stop at exactly 0.050 inches before the dial indicator reads zero. The cam is now at 0.050 inches before its maximum lift. Record the degree wheel reading, which is somewhere after TDC. Now continue to rotate the crank clockwise until you reach 0.050 inches past max lift on the closing flank of the intake lobe and record this reading on the degree wheel. Add the two numbers together and divide by two and you have the location of the intake centerline. For example, you might come up with numbers like 84 and 128 degrees. Add 84 + 128 = 212 then divide by 2 and you have 106 degrees, which would be the intake centerline, which would be ATDC.

While this works, and most cam companies indicate the intake centerline spec on their cam cards, this method does not address the opening and closing points of the intake lobe, which is the real reason you should be checking the cam in the first place. Since the setup for degreeing the cam is the same for either procedure, we generally check the opening and closing points first, then if it's warranted, we'll also go through the intake centerline procedure.

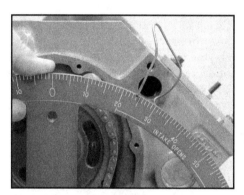

Turn the crank clockwise and record the reading on the degree wheel when the piston hits the stop. This is on the BTDC side. In this case, the wheel reads 24 degrees BTDC.

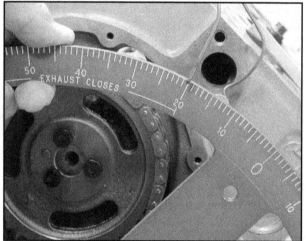

exactly where Number One intake lobe is timed relative to piston Number One and therefore the rest of the engine. Let's say the cam is supposed to open at 34 degrees BTDC and close at 66 degrees ABDC, but your measurements indicate that the cam is actually opening 32 degrees BTDC and 68 ABDC. This means your camshaft is actually two degrees retarded since it is opening and closing two degrees later than indicated on the cam card. Conversely, if your numbers indicate an opening at 36 BTDC and a closing of 64 ABDC, then the cam is advanced by two degrees. Either of these situations is easy to fix.

Now turn the crank counterclockwise all the way around until the piston hits the stop. In this case, the degree wheel reads 20 degrees ATDC. Now we have to move either the degree wheel or the pointer so that it should read halfway in between, or 22 degrees. Then turn the crank back to the other side of the piston stop to ensure it reads 22 degrees. If it does, you have true TDC. Remove the piston stop.

Now we can actually start the degreeing process. Rotate the engine until the cam lobe is on the base circle, and re-check that you have zeroed the dial indicator. Look at your cam card, if the opening and closing numbers are given at a checking height of 0.015 inches for example (this is a mechanical lifter cam), then rotate the engine clockwise until the dial indicator reads 0.015. Then record the number on the degree wheel. In this case, your cam reads 34 degrees BTDC.

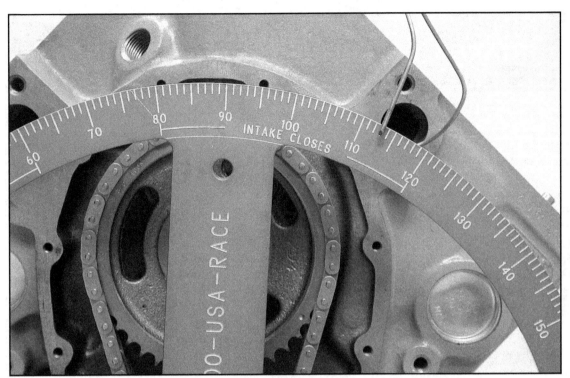

Now we continue to turn the engine over clockwise until you reach 0.015 inches off the base circle on the intake closing side. Our cam card said we should read 66 ABDC, but our degree wheel reads just before 67 degrees, roughly one degree later. Also, note here that 67 degrees is counted backwards from 90. This degree wheel indicates degrees in 0-to-90 segments rather than 0-to-180 or 0-to-360 degree increments. That's the way this wheel works.

Generally, most crank keyways allow a minimum of a 2-degree advance or retard. This also changes all our other openings are closing points. A slightly later intake closing gives us a little more top-end power, so we decided to leave it as is. Always double check your new cam position if you move the crank gear to ensure you moved in the direction you intended.

Let's say you have a timing set equipped with a multiple position crank gear. Most of these, as we saw in the chapter on cam drives, are generally set up to allow you to move the cam in two-degree increments. All you have to do is pull the crank gear, choose the appropriate keyway position, install the gear back on the

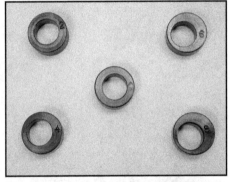

You can also use offset bushings in the cam gear if you don't have a multi-keyway crank sprocket. The trick is to drill the back of the cam gear only deep enough so that the bushing is captured and flush with the back of the cam gear.

crank, and then line up the dots. Here's where you need to be careful since often the marks on the crank gear can be similar in appearance. Plus, you need to know without a doubt what each mark indicates. For example, crank gears are often marked with a circle, square, triangle, and other symbols not obvious of what they represent. The information is usually presented somewhere on the instruction manual. Better timing sets make these symbols more obvious, so be sure you know what you're working with. It's easy to see how each manufacturer may define

these same symbols differently. If you've lost or discarded your instruction manual, you may have to go through the grief of degreeing each location until you discover which one gives you what they want. If you've lost your instructions, you can always go online since most cam companies post instructions on their website. Keep in mind that when you remove the crank gear, this means removing the degree wheel from the crank snout. Even with the pro model snout that locates on the keyway, you must always re-establish TDC just to be sure. Even the pro model snout mount has some slack, and it's best to be sure.

Converting to a Roller Cam

As we mentioned in Chapter 2, Chevy converted from flat tappet hydraulic cams to hydraulic rollers beginning in 1987. We've reviewed the differences, but what's involved with converting a flat tappet over to a hydraulic or mechanical roller cam? You actually have a couple of different options for this, depending upon which cylinder block you are using.

Assuming we're starting with a traditional two-piece rear main seal block, converting this style small-block to a

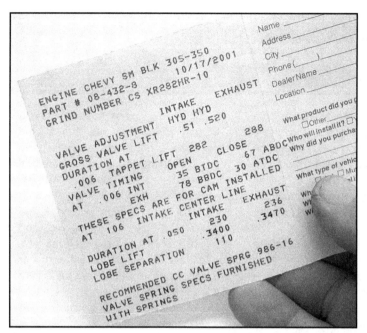

Cam cards come in many different configurations. It's important to know all the nuances so you don't get confused.

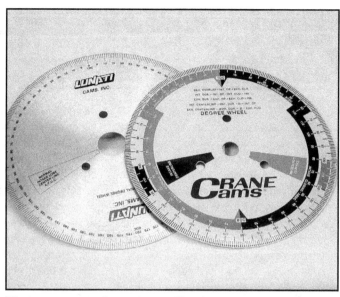

We have seen at least three different degree wheel designs and more probably exist. Be aware that they don't all read out the same way. For example, you may have to count numbers back from BDC to get the numbers you're looking for.

roller cam configuration is not that difficult. The only negative is that this conversion is a bit more expensive. The big cam companies like COMP and Crane both have retrofit cam kits that offer you a cam, retrofit tie-bar lifters, pushrods, roller rocker arms, and better valvesprings. You also need a thrust button to limit cam movement fore and aft, and sometimes these may not be included in the kit. The cool thing about these kits is that most street roller cams, especially the hydraulic roller versions, require no special machine work. Even the cam drive ends up being the same. As we learned in the earlier chapters, street-oriented roller cams employ a pressed-on iron distributor drive-gear and rear cam-journal. This means you can run your standard iron distributor drive-gear.

These retrofit kits are not cheap, with a price tag of roughly around $900 to $1,000 for everything. This is mainly due to the high cost of the new roller lifters. As an alternative, if you intend to use a hydraulic roller cam in a relatively mild 355– or 383–ci small-block, it would be wise to look into building a one-piece rear main seal engine instead. New stroker cranks are cheap now, and the real advantage is that these newer blocks allow you to use the taller, OEM-

style hydraulic roller lifters. Used lifters can be employed on a new cam, or even purchasing new OEM-style hydraulic roller tappets is really inexpensive compared to the aftermarket roller versions. Plus, you don't have to bother with an aftermarket roller thrust button because these late model blocks are already machined for a front camshaft limiter plate that bolts to the block in front of the cam, also requiring a new stepped nose for the cam.

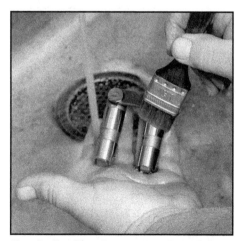

New hydraulic roller tappets should always be thoroughly cleaned before use since they are packed in grease to prevent corrosion during shipping and storage. Good clean solvent followed by a bath in heavy engine assembly oil is the best plan.

Perhaps one of the best deals on the planet for a small-block hydraulic roller cam is the GMPP Hot hydraulic roller cam package that can be purchased in several different configurations. The smokin' deal is to order the GM Hot cam kit (PN 12480002) that includes the

Guideplates are used on the small-block Chevy to line up the rocker arm with the valve tip. You may need to move the guideplates slightly to ensure the rocker lines up with its valve. Worse case, you may have to elongate the guideplate mounting holes slightly.

BREAK-IN PROCEDURES

Once the cam is installed, degreed, and the valvetrain has been lashed to the proper spec, there's still one more important step to take before you can begin to enjoy the power your new cam delivers. For flat tappet cams, you must take the time to break in the new cam. Roller cams, either hydraulic or mechanical, do not require as precise a break-in procedure, although duplicating this step would certainly not detract from their longevity.

For a flat tappet hydraulic or mechanical cam, you must make sure to thoroughly break in the mating surfaces of the lifters and the lobes. This ensures both long life and best performance. If the cam requires a dual spring with high seat pressures, you may want to break the cam in on just the outside springs to reduce the load. One key is to have the engine completely set up and tuned so that it starts very quickly. This also demands oil be in the engine and the cooling system be full of coolant and ready to go. The best approach is to pressure lube the engine before its initial fire-up so that the oil filter is full of oil and the entire engine, all the way up to the rocker arms, is fully lubed. This also requires accurately setting the initial timing at around 12 to 15 degrees BTDC and also having fuel in the carburetor so the engine is ready to run as soon as you hit the starter. This tune-up prevents having to crank the engine over for a long time, something you want to avoid. Excessive cranking tends to wipe the lube off the cam lobes before the engine starts.

With the engine tuned and ready to fire, start the engine and immediately bring it up to at least 2,000 rpm. Some enthusiasts don't like to do that with a brand new engine, but you need to keep in mind that the small-block Chevy lifter-camshaft interface relies solely on splash oiling to lubricate the area between the lifters and the cam. That's why you need to bring the engine up to at least 2,000 rpm and then constantly vary the engine speed between 1,800 and 2,300 rpm for roughly 15 to 20 minutes. Another useful tip is to have the entire exhaust system connected, so that you can more easily hear any potential internal problems. This also means that you should do this break-in procedure either outside with plenty of ventilation or, if indoors, at least where you can plumb the exhaust outside the building.

Varying the engine speed around a 500–rpm spread ensures that all the lifters receive oil as the engine speed varies. Do not merely set the carburetor's fast idle cam at a set RPM and then walk away from the engine and grab a cold drink. This initial startup portion is the most critical time for an engine, and especially for the camshaft. Merely setting the fast-idle cam may result in one or two flat lobes on the cam that were starved of sufficient oil for the initial break-in process. You also want to keep an eye on the oil pressure and coolant temperature to ensure the engine doesn't overheat or suffer from lack of oil pressure due to a leak.

Once you've accomplished the break-in procedure, we recommend driving the car or testing the engine only after all the fluids are up to temperature. Then, change the oil after the first 100 miles. This flushes most of that moly lube out of the engine and filter, as well as getting rid of much of the initial startup junk that inevitably comes out of a fresh engine. Then, after the oil change, you're truly ready to begin enjoying your new engine!

cam, springs, retainers, keepers, shims, and a set of GMPP 1.6:1 guided roller rockers. All you need then is a set of OEM-style hydraulic roller lifters and the appropriate-length pushrods and you're ready to rock 'n' roll. The Hot cam specs at 218/228 degrees at 0.050-inch tappet lift with 0.492-inch lift on both valves with a 112-degree lobe separation angle using 1.6:1 roller rockers. This cam is a proven winner for overall street performance without breaking the bank. At the time of publication, this package runs roughly around $800.

One thing not included in this price is the factory spider and lifter tie-bars, which we assume you would reuse from the original block. If you choose to buy them new, the prices are reasonable.

If you bolt one of these cams into a one-piece roller cam block already set up for factory hydraulic roller lifters, you have a cool setup. And you save money so that you can spend more on the heads and intake! Even if you don't buy the GMPP Hot cam, you can still enjoy the benefits of the one-piece, hydraulic roller cam block by minimizing your investment.

Power Tuning

Since we're dealing with the installation and degreeing of cams, we should also touch on the effects of these changes. While this is a fairly broad statement, advancing a cam opens and closes all the valves earlier in the four-stroke cycle. This tends to create a cam that "appears" smaller to the engine, which improves low-end torque while

Never combine guided rocker arms with pushrod guideplates. This could cause a binding situation guaranteed to cause some destruction and lots of metal filings in the oil.

Setting lifters is easy with the Exhaust Opening/Intake Closing procedure; just remember EO/IC. With EO, set the intake lash, and with IC set the exhaust lash.

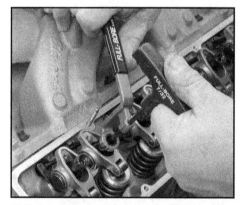

This handy tool allows you to set the lash or preload quickly when using poly locks. Several companies like ProForm, Moroso, Manley, and others offer similar tools.

If you want to use a stud girdle, keep in mind that you have to loosen the girdle bolts in order to change lash and then tighten it back and recheck the lash because lash changes with the girdle tight.

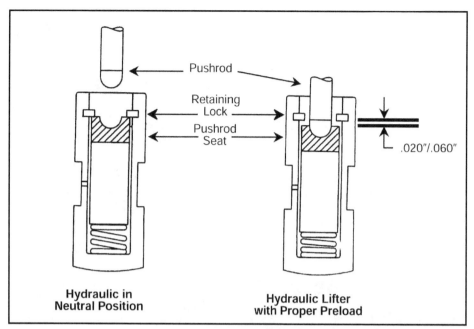

Proper hydraulic lifter preload is important and should be between 0.020 and 0.060 inches. On a 3/8-inch stud using 24 threads-per-inch (tpi), this means that a 1/2–turn on the adjuster from zero lash preloads the lifter by 0.020 inches. For a 7/16-inch stud at 20 tpi, a 1/2–turn is worth 0.025 inches.

sacrificing top-end power. Remember that since intake closing is the most important of the four-valve positions, by moving the cam ahead, we have also moved to an earlier intake closing point.

Conversely, retarding the overall installed position of the cam produces a later closing intake, which reduces low-speed torque while improving top-end power. Generally, moving the cam a few degrees seems to do very little other than slightly moving the power around. While much has been written about fine-tuning the cam position, frankly the best thing to do is run the cam the way it's delivered and then figure out if the cam is the proper duration for your application.

Lash Loops

If you are running a mechanical lifter camshaft, some additional tuning efforts are available that have a significant effect on power. These efforts might also lead you to a better understanding of what your engine wants to make more power. When we advance or retard the cam, we're moving all four valve-opening and -closing points simultaneously. By making independent lash changes first on the intake and then the

exhaust lobes on a mechanical cam, we can separate the intake lobes from the exhaust and tune the engine with more finite control. Here's how it works.

Let's start with the intake lobe on a mechanical flat tappet cam. Let's say the lash spec is 0.020 inches. If we were to tighten the lash by 0.004 inches to 0.016 inches, this has the effect of lengthening the effective cam duration since the lifter has less distance to travel before opening the valve. A crude rule of thumb for lash

A company called Ferry's Aluminum Repair in Dallas, Texas (972/557-3565) makes this unique tool that measures the actual position of the rocker arm tip on the valve face. You can use this tool to establish accurate pushrod length and also to measure total travel of the rocker tip across the valve tip.

Several companies make this on-the-head spring compressor that can also be used as a substitute piston stop when dealing with heads where the screw-in spark-plug-style piston stop won't work. Just be sure to move the valve with the spring as a unit. Also, be careful to just kiss the valve with the piston so you don't bend the valve. Turn the engine gently by hand when using this procedure.

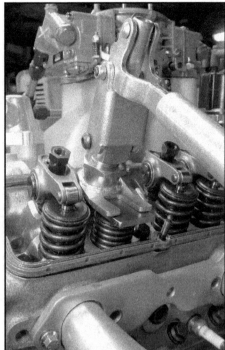

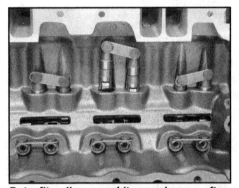

Retrofit roller cam kits employ an aftermarket roller lifter that uses aftermarket-style tie-bars to keep the lifter in line with the cam lobe. Remember that you must also use some type of cam button to prevent cam walk.

But let's not forget the exhaust side of things. Once we've tuned our intake lobe to where we want it, we can now go about tuning the exhaust side. First, return the intake lash back to its original lash spec. This returns the engine to its baseline power level. Now, start by tightening the lash on the exhaust by 0.004 inches (to 0.016 inches total) and evaluate the power. If peak power improves, it's because of the later closing exhaust and increased overlap, which means we probably lost a little

low-speed torque as well. If the power didn't change or we lost some peak power, then we know we don't need more exhaust duration, but there's still one more test.

Let's say we open the exhaust lash by 0.004 inches and the power increases.

changes is roughly 1.5 degrees of duration for 0.001 inches of lash change. This would mean we've added 6 degrees of duration to the cam on just the intake side. With our engine on a dyno, chances are peak power may increase slightly while sacrificing a little power on the low end. If engine power improves throughout the entire power curve, it's clear the engine needs a bigger intake lobe.

Let's say that the power fell off across the board. If so, then we'd want to try increasing lash on the intake side to see what effect this would have on the overall power curve. Super-sizing the lash up to 0.024 inches has the effect of reducing cam duration by roughly 6 degrees, which should improve low-speed and mid-range power, and hopefully not hurt top-end power that much.

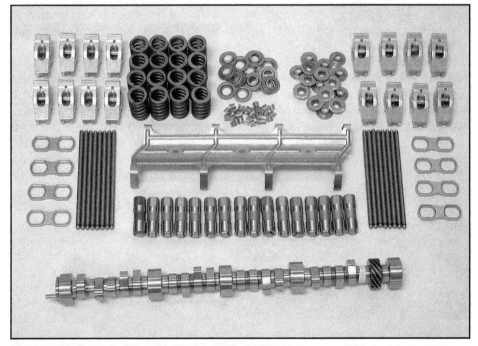

The best buy in hydraulic roller cams is the GMPP Hot cam and kit for blocks that can use the factory hydraulic roller lifters. This kit includes the cam, 1.6:1 roller rockers, springs, retainers, shims, and keepers. All you need to complete the kit is pushrods, assuming you already have the eight factory tie-bars and "spider."

CAM BUTTON INSTALLATION

As mentioned in Chapter 3, roller cams require a button to prevent the cam from moving forward in the engine, retarding the ignition timing. The only button that you should consider is the roller cam button. Several companies sell both aluminum and plastic cam buttons that work, but also experience significant wear very quickly. It should be obvious that once the button wears, the cam is able to walk and the engine begins to experience retarded timing, just what you wanted to avoid!

The beauty of the roller cam button is that it also incorporates tiny internal shims that can be used to set the actual cam thrust clearance. This is generally spec'd at 0.005 to 0.010 inches. Before you embark on this exercise, also consider investing in a heavy cast-aluminum timing chain cover. Since the cam button must press against the timing chain cover to limit thrust, the button needs a sturdy point to press against. The typical stock tin small-block timing cover doesn't offer sufficient resiliency to accommodate the cam thrust forces unless you reinforce the cover with a welded-on plate. If you plan on using a reinforced stock cover, also consider using an aftermarket water pump like the Edelbrock units. The Edelbrock units incorporate a threaded bung that allows you to place a thrust bolt that contacts the outside of the timing cover to assist in limiting cam thrust movement.

This is a lot of extra work when you consider that for a few bucks more you can use a two-piece timing chain cover like the one from Bo Laws that has sufficient strength to handle cam thrust. It also offers a small, tapped hole accessible to a dial indicator to measure cam thrust while assembling the engine. If you don't have one of these covers, you can still measure cam thrust clearance, but this requires placing the dial indicator in line with the cam with the rear cam plug removed. The cam gear limits cam travel to the rear of the block, while the cam button limits forward thrust. The usual procedure is to position the dial indicator and then gently pry the cam forward and back with a long screwdriver to establish total cam travel. Be careful not to nick a lobe. You must also include the timing chain cover gasket when doing your clearance measurements or the thrust clearance increases by the thickness of the gasket.

That means we may have too much exhaust duration. It's possible that an efficient exhaust port in a set of aftermarket heads don't need as much exhaust duration. In fact, they could make more power with a shorter duration exhaust lobe. The cam and head chapter (Chapter 13) touches on more of this. Keep in mind that we can't emphasize enough that these changes need to be made one at a time. If you simultaneously open the lash on the intake and close it down on the exhaust and the power improves, you won't know which change was responsible for the increase. Worse yet, one change may cancel out the other and then you miss an opportunity entirely. So, once you've

The Hot cam is least expensive when using tall OE-style hydraulic roller lifters. These lifters require the use of GM tie bars and a spider. It is possible to use the OE lifters and tie bars in an older 2-piece rear main seal block, but you must drill and tap holes in the lifter valley for the spider, which is a major hassle.

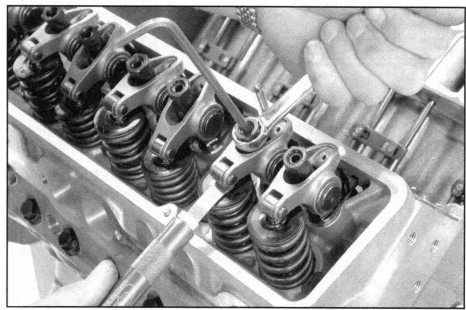

Lash changes to an engine on the dyno point out whether the cam needs more or less valve timing on either the intake or the exhaust sides of the cam. These can only be done on a mechanical lifter camshaft.

The only cam button to use on any roller-cammed small-block is one of these roller timing buttons, like this one from COMP Cams. These slick little pieces also include tiny shims that can be used to establish the proper cam thrust clearance of between 0.005 and 0.010 inches.

established which exhaust lash spec makes the best overall power, now you can go back and go through the intake lash again to be sure the best lash spec still works with the best exhaust lash. If this sounds like a ton of work it's only because it is. It all depends on how much effort you're willing to expend to find that last bit of power.

This lash loop exercise can also be done at the drag strip, but with so many more variables inherent at the track, the only way you can test is by looking at the trap speed power. If MPH goes up, you're working in the right direction. You can also add to this effort by trying 1.6:1 rockers instead of 1.5:1s on either

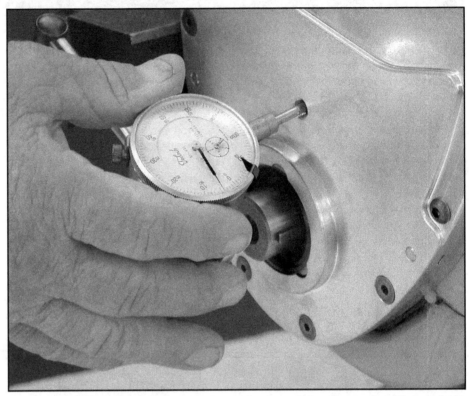

The best procedure for checking cam thrust clearance is to use a custom timing-chain-cover that allows you to place a dial indicator plunger directly on the cam gear. Then merely pry the cam forward and back to check the total thrust clearance.

SETTING LASH

Whether you have a mild hydraulic flat tappet that requires preload or a monster mechanical roller cam that has a hot lash spec, you need to set the lash on your new cam. Since most performance small blocks now run roller rockers, we run through the procedure with those in mind, although the process is the same even for stock rockers.

With many different ways to set the lash on a small-block Chevy, the easiest process we've found can also be used on any four-stroke engine regardless of make. There are only two terms you need to remember—exhaust opening (EO) and intake closing (IC). Here's how it works.

Let's start with cylinder Number One. With the engine warm, valve covers removed, and the entire valvetrain installed, turn the engine until the exhaust pushrod begins to move upward. We call this EO. At this point, set the intake valve lash or preload. In the case of a hydraulic lifter camshaft, once you have found zero lash, add 1/2 turn of preload to the adjustment and cinch the poly lock down. Now, continue to turn the engine over until the exhaust pushrod has gone through its entire lift curve and the intake rocker/valve is on its closing flank, roughly 3/4 closed. We call this IC. Now set the lash or preload

on the exhaust rocker. That's it for cylinder Number One. We then progress right down the side of the engine, doing the odd bank (driver side) first, then the even (passenger side) bank last.

The reason this works is that when the exhaust lobe is on its opening flank, the intake lobe is placed on its base circle. The same situation occurs when the intake lobe is near its closing side, this positions the exhaust lifter on the base circle of the exhaust lobe. These relationships hold true for any four-stroke engine regardless of make and country of origin, as long as the engine has valves that require you to set the lash.

FUN WITH NUMBERS

With all these numbers floating around, we thought we would add a few more to the mix, not to confuse, but to illustrate some typical relationships that can occur with intake and exhaust lobes.

Let's assume you have a camshaft in which you know the advertised duration and the lobe separation angle. Use a hydraulic flat tappet cam with an advertised duration of 292 degrees and a lobe separation angle of 110 degrees.

Intake Opening:
IO = (Adv. Duration / 2) –
   lobe separation angle
IO = (292 / 2) = 146 – 110 = 36 degrees BTDC

When we looked at our timing card for this cam, we noticed that the cam was actually ground four degrees advanced (which is very common with street cams), using a 106-degree intake centerline. We got this number because if the cam is ground straight up, the lobe separation angle and the intake centerline is always the same number, even though they mean different things. So, with a four-degree advance ground into the cam, this means we must add four degrees to the final number to come up with the proper intake opening point, making it:

(292 / 2) = 146 – 110 = 36 + 4 = 40 BTDC

If the cam is ground retarded, then we subtract the amount from the result.

Intake Closing:
IC = Duration – (IO + 180)
IC = 292 – (40 + 180)
IC = 292 – 220 = 72 ABDC

For the exhaust side, the equation looks like this:

Exhaust Closing:
EC = (Duration / 2) – lobe
   separation angle
EC = (292 / 2) – 110
EC = 146 – 110 = 36 ATDC

But again we must compensate for the ground-in advance and this time subtract 4 degrees:

EC = 146 – 110 = 36- 4 degrees = 32 ATDC

Exhaust Opening:
EO = Duration – (EC + 180)
EO = 292 – (32 + 180)
EO = 292 – 212 = 80 BBDC

---

the intake or the exhaust, or both in various combinations to see if additional power is to be found in addition to the lash changes. That keeps you busy for quite a while.

Conclusion

Integration is the key to this combination. Start by installing the cam correctly, then go about using the tools already in place with the engine to fine-tune it to make more power. For years, everyone has been using hydraulic flat tappet and roller cams for the street because they didn't want to be slaves to lashing valves. But from our experience, if the valvetrain is designed, built, and installed properly, a mechanical lifter cam holds its lash for a long time, allowing you the luxury of using lash to fine-tune the engine without having to spend any more money. And it's the smart engine builder who comes out on top in that game.

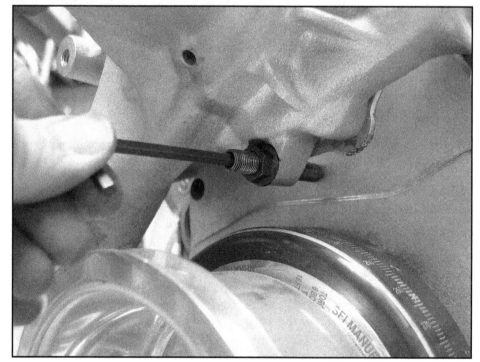

Both of Edelbrock's short- and long-style aluminum small-block water pumps include small bosses that can be used for thrust-limiter bolts to assist a stock tin timing chain cover.

HOW TO CHOOSE A CAM

Choosing a camshaft for street-driven cars is more of a compromise to create more power throughout the power curve while not sacrificing too much low-speed torque so that the car is sluggish and kills the fun factor of street driving.

The lure of a big cam is that, unlike carburetors or intake manifolds, a big cam doesn't cost any more than a conservative selection. Unfortunately, this is when the "bigger is better" theory intrudes.

Now that we have a decent handle on the secret language of camshafts and perhaps an appreciation of what the valvetrain has to endure in a typical street performance engine, it's time to put all this knowledge to work by choosing a camshaft for your next performance small-block. And it is here that many enthusiasts forget what they've learned and go straight to the biggest "lumpy" cam they can find.

Perhaps it is all this complex engineering that sucks the romance out of performance engines. But if you let your enthusiasm, or worse yet—your buddy's Kentucky Windage choice of a big cam to color your decision, then you don't need to read this chapter. But chances are that if you've plowed your way through most of this book to get to this point, you're here because you want to learn. So let's get started.

The first thing we need to do when deciding on a camshaft for any small-block is to honestly answer a few questions about how this cam is to be applied. Being honest here is critical. How is this engine to be used? Is it a mild street engine that is to be driven to school every day with an occasional jaunt down the quarter mile, or is this more of a hot street engine that only comes out on Saturday night and only to impress that snobby cruise crowd at the Boffo Burger? Car weight, auto or manual transmission, rear gear ratio, induction and exhaust system configuration, and a host of other factors all play a part in this concert that's directed by the camshaft.

Once you have an idea of the basic cam specs, you're not done yet. Budget comes into play here since we can go with a flat tappet hydraulic, or mechanical if you're looking to do this on a budget. Or, you could spend a little more cash and step up to a roller. Hydraulic rollers are hot right now, but

our money is on the mechanical roller if you're looking to make power since we can squeeze a good spring on top of this application and make it work. But now we're talking about an engine that probably spends most of its time in the garage and not on the street.

Most of the cam companies address this selection process by jumping right into rear gear ratio and cruise RPM. This is a good first step, but let's take the time to find out why. It's been our experience that guys building engines or even swapping cams tend to overlook a somewhat simple application question. To be honest, your typical street enthusiast wants it all. He wants a cam that makes "big power" and he's willing to sacrifice drivability and fuel mileage to get it. The more enthusiastic yet less informed also want that big power, but they are unwilling to give up anything to get it. Those are the guys who should bolt on a centrifugal blower or nitrous, because they're not going to get that kind of overall performance gain out of a camshaft.

The real question should be: Do you want to build your existing car around the engine, or would it be better to build the engine around the rest of the car? This is an essential question. The problem that occurs almost daily is that many enthusiasts get so excited about building power that they forget that the car is not configured to maximize the engine's potential. Keep in mind here that we are talking about accelerating quickly in a quarter-mile, which is the most common application for a hot street engine.

The Saga of Ricky Racer

Let's get a little deeper into this because it's worth the time. To do this, allow us to introduce you to our pal Ricky Racer. Ricky has a 1968 Nova with a 355–ci small-block that he wants to make "faster." He opens up his favorite cam catalog and instantly goes to the bottom of the page, looking for a "big cam." He chooses a 300-degree advertised duration flat tappet hydraulic cam from Friendly Cam Company and somehow manages to properly bolt it in the engine. Luckily, he changed valvesprings too, so at least the springs won't immediately go into coil bind! Unfortunately, Ricky didn't take into consideration that his Nova is still spinning a stock torque converter, TH350 trans, and a lame 8.2-inch ring gear diameter 10–bolt rear with 3.08 gears. He's got a big dual-

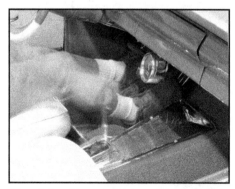

The style of transmission should also be taken into consideration. A lighter car equipped with a manual transmission is much more tolerant of a big cam than a heavy car with a stock converter and an automatic transmission.

plane intake and an even bigger 750–cfm Holley carb on the intake, but he's only planned on a set of headers and an exhaust system. And for now he's saddled with a set of cast-iron manifolds and a dual 2-inch exhaust with hideously restrictive mufflers. Must we go on?

Ricky soon discovers that his shoot-from-the-hip combination is a pig. Not only has it lost all its low-speed torque, but the cam also doesn't "pull" at high RPM either. In his zest to make hero power, Ricky has managed to kill the engine's mid-range torque potential with a long duration cam that includes an incredibly late-closing intake valve. This means all his low- and mid-range cylinder pressure has evaporated. Even better, by the time the engine speed has achieved an RPM where the cam starts working, the exhaust system has long since maxed out, choking any further power. So our pal Ricky is left with a slug that makes less power everywhere. Of course, he blames all this on Friendly Cam Company when all they did was sell him what he wanted!

Ricky has two options to remedy this mess. The first recommendation, if Ricky has the money, is to salvage his cam selection by adding a set of 1–5/8-inch headers, a mandrel-bent exhaust system, and a pair of less restrictive mufflers like a set of Flowmasters. Next, he has to step up to a 12–bolt rear end (why invest money in a spindly 8.2-inch 10–bolt that will never live?) with a set of 3.73 or 4.10 rear gears and a good limited slip unit for traction. Of course, that means a set of sticky tires as well to hook all that torque multiplication. Speaking of torque multiplication, he also needs a 2,600- to 3,000-rpm stall speed converter, and at the very least some type of shift kit to complete the deal. He also needs a better ignition system, as well as roller rockers, and better heads. But let's stop here for the sake of Ricky's ego and his heavily ventilated wallet.

The second recommendation is much simpler and far less expensive, but it isn't what Ricky wants to hear. This involves yanking the cam and putting it on the shelf. Instead, we choose a more conservative cam that works best with a 355–ci small-block with stock heads and

There is an art form to matching torque converters and camshafts. To condense it down to its essentials, a long-duration cam requires a much looser converter than a mild cam in order to take advantage of the engine's higher peak torque point.

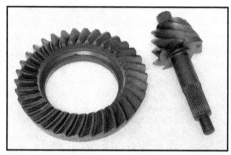

As odd as it sounds, rear-end gears are also part of the camshaft selection equation. Deep gears (numerically higher, like 4.10:1) multiply the leverage factor to get the car moving; so, deeper gears and a longer duration cam are suited to each other. Taller gears (numerically shorter, like 3.08:1) are better suited to shorter-duration cams where the engine makes more low- and mid-range torque.

You certainly can't tell by looking which of these two cams is the bargain basement grind. If you know how to decipher a cam card, the specs clue you in on the right decision.

a mild induction system. Ricky still needs to install a better exhaust system; in fact, he should have done that before he changed the cam. But now, a cam

If you're building a cam for a full-on drag race effort like a Fastest Street Car, then a duration figure in the mid-270 degree at 0.050 might be a good place to start. But if you're building a street engine, you might want to re-think that "bubba" cam.

Even if your street car spends more time on the track than it does on the street, that still doesn't necessarily mean the cam needs to be some monster grind. A cam that improves the mid-range torque always accelerates the car quicker.

around 216/224 degrees at 0.050 with a lift of around 0.460/0.470 and a lobe separation of 110 to 112 degrees would be a good choice. This cam creates decent low-speed and mid-range torque to accelerate the car because it has a tall gear and a stock stall speed converter. It has a dual pattern to "cheat" the exhaust side since it's restricted by the stock heads and iron exhaust manifolds. Even with headers this is still a good cam selection. The down side to this cam is that it doesn't have that drive-in lumpy sound that everybody wants. But since the rest of the car is a far cry from a "fast" car (actually what Ricky wants is a quick car), it doesn't make sense to build the car around the cam.

What we've accomplished here is to choose a cam that complements the existing car. At the least, Ricky shouldn't start the buildup of his fast street machine with the cam. The smarter move would be to start on the exhaust system to get the most from what the existing engine is capable of producing. The problem with that, for many street rats, is that the exhaust isn't nearly as sexy or appealing to his ego as a big, lumpy cam.

Perhaps that was a long way around to make this point, but it makes more sense to configure the camshaft around the existing car combination. Or, at least be willing to spend a lot of money to build the car around the engine. Either way works, and it again comes down to how much money you have to spend and what your ultimate goals are for the vehicle.

Street Compromises

Another big dilemma for a street engine builder is that the entire concept of building a performance engine for the street is absolutely rife with compromises. First, the engine must perform well throughout an incredibly wide RPM band – from idle to 6,500 rpm or more. It must run on pump gas, it better have some type of low-speed torque for drivability, it must be able to have some type of longevity, oh and we don't want to do any maintenance like setting valve lash either. And of course, we don't want to spend $10,000 to build this engine either. In fact, our budget is less than $2,000. But it'd better make a bunch of power!

As we see it, four levels of street engines with an almost limitless number of engine variations fall somewhere in between these categories. At the most conservative end, we have the Computer Controlled engines, which are also emissions-controlled and limited in the amount of camshaft they can sustain, mainly because of idle quality concerns. Next, we have the Mild Street engines that should be constrained by an approach aimed at making as much mid-range torque as possible. Next we have Strong Street engines willing to sacrifice some idle quality and some low-speed torque in search of more power in the mid-range and the top end up to 6,000 rpm. Finally, we have the Big Power engines that are larger in displacement or are willing to spin engine speeds higher than 6,000, don't care about idle quality, and have only a passing interest in mid-range torque below 4,000 rpm.

While these descriptions are about the engines, we're really talking about the cars. The Big Power guys have the money for high stall speed converters, deep gears, light cars, big tires, and the cash to make it all work. Much like the ubiquitous bell curve, the majority of the street engines actually fall into the two middle categories. With both of these two categories, the camshafts should still be considered conservative mainly because we are attempting to create the widest torque band possible. This is probably where you're thinking: "Wait, what happened to horsepower? Where's my big horsepower numbers that I read about in the magazines?"

These are good questions; so let's start by delving a little deeper into Mild Street and Strong Street car acceleration. While we don't want to downplay peak horsepower, it should not be the street-car enthusiast's Holy Grail. We get plenty of opposition to this statement, but the truth is that torque accelerates the car while horsepower creates

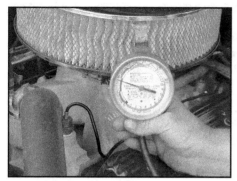

As duration increases, idle vacuum decreases – it's as simple as that. For street engines, a cam with less than 8 to 9 inches of manifold vacuum begins to create several carburetor-tuning issues that may be challenging to resolve.

Big carburetors and long duration cams are obvious common bedfellows, but be careful. Those monster carburetors look sexy, but they were never intended as daily-driven street carbs. You can make them work, but you better know your way around carburetor circuitry. Holley Dominators are notoriously pig-rich at part throttle.

Mild street small-blocks, especially those with cast-iron manifolds, respond well to dual pattern cams with around 210 degrees at 0.050 duration on the intake, and a wider lobe separation angle like 112 to 114 degrees.

Most street cams are created with a built-in intake lobe advance of usually 4 degrees, which is why you don't really need to advance these cams beyond their intended "stock" position. You can tell how much advance is designed into the cam by comparing the intake centerline number to the lobe separation angle. The intake centerline is a smaller number than the lobe separation angle by the amount of advance dialed into the cam.

those big MPH trap speed numbers. The real battle on the torque-vs.-horsepower controversy that everyone argues about is really about separating torque from horsepower. The torque pushers argue that we should have as much torque as possible.

The horsepower heroes all push the analogy that if torque were king, then we'd all be driving low-speed diesel engines.

Our counterpoint is that for street engines, we want both. We want an overall power curve with as much area under the curve as we can get. But we're less willing to compromise torque for the sake of peak horsepower. This is because a street car with less-than-ideal drag strip gearing spends most of its time in the mid-range RPM band trying to accelerate a heavy car in between 4,000 and 5,000 rpm in first, second, and third gears (assuming a typical three-speed automatic). The key factor that drives this point home is that very few street cars cross the finish line at the drag strip at or above their peak horsepower RPM point. A Mild Street engine usually attains peak horsepower at around 5,500 rpm. Yet this same engine in a typical Chevelle or Camaro runs through the traps in third gear at barely 5,000— an easy 500 to perhaps as much as 1,000 rpm shy of its peak horsepower point! This is because most of these cars use 3.08:1 to 3.55:1 gears and relatively tall

JUST FOR FUN

Since we're looking at applications for camshafts in this chapter, we thought it would be fun to take a look at a couple of NHRA drag racing engines to get a feel for what they're doing. You would think that a Top Fuel or nitro Funny Car would use a monster cam to feed that hungry hemi, and you'd be right. According to our pals at Crane, a good "baseline" for a Top Fuel engine would be a solid roller with 298/298 degrees of duration at 0.050-inch tappet lift with an impressive 0.750-/0.726-inch valve lift specs on a 114-degree lobe separation angle.

On the normally aspirated side of things, the 500 ci Pro Stock engines use a somewhat more conservative roller with 276/306 degrees of duration at 0.050-inch tappet lift but they make up for the reduced duration by hitting the lift

curve very hard. Using 1.9:1 rocker arms, these cams start with a lobe lift of 0.503, which computes to a rockin' 1.007-inch valve lift! Keep in mind that these guys are running these engines to 9,500 rpm, which is why you see them return to the pits and immediately inspect their valvesprings after every run and change the springs after a few runs.

Of course, we can't miss an opportunity to mention that unless you're building a record-setting, 9,000-rpm, 500-ci Pro Stock engine, why would you be looking at cams with 270 degrees at 0.050 durations? Makes you think, doesn't it? Especially when you consider that these engine builders could care less what the engine makes below 7,000 rpm since these engines don't see that "low" RPM even on the starting line.

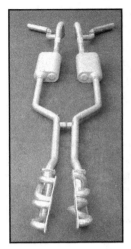

Like induction systems, the exhaust system is also a critical player in performance. A restrictive exhaust system does not allow a long-duration cam to work at higher engine speeds, negating the potential benefits of the bigger cam.

A later-closing intake valve requires that the engine wait longer to make cylinder pressure (until the intake closes). This means the piston moves farther up the cylinder before the intake closes. It should be obvious that this reduces low-speed cylinder pressure. That's why the cam companies recommend more compression for longer duration cams.

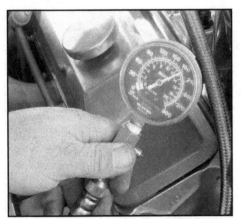

The relationship between compression ratio and intake closing can be easily measured with a cranking compression gauge. The combination of a low static compression ratio with a long duration camshaft shows up as extremely low cranking compression. Shoot for an acceptable cranking pressure of 180 to 190 psi.

CAM CHART

Category	Cam Type	Advertised Duration Range	Duration @ 0.050 Range	Lift Range	Lobe Separation Range
Computer Controlled	Hyd. Roller	245 - 260	192 - 210	0.420 - 0.450	112 - 114
Mild Street	Flat Hyd.	250 - 265	210 - 224	0.450 - 0.480	110 - 112
Strong Street	Flat Hyd.	265 - 285	220 - 245	0.460 - 0.510	108 - 112
Big Power	Mech. Roller	280 - 300	240 - 260	0.550 - 0.620	112 - 114

THE 4/7 SWAP

One of the latest ideas for the small-block Chevy is what is being referred to as the 4/7 swap. The cam grinder merely switches the timing of cylinders 4 and 7 so that the typical small-block firing order changes from 1-8-4-3-6-5-7-2 to 1-8-7-3-6-5-4-2. Then the only other thing you have to do is to remember to switch the order of the plug wires on the distributor cap to match the cam and you're ready to go.

So why go through all this? Many professional engine builders feel that the small-block is hampered by cylinders 5 and 7 firing adjacent to each other in the firing order. By switching the firing order of the small-block, cylinder 5 fires followed by cylinder 4 on the opposite side of the engine. Of course, this moves this adjacent firing sequence to the front of the engine with cylinders 4 and 2 firing alongside each other. We have not performed a comparison test to see if there is a power increase to be had, but according to COMP Cams, there appears to be a "smoothing" of the torque curve with less variation between data points.

This change in firing order does require a 4/7 switch-specific cam blank for a small-block cam, but most of the major cam companies are set up to handle this. COMP Cams has gone one step further and created a line of flat tappet hydraulic and mechanical Xtreme Energy cams that incorporate this 4/7 switch. We've listed a few of the lineup in the following chart.

Cam	Style	Duration @ 0.050	Lift	Lobe Separation
XE274H-10	Hydraulic	230/236	0.487/0.490	110
XE284H-10	Hydraulic	240/246	0.507/0.510	110
XE294H-10	Hydraulic	250/256	0.519/0.523	110

"CHEAP" CAMS

Everybody's always looking for a better deal on parts. One of the more attractive prices is on budget, "no-name" cams from warehouse distributors, mail-order houses, and even from the name cam companies themselves. So what differentiates a budget cam from a brand new line of cams that sells for a bunch more money? The answer is tied up in the price of technology.

Place a budget cam alongside the latest Lobemaster 2000 cam and they look the same. But the art of cam design is continually evolving. As we mentioned in the chapter on cam basics, the level of sophistication has grown substantially in the last 10 years. A cam designed in 1965 might have all kinds of appeal for a nostalgic muscle car resto-fanatic who must have nothing less than that Duntov 30-30 solid lifter cam for his 1969 Z28. But we can guarantee that hundreds of camshafts on the market today are far superior to that Duntov cam in terms of duration versus lift. The same is true with budget cams.

When the cam companies decide to release a whole new line of

camshafts, they don't automatically shelve their previous lineup. The Energizer lineup of cams for Crane and the Magnum series for COMP are still very good camshafts, but the Crane PowerMax and COMP Xtreme Energy cams now attract the most attention. But if you want to seriously compare numbers, take a look at the hydraulic intensity numbers and also the amount of valve lift compared to the advertised duration. Compare the latest designs with cams that are perhaps 10 years old or older. You see some subtle yet interesting shifts in the way cams are designed.

One of the big-name mail-order houses sells an in-house brand of very attractively priced cams at under $50 for a performance hydraulic flat tappet camshaft. That's a screamin' deal. But let's compare the published specs to a current design cam from Crane.

We chose to use 0.050-inch tappet lift as our common denominator. With the later design camshaft, you pick up low- and mid-range torque with a shorter advertised duration and the added plus of more valve lift. If you remember our definition of hydraulic intensity, it is the number of degrees between the advertised duration figure and the duration at 0.050-inch tappet lift. The budget cam specs do not specify a checking height for advertised duration (Crane's is 0.004) so this comparison may not be exactly apples to apples, but the difference in hydraulic intensity is minimal.

Are we bagging on this budget camshaft? Not really. At its under-$50 price, it serves a purpose. Especially if the brand name cam is roughly twice the price or more. The more important point is that you now have a way to evaluate both cams and can use that information to help you make a more intelligent decision when it comes to choosing the right cam for your next engine.

Cam	Adv. Dur.	Dur. @ 0.050	Lift	Hyd. Intensity
Budget Cam	300/300	222/222	0.436/0.436	78
Crane PowerMax	284/284	222/222	0.450/0.450	62

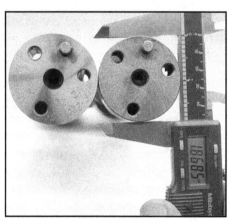

Big roller cams and high RPM means you must increase valvespring pressure. Drag racers have been grinding small-block cams on big-block lobes for years to increase the cam's stiffness and to prevent torsional twist that creates timing inaccuracies in the rearmost cylinders.

How important is cam core diameter on a stock engine? GM engineers decided it was pretty important since the LS1 cam core (right) is substantially larger than the GEN I cam on the left.

tires. So now, why would we want to place more emphasis on making more peak horsepower when it's obvious we can only make use of this peak power in first and second gears? Hmmm…

On the other hand, if we decide to emphasize torque between 4,000 and 5,000 rpm, even if it means sacrificing some peak horsepower to do so, we can now accelerate our mild or strong street car much faster through first, second, and third gears because of this additional torque. So let's choose a camshaft that improves mid-range torque while perhaps not hurting top-end power. Let's also keep in mind that we don't want to spin the engine too slowly since RPM is horsepower. But if we choose a cam with too much duration, we begin to lose mid-range torque. That's because a longer duration cam merely shifts the engine's torque curve higher in the engine RPM range. Can you begin to see how building a street engine is a giant set of compromises?

In an incredibly long equatorial route of circular logic, this brings us back to why the cam companies start their cam recommendations with asking what weight, rear gear ratio, and transmission equipment is present in the car. Their focus is to determine a highway-cruise RPM and then select a camshaft based on that simplified number. This has its advantages, but unfortunately most cam company recommendations end up being conservative ones that most enthusiasts don't want to hear.

Take a look at the cam chart that we created. It makes some very general cam recommendations based on our four types of street small-block Chevy engines that take into account all the things we've mentioned up to this point. Now, the problem with generalized charts is that they're just like universal parts—they don't universally fit anything really well. But if you're looking for some ballpark areas to work around, then this chart helps. You may notice that many of the cam specs overlap from one category to the next. This is because a slightly more muscular mild street engine could also be a conservative strong street small-block. The idea here is to create some general starting points without getting bogged down into incredibly long and boring descriptions of hundreds of individual engine combinations.

Duration Facts

One key to understanding the effect of cam timing on an engine is to not necessarily think in terms of duration, but rather in terms of when the intake valve closes in the intake cycle. A longer duration intake lobe opens the valve sooner in the cycle and closes it later. While the sooner-opening intake tends to increase overlap, it is the later-closing intake valve that has the most telling effect on the power curve. Think about what effect this later closing intake has on lower engine speeds. As the piston begins to move upward in the intake-closing portion of the four-stroke cycle, and as the valve remains open, the piston at some point begins to push fresh air and fuel out of the cylinder because the valve is still open. The cylinder cannot begin to build pressure until the

Long duration cams also mean later closing intakes. At low speed, lots of overlap and a late closing intake can conspire to create serious reversion in the intake tract. If your carb or the inside of your intake appears black and sooty, the engine's trying to tell you something. Exhaust gas doesn't burn—it's like built-in EGR, which isn't good for performance.

When choosing a cam for a later-model car or truck with EFI, even a mild TBI combination responds best to a mild-duration cam with wide lobe separation angle to create a near-stock idle condition. Keep in mind that a significant cam change on a computer-controlled car probably requires computer reprogramming in order to optimize the power offered by the cam.

Big cams and high engine speeds require big, stiff valvesprings that are brutal on parts. Attention paid to proper installation minimizes the chances of serious damage.

All the dyno testing that you read in this book and any magazine story all reference wide-open throttle power only. Very little has been written about the effect of big duration numbers and tight lobe separation angles on part-throttle efficiency, which is why cam selection is such a mysterious topic.

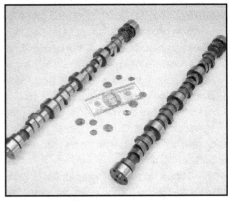

Don't overlook the cost factor of those romantic roller cams and valvetrains. Granted, rollers make more power, but for many average street engines, a flat tappet mechanical cam can probably produce all the power you need for a significantly less amount of cash.

Broken valvetrain parts are the most common cause of engine problems with high-strung street and race engines, which is another reason to be conservative when choosing a camshaft. A dropped valve can ruin your whole day.

Don't be afraid to spec out your own custom cam if you don't see what you want in the catalog. All the major cam companies offer custom grinding services that can often be accomplished in very short order.

intake valve closes. The net result is lower cylinder pressure at lower engine speeds, which means reduced power and a sluggish engine (see "Cranking Compression" sidebar).

The advantage of the later closing intake is that the inertial forces and higher inlet air speed of the inlet system at higher engine speeds continue to fill the cylinder with that later closing intake valve. This works because the air and fuel are rushing in at a high enough speed to cram more air and fuel into the cylinder even when the cylinder is at or above 100 percent volumetric efficiency. This is also due to the fact that the high engine speed does not allow the air and

OF LUMPY CAMS AND OVERLAP

We must acknowledge that many street-performance camshafts are purchased strictly based on how radical the camshaft sounds in the car and that ultimate power is not really all that important. The typical route to get there is a long duration camshaft with lots of overlap. If, for example, a 268 Xtreme Energy COMP Cams grind would be a good overall choice, some enthusiasts choose an Xtreme 294 instead, just to make sure that their idle quality sounds more like a Pro Stocker than a pure stocker.

We'd like to propose a different approach. As we learned in the cam basics chapter, that hard-core idle quality is a direct result of the amount of overlap between EC and IO. All Xtreme Energy cams come with a set lobe separation angle of 110 degrees. Given that, as you add duration, this automatically increases the number of degrees of overlap. The combination of a later-closing intake with much more overlap on an overly large camshaft absolutely kills low-speed torque and, to a lesser extent, mid-range power. What we need is a different approach.

The following charts list the cam specs for the both the COMP Cams Xtreme Energy 268 flat tappet hydraulic and the 294 Xtreme Energy cams. Our

idea is to create a lumpy cam idle sound without sacrificing power in the mid-range. The plan is merely to tighten the lobe separation angle on the smaller cam by four degrees. This creates more overlap, which creates less manifold idle vacuum, which makes the engine idle lumpier. If you like the idea of more valve lift, we've accommodated that as well with a 1.6:1 rocker ratio that creates almost the same lift as the larger cam. Clearly, the larger cam has much more overlap than the equivalent of moving the lobe centers on the 268 cam closer by four degrees, but the idea is that the idle still generates that distinctive lope while the engine is much more throttle responsive, while also making more power in the mid-range. Plus,

with the 268 cam's much shorter duration numbers, peak power occurs at a more streetable RPM. The larger 294 cam requires much more engine speed to attain ideal peak power.

The only hitch in this plan is that this would require a custom camshaft with the tighter lobe separation angle. But that's the only change to this otherwise off-the-shelf cam. COMP and Crane can do this in a day or so, which means you don't have to wait a month to get this cam. This is mainly another idea to get you to think about intake and exhaust lobe relationships and how camshafts operate. If we've got you thinking, then we've done our job.

Camshaft Comparison

Cam		Adv. Dur.	Dur. @ 0.050	Lift	Lobe Sep.
Xtreme 268, Int.		268	224	0.477	110
Exh.		280	230	0.480	
Xtreme 294, Int.		294	250	0.519	110
Exh.		306	256	0.523	
Xtreme 268,	Int.	268	224	0.508	106
Custom 1.6 rockers	Exh.	280	230	0.512	

fuel time to bleed back into the intake port. The net result is higher cylinder pressure and more horsepower at higher engine speeds.

The trick is to close the intake valve at the precise moment and RPM when you can ideally fill the cylinder to maximum volumetric efficiency. This is the peak horsepower point. A higher engine speed does not help fill the cylinder any better, and more duration only hurts the volumetric efficiency of the existing engine combination.

The point of this discussion is to drive home the idea that additional duration means a later closing intake and higher engine speeds that may not be safe for your engine combination, so additional duration is not always the answer. Each engine combination has its own particular amount of duration and lift that makes the best power. The trick is to build that exact combination, and that's what

Cylinder heads also are a critical part of the camshaft selection process. As performance heads become better and more affordable, choosing the right cam is critical.

CRANKING COMPRESSION

One slick way to measure how well your street engine runs is by testing cranking compression. The cam companies generally incorporate compression ratio in with many of their cam recommendations. The main reason for this is that, as we explained in the main body copy, cylinder pressure drops off at low engine speeds with a later-closing intake valve that is the result of a long duration cam. Cranking the engine over, cylinder pressure cannot begin to build until the intake valve closes. Therefore, the longer the duration (and the later the IC), the lower the cranking compression, given the same static compression ratio. So, for a longer duration cam, it's best to have more static compression ratio to make up for the loss in low-speed torque.

To see how this works, merely start with your basic cranking compression gauge. While most mechanics use it as a comparator between cylinders, looking for the weak points, we use the same tool as a tuning device. The standard for pump-gas street-

engines is usually around 185 to 190 psi cranking compression. If you are really serious about testing, the best procedure is with a warm engine: Remove all the spark plugs, disable the ignition system, prop open the carb or fuel injection throttle so there are no restrictions, and then crank the engine over for about three to four revolutions. The compression gauge delivers the cylinder pressure reading.

Generally, any pressure below 180 psi means you either have a low static compression ratio compared to the cam you're using, you have serious leakage past the rings or valves, or a later closing intake valve from a long duration cam. The way to evaluate poor ring seal is with a cylinder leak-down gauge that pumps pressurized air into the cylinder and delivers the amount of leakage as a percentage. Don't fall into the trap of believing you must have less than 10 percent leakage to make power. A decent street engine might leak as much as 15 percent and still have good power, so don't freak out over leakage numbers below 20 percent.

Of course, there are limitations on this cylinder pressure theme when using pump gas. Our experience is that any cranking cylinder pressure readings in excess of 200 psi are probably going to generate detonation problems on pump gas, especially on warm days or at elevated engine temperatures. We have had experience with a 383-ci small-block with 200-psi cranking pressure with 34 degrees of lead that made close to 500 hp and over 500 ft-lbs of torque with aluminum heads that rarely exhibited detonation problems on pump gas. The good chamber design probably did much to prevent detonation sensitivity.

So, this should give you a range of cylinder pressure to use to evaluate your street engine and how well it compares to these levels. Obviously, the higher the cranking cylinder pressure, the better your street engine runs—it's as simple as that.

CAM MATH

Camshaft specs are all about numbers. But despite the fact that we're dealing with an eccentric shape, these shapes do follow a few simple rules. Once you understand them, you can apply these rules to help you discover more about any camshaft. Let's start with some basic moves. After having digested our cam basics chapter, you know that adding the IO and IC figures along with 180 degrees gives the cam's duration. Of course, this figure is accurate only for the specific opening and closing checking points, either at advertised duration (such as 0.004-inch tappet lift, for example) or at 0.0050-inch tappet lift. Let's look at an example for a cam at 0.050 inches:

IO = 16 BTDC   IC = 48 ABDC
16 + 180 + 48 = 244 degrees of intake duration at 0.050-inch tappet lift

The same procedure holds true for the exhaust lobe:

EO = 63 BBDC   EC = 11 ATDC
63 + 180 + 11 = 254 degrees of exhaust duration at 0.050-inch tappet lift

Now that we know how to determine duration, we can use these figures to calculate intake and exhaust centerline. For the intake lobe, we divide intake duration by 2 and subtract the intake opening point from the previous figure. If you're working with a stock or near-stock camshaft with very short duration numbers where the IO is ATDC, then add the

IO figure to half of the duration. The result of these calculations is the intake centerline ATDC. It's important to note that this is probably not the cam's maximum lift point, especially if the cam is asymmetrical. Let's look at an example of how this works:

Intake Duration: 244 degrees / 2 = 122
122 − 16 = 106 degrees intake centerline ATDC

To find the exhaust centerline, we use a slightly different equation. This time, we again divide the duration in half, but subtract the EC from that figure. If the EC is from a very short-duration camshaft where the EC is listed as ATDC, or is listed on the cam card with a minus sign in front of it, then add the EC number to half the duration. Here's an example:

Exhaust Duration: 254 degrees / 2 = 127
127 - 13 = 114 degrees BTDC

Now that we know the intake and exhaust centerline positions, we can use those figures to help us determine the lobe separation angle. This again is pretty easy and you may have already guessed how to get there since all we have to do is add the two centerlines together and divide by 2. Using our previous examples, it works like this:

Intake Centerline 106 + Exhaust Centerline 114 = 220

220 /2 = 110 degree lobe separation angle

These simple formulas can help you see how camshaft companies come up with the numbers used when comparing camshafts. One caution to this: Some cam companies express a different cam opening or closing point by placing the degrees in parenthesis. As an example: EC (6) BTDC. This means the cam actually closes at 6 degrees After TDC (ATDC) rather than before, even though the tag next to the figure says BTDC. The cam companies do this so that a separate cam card reading ATDC does not have to be printed for these short duration cams since most cams close the exhaust ATDC.

Another interesting side note is that if a cam is ground "straight up," the intake centerline and the lobe separation angle are the same figure. In our example, the intake centerline is at 106 degrees ATDC, while our calculated lobe separation angle is actually 110 degrees. This is because most cam companies grind a majority of their street camshafts advanced. In this case, the cam company advanced the cam four degrees so that the intake centerline moved from 110 degrees to 106 degrees. The cam companies do this on longer-duration cams to improve low-speed torque. Of course, this also moves the intake closing point four degrees ahead, which would tend to hurt top-end power. This is another reason to really look at the IC point and not the total duration figure when determining which cam to run. It's just another detail to use when deciding which cam is best for your engine.

engine builders have been striving after for over 100 years of building performance engines.

By remaining conservative with duration figures, this improves the engine's overall torque curve, since a long duration cam with a later closing intake means that the engine is sacrificing cylinder pressure all the way

through the RPM curve in order to create the ideal conditions to make peak horsepower. For street engines that spend a lot of time in the midrange RPM, making more power—up to a point—is always beneficial. Of course, there comes a point with perhaps a big cubic inch engine where you make enough torque that you can't hook

the tires to the track and the car just spins the tires. Then you can consider closing the intake valve later to help make more peak horsepower while not hurting acceleration since you eliminate tire spin as well. All this can get complex, but if you think it through, it all does make sense.

SUPERCHARGER, NITROUS, AND TURBO CAMS

It's impossible to walk through a car show or even a Wednesday night cruise and not witness several different approaches to what has been dubbed "power adders" by those in the know. This arena has grown radically in the last decade or so with the development of better and more efficient superchargers like centrifugal blowers, screw superchargers, and of course turbos. The nitrous circus also continues to evolve with both smaller and easy-to-install street systems and those outrageous multi-stage nitrous oxide systems that seem to get more complex by the week.

With the expansion of not only large cubic inch small-blocks as well as these power adders, horsepower has never been easier to make. The old standard for small-blocks used to be 400 hp. That has now gradually grown to 500 hp as the mark you need to achieve just to keep up with the other Camaros on the boulevard. But now with superchargers and better cylinder heads, 800 hp is not unusual for a big-inch nitroused small-block. For a 400–ci small-block, 800 hp is 2 hp per ci (hp/ci). Not long ago, that number would have made the cover of several magazines and earned the engine builder entry a first floor spot in the Small-Block Haul of Fame. But today, 800 hp is almost standard fare. If you want stupid-big numbers, let's talk about a 287–ci turbocharged small-block Chevy that powers Ken Duttweiler's Comp Eliminator car that with a single, monstrous tur-

Roots superchargers have been a perennial favorite with hot rodders for decades. Many enthusiasts choose a Roots blower as much for its sticking-through-the-hood impact as for the power increase.

bocharger is capable a jaw-dropping 1,600 hp that equates to a stupefying 5.5 hp/ci.

So now that we've established that power numbers are easy to make, let's look into how the camshaft relates to each of the big three power adders – nitrous, superchargers, and turbos. We give you a quick overview of each and then address how cam timing relates to all three.

Nitrous

Nitrous oxide is an odorless, color-less gas consisting of two parts nitrogen and one part oxygen atom to create a compound that appears as N_2O. Nitrous oxide is compressed into a liquid so that it can be easily stored in a small contain-er under extremely high pressure, usual-ly around 900 psi. When released in your engine, the first thing that occurs is that the energy used to compress the gas into a liquid is released during the change from a liquid to a gaseous state, reducing the inlet air temperature in the intake manifold by roughly 65 degrees F. This temperature reduction alone is worth roughly 6 percent power, even if the

Centrifugal superchargers can be thought of as belt-driven turbochargers. The design of the compressor side is very similar to a turbocharger. The big difference is that centrifugal blowers require massive amounts of shaft horsepower to drive them compared to a turbo.

nitrous didn't contribute to the combustion process—but it does!

Next, nitrous oxide is a fairly stable organic compound, which means it doesn't release its combined oxygen element easily. In this particular case, nitrous requires a combustion temperature of 575 degrees F before the oxygen is available to contribute to the combustion process. But once this temperature occurs, it certainly lives up to its nickname as supercharger in a bottle. Since the idea of any normally aspirated engine is to stuff as much air into the engine as possible, injecting nitrous into the engine at a finely tuned rate can do wonders for power. Of course, this means you must also inject a given ratio of fuel along with the nitrous to prevent the combustion process from running excessively lean and melting all those pretty pistons you invested so much money to buy.

The beauty of the nitrous oxide compound is that the two parts nitrogen also play a part by contributing to slowing the burn rate of combustion from the additional oxygen. This is why no one injects pure oxygen into an engine, since the burn rate would basically turn into a true explosion with devastating consequences to an engine.

One of the reasons that nitrous is so popular is because a basic 150-hp nitrous system is an external bolt-on kit that can be installed on almost any car in a few hours and requires no special internal or external components to make it work. As

Another, more efficient supercharger that has yet to catch on with the street set is the screw supercharger. Whipple markets this Swedish-built screw supercharger that is roughly equal to the centrifugals in efficiency. The difficulty comes in that the Swedes don't build a blower big enough to move enough air to make decent horsepower.

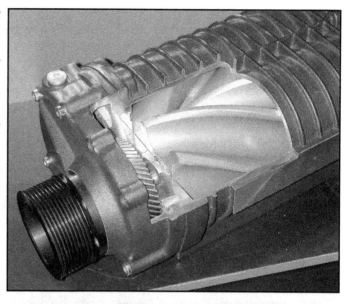

Centrifugals have been around for decades. The old McCulloch centrifugal with straight inlet blades used on the 1957 T-bird have evolved into impressive belt-driven superchargers like this ATI ProCharger that can push close to 1,000 hp out of an aggressive big-inch small-block.

long as your engine can produce at least 4 to 5 psi of fuel pressure under load with the nitrous engaged, these nitrous kits are exceptionally easy and fun to use. The down side to nitrous is that even a 15-pound bottle doesn't last long, which means you become close friends with your nitrous supplier since he sees you often, and at $3 per pound nitrous is anything but free. But it sure is fun.

Supercharging

This power-adder takes a little more space to cover since we now have several variations of what used to be a one-horse town. The two basic styles of

supercharging are positive displacement and non-positive displacement superchargers. Positive displacement superchargers encompass Roots-, screw-, and piston-style compressors. The most popular is clearly the Roots blower, using a pair of either two- or three-lobe rotors that turn inside a case to push air into the cavity above the intake ports. A Roots blower really isn't a true compressor, but rather an air mover. It just moves air faster than the engine can use it, creating pressure in the intake manifold.

A screw-type compressor such as the Lysholm style units sold by Whipple Industries is a true compressor that squeezes air between twin screws.

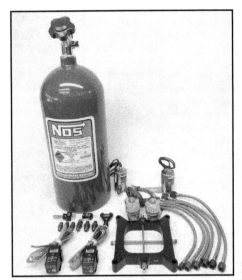

Nitrous is by far the simplest and easiest of the power-adders. This is a Nitrous Oxide Systems two-stage 250 to 500 hp "Double Cross" plate system. These bolt-on systems work extremely well and make tons of torque along with the horsepower as long as they are installed properly and the electrical connections are rock solid.

Because the screw compressor is a true compressor, its adiabatic efficiency (see sidebar) is better than a Roots. While the screw compressor is more efficient, it hasn't been highly successful for street performance use, mainly because the Swedish company building the compressors has yet to build a large enough compressor to move enough air to make serious horsepower. But for smaller displacement applications, these are excellent superchargers.

Centrifugal superchargers are much more similar in design to what you could call a crank-driven turbocharger. The compressor wheel is driven by a two-part

step-up ratio in order to generate the high compressor wheel speeds necessary to make these radial-flow superchargers work. The first step-up ratio is between the crankshaft drive pulley and the supercharger driven pulley. Then, a gear-drive step-up ratio occurs inside the supercharger to pump the speed up again to roughly an overall ratio of around 7:1. This means that if the engine is spinning 6,000 rpm, the compressor wheel is actually spinning at roughly 42,000 rpm. It is this immense speed that centrifugally compresses the air as it travels through the snail shell of the supercharger.

One downside to engine-driven superchargers is that each blower requires a significant crankshaft horsepower to drive. Even for a mild street engine, we're talking about 35 to 50 hp required merely to drive a supercharger that may only then deliver an increase of 200 hp to the crank. If there was some alternative way to drive these blowers, a supercharger could gain an additional 25 percent power increase with no other changes.

Turbocharging

Many enthusiasts consider the exhaust-driven turbocharger to be "free" horsepower since it has no direct connection to the crankshaft. While it is true that "waste" exhaust energy in the form of heat and pressure are used to turn the turbine wheel, this is not exactly a free lunch. Generally, some pumping losses are involved with piston effort required to push the exhaust gas past the turbine wheel, but these loses, while real, are substantially less than those required at the crankshaft to spin a Roots or centrifugal supercharger.

Multi-stage nitrous kits are best left to enthusiasts with more nitrous experience. These systems can be complex and difficult to tune if you have only a limited amount of nitrous experience. But these kits do make serious power when it all works properly.

The advantage of turbocharging is that it offers tremendous power advantages without necessarily overstressing the engine. The disadvantage to turbocharging in the past had to do with the poor combination of carburetors and turbos, and few ever really came up with a simplistic accomplishment of that task. But with the advent of electronic fuel injection (EFI), now the engine can be fed the proper ratio of air and fuel that can be finitely controlled to ensure the engine never suffers from poor mixture distribution, which creates lean conditions in certain cylinders, usually followed by a burned piston!

Recently, turbo technology has improved to the point where the big problem of "turbo lag" has also been eliminated. Even very large diameter single turbo applications can sit at the starting line of a drag strip and create boost based strictly on engine speed and not load. This means that you can now use a manual transmission with a turbo, sit there at the starting line with the clutch in, and make as much boost as necessary to launch the car. This new generation of turbos eliminates the need to run an automatic transmission and brake stall for the engine to make boost.

The bottom line is that turbocharger systems are becoming increasingly popular although their price is still well above those more traditional supercharger kit prices. A typical small-block EFI-packaged small-block also requires more custom fabrication than supercharger systems, but this may change as turbos enjoy increasing popularity.

Power-Adder Cams

According to the engine builders that we've interviewed, you can basically treat turbocharged, supercharged, and nitroused camshafts all the same way. Cam selection for these applications deals with taking into account the basic "funnel theory" of power-adder engine tuning. The funnel theory suggests that any power adder is like a funnel, in that it enhances the efficiency of the inlet side, but the outlet side of the funnel remains somewhat restricted. For example, if the cylinder heads remain the same but we pressurize the inlet side, it's like adding a funnel to the inlet side of the engine.

Turbochargers are by far the most efficient of the engine power-adders. While complex to install and expensive, they require the least power to drive, offer excellent efficiency numbers, and require the least radical engine setups. The key is properly matching the turbo to your application.

The key to cam timing for any power-adder is maximizing the potential of the overlap cycle. For boosted engines, reduced overlap minimizes the amount of time available when high-pressure inlet air can escape past the exhaust valve.

The difficulty with nitrous engines is that the place where you make the most power is right on the ragged edge of detonation. It doesn't take much for the engine to rattle slightly and knock a ring land off the piston. This is common with any boosted engine.

Since the outlet size (the exhaust port) does not change, we need to come up with a way to enhance the exhaust side in order to make maximum power.

The reasoning for this is simple. If you cannot purge the cylinder of the remaining exhaust gas at the completion of the exhaust stroke, either because of a restriction or insufficient time (in this case, degrees of exhaust duration), then the next inlet stroke still contains the remnants of the previous exhaust stroke. As the intake valve opens, the exhaust gas pressure remaining in the cylinder may be slightly higher than the intake manifold pressure, so the exhaust could (and will) easily travel up the intake tract. At the very least, it is eventually pulled back into the same cylinder. At worst, this exhaust gas, commonly referred to as reversion, mixes in the intake manifold plenum with the incoming gas for other cylinders. Since this exhaust gas does not burn a second time, reversion has hurt the volumetric efficiency and killed power because we've created a built-in exhaust gas recirculation (EGR) device. That's hardly the way to make good power.

This process is easily seen when you look at an engine that first runs normally aspirated and then is quickly converted over to a supercharger with no other changes. Let's say our normally aspirated engine achieved 400 peak horsepower at 6,500 rpm. Adding a

TORQUE TALK

A rarely recognized, yet crucial, benefit of nitrous is that while most kits are rated by their peak horsepower potential, few enthusiasts realize the massive torque gains that nitrous contributes. As an example, let's take a typical 125 hp plate kit system. This rating is generally the peak horsepower the kit delivers, and most kits are usually very close to their rated figures. But since the kit is delivering this "horsepower" through a fixed orifice, it is subject to the classic horsepower and torque formula, which for those of you who'd like to write it down somewhere (like stenciled across your forehead) is:

Horsepower = Torque x RPM / 5,252

Now, using our limited high school algebra, we can convert this formula to find torque, which ends up looking like this:

Torque = Horsepower x 5,252/ RPM

Perhaps you've already guessed what comes next. Most nitrous instructions suggest that even mild nitrous kits like our 125-hp kit should only be engaged at 3,000 RPM or higher. If you plug the 125-hp kit into the torque formula, you'll see why:

Torque = 125 hp x 5,252/3,000 rpm
Torque = 218 lb-ft

This means that when you hit the 125–hp kit button at 3,000 rpm, the engine instantly gains well over 200 lb-ft of torque. Since a mild street small-block makes roughly 300 lb-ft normally aspirated, that's an instantaneous torque increase of 66 percent! That's why nitrous is such a literal kick in the pants. This is also why the nitrous companies warn you to not engage even a small 125–hp kit below 3,000 rpm, since at 2,000 rpm this represents a massive 328 ft-lbs of torque gain. Especially with a cast-piston engine, that huge cylinder pressure hit knocks ring lands off the pistons–or break the pistons altogether. This concept is also why large nitrous systems are staged, to gradually bring in the massive power levels since dumping all that nitrous into the engine all at once would probably either push the pistons out of the engine, or at least put the tires up in smoke. Nitrous is a great power-adder, but like everything else, you have to know how to use it to prevent catastrophic engine damage.

ADIABATIC EFFICIENCY

The direct result of any attempt at making pressure is an increase in discharge temperature. As we all know, higher inlet air temperatures reduce air density, which reduces power. The trick is to compress air with minimal temperature rise. Roots blowers don't do a real good job of this, which is why they don't make as much power at the same boost level as a turbocharger.

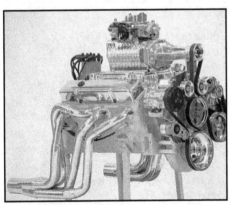

An interesting twist on the Roots blower is the Magnacharger that employs the Eaton-style supercharger that gained fame in production use in various mild performance applications. The company made a name for itself adapting this durable air mover on to late-model performance cars. The latest venture is carbureted small-block conversions.

Anytime you deal with compressing air to increase its pressure, you end up dealing with a phenomenon that was originally defined by two guys, Robert Boyle (1627–1691) and Daniel Bernoulli (1700–1782), who together helped create the kinetic gas laws that we still use today. While we're not physicists, it's still worth considering how physics relates to supercharging. What all this comes down to is that pressure and volume are inversely proportional—meaning that with a given pressure, if you increase the volume, the pressure is reduced. Or, if the volume is decreased, the pressure increases.

Positive-displacement superchargers are the easiest to deal with in this case, since they merely squeeze air into a tighter space, thereby increasing pressure. But this is no free lunch. First, it takes power to perform this operation. Second, while the pressure increases, so does temperature. For each gas, like air, a given amount of heat increase accompanies what can be called the perfect compression of this gas. So, it follows that as we compress air (regardless of the style of compressor we're using), the air temperature rises. The simplest example of this is a normal shop air-compressor. Place your hand on the tank when the compressor is running and it is warm to the touch.

There is also a secondary increase in the air temperature since our compressor methods are never perfect. This means that the device by which we compress the air also contributes to the temperature rise of the compressed air. Now we can get into what physicists call adiabatic efficiency, or

the rating system of how well our air compressor performs its job. This comes down to a somewhat simplistic definition that the more efficiently we compress air, the less heat we contribute to the process and the closer we can get to perfect compression of air—or 100 percent adiabatic efficiency.

You see references to this in discussions of the relative performance of all the different superchargers. The older-style Roots superchargers, while positive displacement, were not originally intended as air compressors, but rather as large air movers. Because of this, these blowers are not as efficient. We often see references to Roots blowers as having adiabatic efficiencies of around 50 to 55 percent compared to turbochargers rated as high as 70 to 75 percent. All this means is that the discharge air temperature from a turbocharger (at its peak efficiency) is lower than the same pressure rise generated by a Roots-style supercharger with all other variables being the same.

Other superchargers tend to fall in between these two extremes. For example, centrifugal superchargers are roughly equivalent to turbos, while screw superchargers are more efficient than a Roots, but not quite as good as a turbocharger. Design differences between styles of superchargers also affect these ratings. For example, the older compressor wheel designs of the original centrifugal superchargers designed by McCulloch and Paxton pale in comparison to the much more efficient centrifugals designed today by ATI ProCharger, Vortech, Paxton, and the rest.

centrifugal supercharger to this engine and running it again with no other changes creates a big peak power improvement by 40 percent—now we're making 560 hp. But a funny thing has also happened, peak horsepower normally aspirated was at 6,500 but now the engine makes peak power at 5,900, which is 600 rpm lower than the normally aspirated peak.

Several things are happening here. First off, we're probably paying roughly a 40 to 50 hp penalty to spin that centrifugal blower at 6,000 rpm. That's a big reason why peak horsepower didn't occur at a higher engine speed. But it's also entirely possible that the exhaust side of our engine is less efficient now at evacuating the entire exhaust load since the cylinder is now operating at a much

higher pressure and with more mass to purge. In this particular example, the crossover point is probably around 6,100 or 6,200 rpm where the engine no longer makes more power because the exhaust side can no longer efficiently evacuate the cylinder.

But let's look at our engine a little more closely. Let's say that our small-block is running a single pattern cam

EXHAUST SIDESHOW

Talk to any performance engine builder who builds, tests, and repairs supercharged or turbocharged engines and eventually the subject of abused exhaust valves and valvetrain parts surfaces. If you ponder the whole process of a supercharged engine, this somewhat puzzling phenomenon begins to make more sense.

Let's say we have a typical centrifugal supercharger running a serious small-block that's making 850 hp. This creates some crank-turning cylinder pressure to make this kind of power. Since we don't need a day-long duration cam and tons of RPM to make this kind of power, this means that the exhaust valve needs to open against pretty stiff cylinder pressure as well.

Let's estimate the cylinder pressure at 100 psi just before the piston reaches BDC. Assuming we have a 1.60-inch exhaust valve, this means we have 2.01 square inches of valve area working against this 100 psi. Multiply those two figures, and we end up with a force of 200 pounds. This is the additional force the rocker arm tip has to overcome merely to push the exhaust valve open. But wait, this scenario gets even worse when you calculate in the rocker arm ratio. Even with a 1.5:1 ratio, this means the pushrod must be able to withstand 300 pounds of force! It's no wonder that we often hear about a turbocharged small-block bending all of its exhaust pushrods or snapping an exhaust rocker stud.

So what can be done besides adding larger, heavier pushrods? The current conventional wisdom starts with reducing the exhaust valve head diameter. Merely using a smaller 1.5-inch diameter valve reduces the exhaust valve head area to 1.76 square inches, which is a 12 percent reduction in area from 2.01 square inches. Other ideas include adding exhaust lobe duration to compensate for the smaller valve and also reducing the rocker ratio from 1.6:1 to 1.5:1.

Of course, these are recommendations that assume a very serious engine making mondo cylinder pressure. If you have a mild street engine, these are probably not situations you need to worry about. But if you're contemplating a killer turbo or supercharged engine, at least you know what to expect!

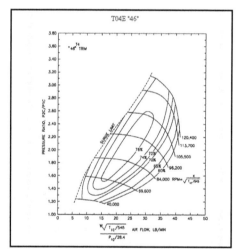

All turbo companies produce what is called a compressor map. The vertical scale is the pressure ratio, while the horizontal scale is the amount of airflow in pounds per hour. The "island" in the center of the map is where the turbo is most efficient, in this case 75 percent adiabatic efficiency. A good turbo offers a large efficiency island in the area where you want to make power.

by six or eight degrees in order to give the engine more time (in degrees of duration) to evacuate the cylinder and allow the engine to make more peak power.

Timing of these events is important since we don't want to rob the engine of the potential to make power by opening the exhaust valve too soon. This merely hurts peak power since pressure is still pushing the piston down, contributing to power. But we also don't want to open the exhaust valve too late, or we run the risk of running out of time on the closing side. On the other side of the lobe, we also don't want to close the exhaust valve too late, since that adds overlap. But the early closing exhaust valve is probably why our engine example couldn't make more power above 6,000 rpm. The key here is to extend the exhaust event duration by just the right number of degrees of duration while also opening and closing the valves at the precise moments.

The overlap portion of the cam timing-curve, between intake and exhaust, is the most critical element for a supercharged or turbocharged engine. The overlap portion is where the exhaust valve is just closing while the intake valve is just opening. Since we're using pressure to force fresh air and fuel into the cylinder,

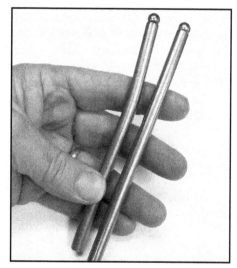

High cylinder pressures, especially with turbo engines, can experience enough residual cylinder pressure at exhaust valve opening that the engine may experience exhaust valvetrain problems like bent pushrods and bent valves. Stronger pushrods and later-opening cam timing are ways to prevent these problems.

where the intake and exhaust lobes are the same duration and lift. One quick way to crutch our engine and fool this air pump into thinking that it has bigger heads is to increase the exhaust duration

the overlap cycle (while still important) becomes less critical. In normally aspirated engines, we rely on that negative pressure pulse reflected from the end of the header collector to create a greater differential in

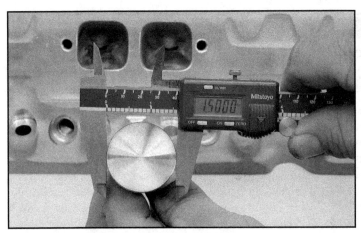

Perhaps the biggest player in determining cam timing for a supercharged or nitrous engine is to pay attention to exhaust port efficiency. One way to do that is to look at the exhaust-to-intake relationship. A head with only 60 percent exhaust-to-intake flow at 0.450-inch lift will not perform as well as an exhaust port that flows well into the 80 percent area.

Current turbo engine technology is also moving toward smaller exhaust valves in an attempt to minimize exhaust-side problems with turbo engines.

the cylinder, which adds more fresh air and fuel from the induction side of the engine. But with a turbocharged engine as an example, a turbine wheel is in the way of this pressure excursion before it can get to the cylinder. This is not the case with a supercharged engine, but again, the pressure on the intake side is generally so great that the effect of this negative pressure pulse is not nearly as critical.

The critical concept about overlap is to limit the duration of the overlap function to help prevent pushing fresh air and fuel directly out the exhaust valve during the overlap period. Generally, an earlier closing exhaust valve followed by a slightly later opening intake valve reduces the effect of the intake charge shooting right out the exhaust. This basically creates a lobe separation angle for supercharged and turbocharged engines of around 112 to 114 degrees of lobe separation angle.

This is somewhat simplistic since longer duration cams may actually require even wider lobe separation angles, but if you look in the Comp or Crane catalogs, the supercharged and turbocharger cams most often fall into this area.

So if we put the two concepts of longer exhaust duration along with a wider lobe separation angle, we have the makings of a decent supercharger or turbocharger engine camshaft. Since we already established an intake closing point (and therefore have a good idea of the intake duration), we have most of what we need to create a good blower cam. While a custom cam has never been easier to come by, wait before you run off in search of your local cam grinder's home number. It's possible that the major cam companies already have what you're looking for.

Let's take a typical street engine and bolt on a big 8-71 supercharger. It could also be a large centrifugal, but let's stick that blower right through the hood. We have a 383-ci small-block with a good bottom end, a 4340 steel crank with

high-quality aftermarket rods, and very good cylinder heads, like a set of Air Flow Research 210-cc aluminum heads. Now all we have to do is pick a cam. Let's take a look at what would work.

Since this is a street engine, we don't want to spin it much past 6,500 rpm. So let's stick with a cam with duration at 0.050 of less than 240 degrees. We looked through several cam catalogs since we decided we wanted to stick with an off-the-shelf camshaft. The selections were limited compared to the normally aspirated cams, but we came up with a Crane mechanical flat tappet cam that looked very promising. The Crane F-278-2 lists in the cam spec box with 238 degrees of intake duration and a nice 10 degrees of additional exhaust duration to help blow down the cylinder at higher engine speeds. Plus, the cam also offers decent lift of 0.500 inches on the exhaust side with an excellent 114-degree lobe separation angle.

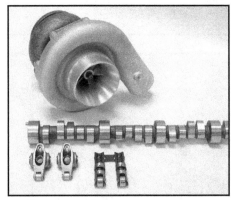

The beauty of turbocharged engines is that the engine doesn't need radical cam timing in order to make power. So the engine builder can spec a valvetrain that is much more conservative while still making great power.

Roller cams offer slightly more power potential than a flat tappet cam. But you can still make excellent power with a flat tappet mechanical cam and save some money in the process. Plus, the mechanical cam offers tuning opportunities the hydraulics can't match.

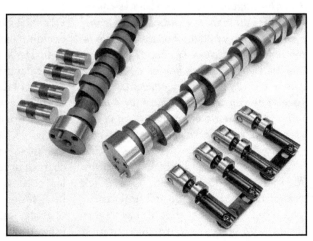

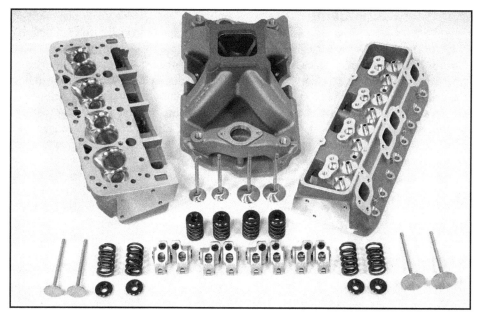

Always think of an engine as a complete system. That means carefully matching the intake manifold, carb, cam, heads, compression, and exhaust as one unit and the engine generally runs better than an engine that has been cobbled together. These are Dart 18-degree heads along with their required valvetrain and intake. These alternate valve angle heads used to be considered exotic race-only pieces, but they do show up on the street on rare occasions.

One way to effect tuning changes with a power adder is to not ignore the exhaust side of the engine. Consider changing an exhaust rocker to a 1.6:1 ratio to see if additional lift and duration helps the power.

Once we've chosen the camshaft, we are not limited to just this configuration. Let's say we have a chance to run our engine on the dyno and we start with the standard lash of 0.022 inches. For our first experiment, let's say that we tighten the exhaust lash to 0.018 inches and run the engine again. We discover that the top end power improves slightly, but we lose midrange torque as a result. By tightening the lash, we added exhaust duration and overlap, which helped the top end power, but the increased overlap cost us more than we wanted to give up in the midrange.

We then decide to return the exhaust lash to the stock spec and instead add a 1.6:1 roller rocker to the exhaust side and try that. This time, the power improves slightly throughout the entire RPM curve. This change added 0.033 inches of valve lift throughout the entire RPM curve as well as a slight amount of duration, which helped improve power throughout the entire curve. These are ways to improve the power without having to go through the expense and effort of swapping cams when the results may only be minor changes in power. If we

SUPERCHARGER, TURBOCHARGER, AND NITROUS CAMS

The following chart lists a few off-the-shelf turbo, supercharger, and nitrous camshafts from a couple of major cam companies. Note that all these camshafts do the two major things that a good blower cam must accomplish – increase exhaust duration and widen the lobe separation angle compared to a camshaft for a normally aspirated engine. The differences are not that great, and it's possible that these blower cams would also work very well in a normally aspirated engine. These are all flat tappet camshafts, but the idea would be the same for a roller.

Crane lists a separate page for nitrous camshafts, but if you compare the numbers, everything (including the part number) is the same. The same cam is also listed under the mechanical lifter normally aspirated camshaft section as well, and with the right combination of other parts would probably work well.

Cam	Style	Company	Duration @ 0.050	Lift	Lobe Separation Angle
268AH-14	Hyd.	Comp	222/226	0.464/0.464	114
290AS-14	Solid	Comp	255/265	0.540/0.563	114
F-278-2	Solid	Crane	238/248	0.480/0.500	114
F-288-2	Solid	Crane	248/258	0.500/0.520	114

The key to making great power with a turbocharger is electronic fuel injection. But nitrous can also be more accurately controlled and implemented with a good nitrous control package like the system included with every ACCEL/DFI GEN VII EFI package. The system allows you to control more closely the amount of nitrous, the amount of fuel, and how much timing needs to be reduced in order for the engine to make excellent power and live.

had added duration by tightening the lash on the exhaust and seen a major power increase throughout the entire RPM curve, then it would have been obvious that we would need a new cam with more exhaust duration.

Nitrous Cams

Up until now, we haven't mentioned nitrous cams specifically since in many ways they operate much like a supercharged or turbocharged application. However, with nitrous the inlet tract is not pressurized like it is in either of the other two applications. As such, we could get off on a wild tangent and begin the discussion by suggesting that nitrous cams could still benefit from additional overlap and that the slight amount of residual cylinder pressure still present when the intake valve opens is not nearly as critical as with a supercharged engine. The big determiner in this situation is probably how efficient the exhaust ports are on your nitrous engine.

Many nitrous engine builders we've spoken to end up tuning their engines more like a normally aspirated engine than a supercharged engine. This could be because they are already using heads with excellent exhaust ports, or because the overlap period is the critical function of the combination. You can choose your favorite theory, but it appears that treating the engine as if it were a normally aspirated engine seems to be winning at least at the present time. So basi-cally, you would choose a cam with an intake duration and intake closing point that would support your peak horsepower RPM point, and then spec the cam based on how well you think your cylinder heads will flow when hit with the additional power.

It's also worth mentioning that the amount of nitrous you hit the engine with plays a big part in determining how well the camshaft plays in this power game. Those small starter nitrous kits that pump in between 125 and 150 hp respond the least to major camshaft tuning changes. It's really only as you get into the big-load 250- to 400-hp kits that nitrous cam tuning becomes critical. The point here is that the returns on nitrous tuning with cam timing on a mild 125 hp kit is probably minimal while the larger kits respond more favorably.

Tuning for supercharger, turbos, or nitrous really isn't that difficult. Paying close attention to the engine's basic requirements and then giving the powerplant what it needs always pays off in terms of more power. That's where the concept of believing your testing comes into play. If you've got a favorite theory, but your testing doesn't support it, believe your testing and invent a new theory.

THE PRESSURES OF SUPERCHARGING

Positive intake manifold pressure for a boosted engine, either supercharged or turbocharged, adds another element to consider when dealing with a street engine. Let's say we have a small-block with a strong hydraulic camshaft mixed with a monster centrifugal supercharger that an over-the-top tuner has spun up to an impressive 15 psi of boost measured in the intake manifold. This pressure is also the same on the back side of the intake valve. If we're sporting 2.02-inch intakes, the valves measure a total of 3.2 square inches of area on the back side of the valves. Now, let's say we're running some middle-of-the-road valvesprings that only generate 110 pounds of seat pressure. If we multiply 15 psi of boost pressure times this valve area of 3.20 square inches, we come up with 48 pounds of force that is trying to push the valve open. Subtract that from our 110 pounds of static seat spring pressure, and we're left with 62 pounds of pressure attempting to hold the intake valves closed. Now think about whether 62 pounds keeps the intake valve from bouncing at engine speeds approaching 6,000 rpm. If this sounds like insufficient spring pressure, you are right. With hydraulic lifters, it's possible that the lifter sees valvetrain separation, the lifter pumps up, and power goes right out the window. So perhaps that peak RPM point is really limited by the valvetrain rather than by the cam timing or insufficient airflow through the engine. Makes you think, doesn't it?

Hydraulic lifters don't respond well to high valvespring seat or open pressures since these pressures tend to compress or "pump down" the lifters, which creates excessive lash in the system at high speeds, which kills power and creates all kinds of clearance in the valvetrain. This is especially hard on hydraulic lifters since the small internal pistons then crash into the lifter retainer rings. These retainers can pop out, allowing the lifter to come apart. We've seen these retainers then work their way right into the oil pump, seizing the pump and shearing off the distributor gear pin, which (thankfully) kills the engine.

The solution to this dilemma is to step up to a mechanical lifter camshaft that can withstand higher spring pressures on the seat and the nose. This affords more valvetrain control over the valve and perhaps even adds some power.

CHAPTER 12

VALVETRAIN DYNAMICS

When NASA decided to build the Space Shuttle, one of the reasons for going with a high-tech approach was to use government money to create new processes and new materials that would be needed in the space program. These new ideas and materials were then open to the business world to use without having to pay royalties. In a way, the world of drag racing, circle track, and road racing is doing the same thing for the street market. The demands of racing continuously push the envelope when it comes to extracting increasingly greater power levels out of the classic small-block Chevy.

This trickle-down effect perhaps benefits the street performance engine builder and enthusiast the most. Roller cams and relatively affordable shaft rocker systems are just a couple of examples that support this theory. Another benefit of continual research in the racing world is the research going on in the wild world of valvetrain dynamics. Camshaft manufacturers are constantly looking for new ways to make power for racers, and this has funded a tremendous amount of research into what really goes on in the valvetrain, especially at increasingly higher engine speeds. The classic horsepower formula clearly indicates that if you can make torque at a higher engine speed, the engine makes more horsepower. To that end, NASCAR has only recently placed a limit on engine speed, but up until that point NASCAR teams were on their way to spinning engines in excess of 10,000 rpm and making the valvetrain live at that stratospheric RPM for 500-plus miles.

At these speeds, a pushrod valvetrain system does not necessarily perform the way it maps it out when degreeing a camshaft or measuring valve-to-piston clearance. The point is that a street engine that sees even a mere 6,000 rpm can easily experience valvetrain dynamic difficulties that not only kills power, but could also ultimately create a situation that would destroy an engine. A dropped valve at 6,000 rpm can be catastrophic. So let's get into what causes valvetrain distress and how to effect remedies.

One key to understanding valve dynamics is to always remember that

The valvespring is one of the most over-stressed and under-appreciated components in an internal combustion engine. Pay attention to how your valvesprings perform, and there's horsepower to be made on any engine.

CONTRIBUTORS TO VALVE FLOAT

The following items can be considered enablers to valve float. The small-block Chevy tends to be able to avoid float better than its big-block cousin, which seems to be much more easily afflicted with valve-float difficulties.

• More RPM
• Higher rocker ratio
• Aggressive cam profile
• Flexing pushrods

• Weak or misapplied springs
• Heavy valve
• Heavy spring
• Heavy retainer
• Poor geometry
• Valvetrain "fuss point"
• Loose spring seat
• Heavy lifter (hydraulic roller)
• Acute pushrod angles
• Mismatched components

One of the more fascinating research tools to come out of engineering development is the valve motion machine. The most popular of these machines is called the Spintron, which uses a large electric motor to spin the entire crank, cam drive, cam, and valves on an engine at high RPM while simultaneously measuring the forces exerted on the valve to study what occurs during valve float.

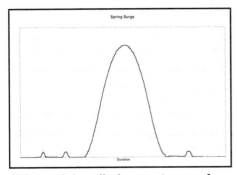

This graph is a displacement-versus-force diagram with valve duration across the horizontal axis and valvespring force plotted in the vertical. The small "bumps" when the valve is supposedly "at rest" on its seat indicates spring forces that travel through the spring. These excursions are what eventually reduce the spring's durability.

SOLUTIONS TO REDUCE VALVE FOAT

- Less RPM
- Lighter valvetrain components
- Reduce deflection in valvetrain
- Stronger pushrods
- Smoother valve action
- Less rocker ratio
- Shaft rocker system

Simply put, a lighter valve is easier to control than a heavy valve. A lighter valve requires less valvespring pressure, which creates less deflection in the rest of the valvetrain.

The next best approach to helping to control the valvetrain is to lighten the retainer. Steel valvespring retainers, especially for large diameter dual springs, can be heavy. As the demand for titanium retainers increases, the price continues to become more affordable. A titanium retainer can increase RPM potential by 100 rpm in many cases.

this is a dynamic system and should be thought of as a whole, rather than a bunch of separate components. The valvetrain is a connection of individual components that creates its own overall resonance point based on this assemblage of parts. To make matters more complex, the resonance point varies with a change to any component in the system. Each individual piece has its own resonant frequency, but this vibration also affects those other parts within the valvetrain. As one engineer put it, "You cannot get rid of harmonics, you can only move it

around a little." Think of the valve system for one valve as a bunch of interconnected springs and you begin to get the idea of the complexity of the interplay within the valvetrain as engine speed changes.

Valve Float

If you spend any time around high-performance street or race engines, you have no doubt run across evidence of an out-of-control valvetrain. Racers and enthusiasts universally call this condition valve float, and there's much more to this condition than this simplistic term might imply. A more precise explanation would be a loss of control when the valve no longer follows the course prescribed by the cam lobe. To entry-level enthusiasts, the term indicates that the valve "floats" off the lobe across the

nose of the lobe, which is more accurately described as valve toss or valve loft. This is a very real condition, but there's also much more to the story.

First of all, we need to emphasize that much of the discussion in this chapter is directed toward what occurs at the valve. Many situations contribute to what happens at the valve, which is ultimately most important in the valvetrain. To bore into what's really going on with valve toss, the situation becomes a bit more clear when you realize that once lifter acceleration on the opening flank transitions from positive to negative, as it approaches the nose, the valvespring is

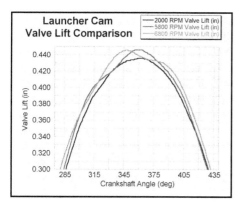

Valve toss can be designed into a lobe to occur intentionally. In fact, COMP offers just such a cam design for those circle-track engines that have a valve lift rule. These lobes are designed to toss the lifter and increase valve lift to make more power while still checking legal during a static lift inspection.

Rocker arm ratio has a major impact on valve motion. Increasing the ratio demands that the valve accelerate faster to achieve the greater valve lift. Often an engine that is perfectly happy at a given RPM with a 1.6:1 rocker ratio experiences severe valve float if the rocker ratio is bumped to 1.7:1.

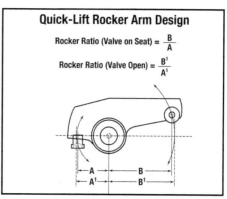

Crane Quick-Lift rockers appear to offer potential advantages but may only create power in the lower engine speeds with milder camshafts. Resultant high closing acceleration rates at valve closing could also cause valve bounce problems at higher engine speeds.

100 percent responsible for controlling the valve. Several hidden meanings reside in this statement since the valve velocity and acceleration rate, up until that point, helps determine how much stored energy is in the valve and spring assembly once the valve reaches this crossover point.

But once this occurs, the spring's open load values must be matched to the negative acceleration area of the valve motion curve. Therefore, if you are planning a serious street or race engine, it pays to actually measure your valvesprings beyond max valve lift values to determine if the springs are in fact delivering their rated load. This means measuring spring loads within 0.050 to 0.030 inches from coil bind to establish maximum spring force. Of course, it is also worth mentioning that at static valve lift, spring clearance to coil bind should ideally be 0.100 inches.

For the last decade or so, many cam companies have embarked on a serious research effort to identify and remedy valve float problems. The most important tool in their arsenal is a valvetrain spin machine that uses a massive electric motor to spin a crankshaft, cam drive, cam, and one or more valves along with their attendant components at high engine speeds. The most popular machine in this family is called a Spintron. This machine uses a serious electric motor to spin a mock-up engine fitted with a single

cylinder's worth of valve gear. The Spintron uses a high-resolution rotary encoder to establish crankshaft position, while a laser is used to accurately plot valve lift relative to crank position. From this machine, exceptionally accurate graphs can be plotted showing valve lift versus duration curves to measure actual valve position relative to the lobe design. Some researchers go even further by adding a load sensor under the valvespring to measure spring loads versus valve position at a given engine speed and piston position. The data generated from these graphs is essential to understanding how the entire valve system works at stratospheric engine speeds.

Previous to the popularity of the Spintron was a machine called the Optron, which used a high-speed camera to capture valve motion that could be played back in slow motion to study valvespring stability. While this machine generated some fascinating footage, the information was less reliable and could in fact be misleading.

One of the more interesting facts that have come out of this research is that different levels of difficulties are associated with valve float. In addition to valve toss, there is also a condition known as valve bounce. Often, the first indication of a loss of valve control occurs at valve closing, usually with the intake valve since it is larger and heavier. At a given RPM, the valve hits the seat

with enough force that the spring is not able to prevent the valve from bouncing off the seat. If you think about our earlier discussion about the four valve events (intake opening, intake closing, exhaust opening, and exhaust closing), intake bounce affects the most important of these—intake closing. Since the cylinder cannot begin to generate pressure until the intake valve is seated, this bounce allows cylinder pressure to escape back up the intake tract. This causes a significant loss of power, not to mention pressure wave excursions in the intake tract, which are also unfavorable.

The onset of valve bounce can be costly in terms of power. According to COMP Cams research, as little as 0.005- to 0.020-inch valve bounce can cost 10 to as much as 50 hp. More serious valve

Manley is just one company that offers something like six different valve material choices in stainless steel valves for the small-block Chevy. Valve size, weight, stem diameters, undercut stems, radius dimensions, price, and several other variables can make the choices difficult.

The latest innovation in spring design is the conical or beehive spring that reduces not only the retainer diameter and weight, but also the actual spring's mass itself, making it easier to control the valve while requiring less spring force to do so.

Ovate wire is another valvespring trick that allows the spring designer to increase the spring's capacity to accommodate more lift before coil bind.

bounce problems with values of over 0.020 inches also expand the duration of the time the intake valve is off its seat. This can kill as much as 100 hp! Plus, this kind of bounce also contributes to broken parts. At the very least, mild bounce causes additional wear on the valve seat since now the valve is hitting the seat multiple times per cycle instead of just once. Of course, in most cases, the driver is not aware this is occurring. If engine speed continues to climb, this bounce condition is only aggravated. Eventually, the engine begins to pop and bang out the exhaust and sometimes even through the intake when conditions become bad enough that both valves are open when they should be closed.

Novice engine builders often attribute this to a poor ignition system, but assuming the ignition system is some-

thing more than a set of points and a stock coil, looking more closely at the valvetrain would certainly a good place to start after ensuring the ignition is in good shape. Often, valve float exhibits a less obvious situation where the engine does not misfire, but is rather just unwilling to RPM past a certain point, almost as if controlled by an electronic rev limiter. This is also misdiagnosed as an ignition problem when in reality weak valvesprings are the real cause of the difficulty. It appears that the pushrod may play a serious part in this situation along with the weight of the valve, and certainly spring load.

Valve Toss

As we mentioned earlier, the original concept of the valve being launched or catapulted off the nose of the cam lobe has a certain amount of validity. This situation occurs when the engine reaches a certain RPM when the valvespring can no longer control the inertia of the valve and its spring assembly and the valve begins a trajectory that, like valve bounce, no longer follows the lobe of the cam. However, this situation occurs on the opening side of the cam lobe and across the nose. As the lifter accelerates past the opening flank of the lobe and approaches the nose, the lifter begins to slow down in anticipation of reaching the nose, where it stops its ver-

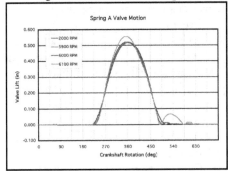

Note how through 6,000 rpm in this Spintron graph of this valvespring that the trace indicates that other than mild valve bounce at valve closing, the spring is doing a good job of controlling the valve. But by 6,100 rpm, valve toss over the nose and valve bounce at closing is clearly evident as well as how much deflection exists on the opening side.

tical rise and begins an equally quick descent toward valve close. At high RPM, the valvespring has insufficient force to control this motion, allowing the valve to begin a ballistic type curve dictated by the force created by its mass (weight) multiplied by its acceleration.

If you look at our accompanying graph ("Spring A Valve Motion") you can see that more RPM merely lofts the valve both earlier in the lift curve and slightly higher in terms of additional valve lift. This graph indicates the motion of the valve, but there's more to this story than just what happens at the valve. Valve toss can begin at the lifter-lobe interface, but it can also occur as a result of several other factors including insufficient spring pressure, a heavy valve and retainer assembly, a too-steep rocker ratio, pushrod deflection, or any one of several combinations of these factors. If this sounds complex, it's only because it is. Let's take a closer look at many of these factors and ways to minimize their contribution.

Lobe Design

The history of cam lobe design has been a continual battle of balancing the forces of mass, acceleration, and velocity with the current limitations of metallurgy and making all those parts live for more than a few seconds at a time. It appears that high peak-acceleration rates can cause serious valvetrain problems. The better approach is to look for a cam with high average acceleration rates that tend to be much more durable and not cause problems in the valvetrain. In essence, the valvetrain design situation boils down to the struggle between cam lobe designer and spring engineer. Within this tug-of-war, the cam designer is the heavyweight. It is well within his ability to design a cam that generates brutal acceleration and/or velocity rates. But this pays few dividends if his compatriot spring designer cannot control those valve actions with a spring. So the creation of a new cam lobe is really a compromise between the cam designer's wish-book aspirations and the reality of what the spring engineer down the hall can come up with.

To prevent spring surge problems that can lead to valve float, almost all single springs use a flat wire damper. The damper fits tightly up against the inside of the spring to minimize oscillation at the spring's natural frequency.

The inner spring on a dual-spring system actually performs two functions. Primarily, the second spring adds load, but it also serves as a secondary damper for the primary spring.

Pushrods have become much more critical in the game of preventing valve toss and valve float. It's a good idea to ensure that all pushrods are indeed straight. This Proform tool uses a dial indicator to measure the pushrod rather than rely on the old trick of rolling across a piece of window glass.

Race engine development pushes this continual give-and-take engineering exercise, which also turns out to be a benefit for the street engine builder since this engineering eventually trickles down to the catalog level. One of the latest race concepts that could eventually find its way onto the street is mechanical roller lobes designed to be used with rocker ratios as high as 1.8:1 for the small-block. The lobes feature much slower lifter velocity rates in order to accommodate the higher valve velocities created by the more aggressive rocker ratio. This also allows the cam builder to grind the lobe with a larger base circle as compared to a standard roller cam.

The subject of lobe design is best left to the rocket scientists and the math geniuses since this goes far beyond the scope of this humble book. However, no discussion of valve float and the vagaries of uncontrolled valve action would be complete without the necessary caveats tossed in about radical profiles and their effect on the valvetrain. This goes way beyond the usual specs called out on a cam card. For example, many cam companies offer both street roller and drag race roller profiles. A measurable difference in power between these two lobes exists, but it is not tremendous. The more important point is that the drag race lobe is much more violent and therefore more abusive

on valvesprings. Can you run a street engine with a drag race designed lobe profile? The answer is yes, but be prepared for the cost. The result is a drastically reduced valvespring lifespan. Spring pressure falls off very quickly, followed by actual spring failure as the radical acceleration rate (even at much lower engine speeds) takes its toll on even the best valvesprings.

It's also important to note that just because a 1.8:1 roller rocker arm is available doesn't mean it's always a good idea. Considering that the stock rocker ratio for the small-block is 1.5:1, a 1.8:1 rocker arm ratio on a very fast ramp cam would probably be a disaster at higher

THE VALVE TOSS CAM LOBE

For the most part, lobe loft or valve toss would appear to be an undesirable situation. But that's not always the case. Many years ago, NHRA Stock Eliminator racers looking for a competitive advantage over their competition began looking into ballistic valve curves by having their cam grinder design a cam lobe that would do exactly that. While NHRA now forgoes the point of checking duration, they still check valve lift to ensure the racers adhere to the OEM lift specs. But by maintaining a high lifter velocity as the opening flank approaches the nose, it is relatively easy to launch the lifter right off the nose, creating additional valve lift.

This technology exists today, even going so far as cams for oval track "lift rule" camshafts. Many local oval track classes attempt to minimize engine costs by specifying maximum valve lift figures, ranging from 0.400 to 0.470 inches. COMP Cams

now makes a series of Low Lift Oval Track cams that, contrary to their name, create as much as 0.050 to 0.070 inches more valve lift than what statically measures at the valve. The following chart lists the specs for two of these cams.

Cam		Advertised Duration	Duration @ 0.050	Lift (1.5:1)	Lobe Separation
12-521-5,	Int.	297	246	0.420	106
	Exh.	299	250	0.420	
12-522-5,	Int.	293	242	0.450	106
	Exh.	300	255	0.453	

Don't assume that a bent pushrod is merely a result of a mechanical misalignment. It could be the result of serious loads deflecting the pushrod and causing permanent damage.

Heat is the big enemy of valvesprings. Many circle-track and road-race engine builders incorporate spring oilers in their valve covers to squirt cooling oil on the springs to maintain their durability.

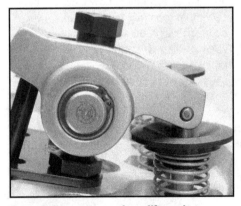

Comparing max valve lift using your springs versus measuring max lift with checking springs is a good way to evaluate the amount of deflection in the valvetrain.

THE CONE ZONE

Conical or beehive springs were first developed for use in restrictor plate Winston Cup racing. The design was so successful that it didn't take long before even the OEMs were using them, including the springs you now see on the GEN III engines all the way up through the radical 500hp LS7 engine. Conical springs offer tremendous opportunities for several reasons.

The first and most obvious advantage of a conical spring is that it requires a very small-diameter retainer, which is also much lighter. Factor in a titanium version of this retainer and the weight savings is more than significant. Less readily apparent is that the retainer and the upper half of the spring is the portion of the spring that travels the greatest distance during valve lift. The conical spring reduces not only the weight of the retainer, but also the spring itself, which means less mass accelerating on both the opening and closing sides of the valve lift curve. That means there's less mass to control across the nose of the cam as well as on the closing side where bounce can be a problem. More importantly, these springs are asymmetrically wound with a different diameter for much of the spring top to bottom. Because each wire

has a different diameter than the coil above and below it, they all have different natural frequencies. This makes the conical spring much more forgiving in terms of harmonics compared to a more traditional spring.

One limitation on this design spring is that its shape precludes the use of an inner spring that could be added to increase the overall spring pressure. COMP Cams offers several versions of the conical or beehive spring that could be considered for 400- to 500-hp small-block applications and all are constructed of ovate wire. The 26595 spring is also designed to handle high-lifts of over 0.700 inches. This is an area targeted for even more development in the future, so don't be surprised to see even more conical spring applications as acceptance of this part of the valvespring market gains momentum. In the chart, we listed a selection of COMP Cams conical springs, including the 26120 spring that was originally designed for big-block applications but could also be used in a small-block application. We've also listed a typical COMP Cams dual spring PN 986 for comparison.

Part Number	Description	Seat Load	Open Load	Coil Bind	Rate
982	1.250 Seat Dia. Conical	100 @ 1.750	286 @ 1.250	1.135	362 lbs./in.
26918	1.290 Seat Dia. Conical	130 @ 1.800	318 @ 1.200	1.085	313 lbs./in.
26915	1.290 Seat Dia. Conical	105 @ 1.800	293 @ 1.200	1.085	313 lbs./in.
26120	1.445 Seat Dia. Conical	155 @ 1.880	377 @ 1.280	1.230	370 lbs./in.
26595	1.589 Seat Dia. Conical	150 @ 2.000	370 @ 1.250	1.110	293 lbs./in.
986	1.430 Seat. Dia. Std. Design	132 @ 1.750	280 @ 1.25	1.150	296 lbs./in.

THE PUSHROD LINK

The game of controlling valve float has also brought attention even to the lowly pushrod. In a game where less weight is better when it comes to controlling valve motion, the pushrod may be the one exception where a stronger pushrod that actually weighs more is a benefit.

Just like a pole-vaulter's fiberglass pole at a track and field event, a weak pushrod tends to deflect at higher engine speeds when asked to accelerate a valve, spring, and retainer combination at high RPM. As the lifter approaches the nose on the opening side and begins to decelerate, this stored energy in the deflected pushrod can easily "launch" the valve into much higher valve lifts prescribed by the cam. In some ways, this is good and can actually improve engine power. But if clearances do not allow this amount of valve toss, then piston-to-valve interference problems are quite costly. Plus, the impact loads imparted on the lifter and cam, when the lifter again comes in contact with the lobe, are usually excessive

and abusive. In addition, Spintron testing also shows that weak pushrods can also contribute to valve bounce on valve closing that can occur over many degrees of crankshaft rotation after the valve was supposedly closed. The ideal solution is a stronger and sometimes heavier pushrod that either eliminates or at least limits the amount of deflection to a more manageable amount. Many companies now offer professional-level 4130 steel, 5/16-inch diameter, 0.080-inch wall thickness pushrods that are many times stronger than stock-production pieces and come in 0.050-inch length increments. If that's not enough, 3/8-inch diameter pushrods are also available for the small-block also of 4130 steel with a 0.080-inch wall thickness. Our sources tell us that adding a small amount of weight on the lifter side of the valvetrain with heavier-wall or larger-diameter pushrods is not necessarily a bad thing. The pushrod is the one place where adding mass can improve the valvetrain stiffness by reducing deflection, even though these pushrods are heavier.

Spring cups are critical to maintaining control over the valvespring, especially during periods of spring surge by accurately locating the spring to prevent "migration" at higher engine speeds.

One relatively easy and inexpensive way to improve valvetrain stability on any small-block is to reduce weight at the top of the valvespring, especially those heavy steel large-diameter retainers. A titanium retainer is worth as much as a 40 percent reduction compared to a steel retainer on a dual valvespring.

engine speeds. The much higher rocker ratio would push the valve far beyond the spring's capacity to control the valve. This is another reason why it's always a good idea to think of valve timing numbers in terms of what happens at the valve rather than the lobe design numbers. A cam lobe that would otherwise be perfectly happy at 6,500 rpm with a 1.5:1 rocker ratio might be an absolute disaster at 6,000 or even 5,500 rpm with a 1.7:1 rocker ratio, all other components in the engine being equal.

Crane has recently developed a new line of Quick-Lift rocker arms that develop a slightly higher effective rocker ratio up to around 0.200 inches of valve lift. So if you are using a Quick-Lift roller rocker with a stated 1.5:1 rocker ratio, the effective ratio is actually closer to 1.6:1 within the first 0.200

inches of valve lift. While this is a slick way to kick the valve up off its seat at low lift numbers, and could be beneficial on the exhaust side to get the valve open to a greater lift to help scavenge the cylinder, some risks are associated with this type of rocker. On the closing side, this effective higher ratio tends to accelerate the valve faster toward valve closing, which could contribute to valve bounce. Having said that, with a lighter exhaust valve, the spring might still be able to control this higher closing speed. The only way to know for sure is to test it. Remember that each application is different. The point here is that it's always best to look at the entire system of the valvetrain rather than placing too much emphasis on one system. A Quick-Lift rocker system would work very well with some situations, while in others it would not work at all.

Mass Attack

Valvetrain weight has always been an issue with race and performance engine builders since additional weight (or mass) is always more difficult to control. While lighter is always better, lighter is also more expensive and, in many cases, lighter components may sacrifice strength to achieve that reduced weight. A few decades ago, drag racers tried using aluminum valvespring retainers to replace those anchor-heavy steel pieces. While aluminum is lighter than steel, it's also not as durable and it wasn't long before those aluminum retainers were failing due to the cyclical nature of the force applied to them.

The obvious places to reduce weight are with the valve, retainer, and also with the spring itself. Titanium retainers have become popular enough

Perhaps one of the most important points to remember here is that the valvetrain should be viewed and tuned as if it was a complete system instead of a collection of individual parts. Taking a systems approach to evaluating a valvetrain is always the right way to go.

One further advantage to rocker shaft systems is that their reduced deflection also means that the valve is more likely doing what the cam tells it to do rather than what the deflected components are dictating.

A good way to see if a valve float condition has affected your springs is to remove one and check it against its new rated load. Springs that have been floated generally lose a big portion of their rated load, which is why the engine has lost power and RPM potential.

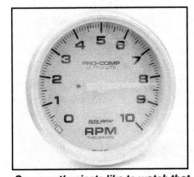

that many aggressive street engines are now hitting the boulevard with these parts in place. A steel retainer for a 1.430-inch dual valvespring weighs around 28 grams, while a titanium version of the same retainer weighs a mere 17 grams. This may not sound like much, but that represents a 40 percent reduction in retainer weight, which at 7,000 rpm can be a significant amount of force that the spring no longer has to control. As a rule of thumb, a set of titanium retainers increases engine speed roughly 100

Perhaps the worst-case scenario is an engine with serious pushrod angles combined with major valvetrain deflection difficulties. This unfortunately describes the big-block Chevy engine, which may be why it has so many valvetrain problems.

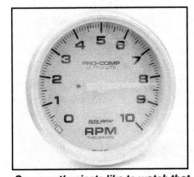

Some enthusiasts like to watch that tach needle spin around to 7,500 or 8,000 rpm, but you could just be killing your valvesprings in the process, especially if your engine makes peak power at 6,000 rpm.

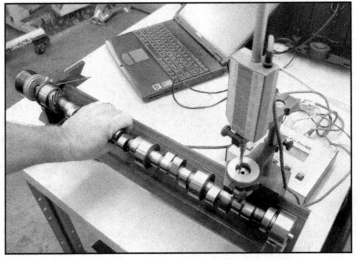

Base circle runout is not something you hear much about, but if you are serious about valvetrain stability, a cam measurement machine like a Cam Pro unit from Audi Technology can measure it. Anything more than 0.001 inches of runout means you should return the cam to the manufacturer.

NATURAL FREQUENCIES

If you've ever played around with a tuning fork, then you've experienced a piece of steel that resonates. This resonance is the result of both the shape and the design of a given component that, if struck, generates a natural frequency. In fact, one way that the OEMs validate their valvetrain designs is by assembling a given valve, spring, retainer, keeper, rocker arm, pushrod, lifter, and camshaft in an engine and then lifting the valve off its seat. Then they literally strike the rocker system with a hammer and carefully measure the entire system's natural frequency. A rigid, high-strength system generates a higher natural frequency.

A valvespring can also be viewed in this same context. During engine operation, the spring is compressing and expanding hundreds of times per second. High-speed photography of valvetrain operation on an Optron is amazing to watch since it presents the opportunity to see subtle actions that are impossible to see otherwise. With the engine at

a given RPM, it's possible to see a pressure "wave" travel through the body of the spring once the valve closes. All of this is occurring while the spring is supposed to be at rest. This wave can also occur when the valve is opened, creating a situation where the wave is moving at one speed while the spring is closing or opening at yet another speed.

Each valvespring also has a natural frequency that generates a resonance, like a tuning fork, at a certain RPM. This frequency can be related, in part, to the spacing of the wire coils. Part of the design requirement of any spring is to ensure that this spring's natural frequency does not occur within the operating speed of the engine. The reason for avoiding or at least dampening this natural spring frequency is so that the spring is not forced to control the usual load of the valvetrain while simultaneously also dealing with its own natural frequency adding to the load on the spring. If you put more energy into the spring than it can handle, it goes into res-

onance. This high-speed vibration, if allowed to continue, rapidly fatigues the spring. Once this occurs, the spring's rate also diminishes, the spring begins to harden, loses its structural integrity, and eventually fails.

One easy way the spring designer can combat this problem is by adding a flat wire damper to the inside of the spring. This damper is not designed to increase the load capability of the spring, but, as its name implies, dampen the main spring's natural frequency at a specific engine speed that would otherwise cause valve control problems. With dual springs, the second, inner spring often acts as a damper since the interference fit of the inner spring tends to dampen the natural frequency of the outer spring. The key to this is to maintain contact between these two springs, but minimize it to limit heat and wear, which are two situations that have a negative effect on valvespring durability.

---

rpm more before the engine experiences valve float problems.

Other tricks include hollow stem valves and reduced stem diameter valves. One advantage of choosing to build a small-block Chevy is the incredible breadth of choices available when it comes to valve selection. For example, the Manley catalog has nine different styles of stainless steel valves from budget replacement to Extreme Duty. That excludes the two different titanium valves that Manley also offers! While the weights of each of these valves differ, the point is that you should be able to find a compromise between weight, strength, and price that allows you to be more selective in valve choice rather than merely accepting what the cylinder head manufacturer offers. For example, reducing a valve weight from 100 grams to around 78 grams is worth a 22 percent reduction

MEASURING DEFLECTION

Here's an easy way to measure the total amount of valvetrain deflection present in your serious street or race engine that uses relatively big valvespring numbers. First, mock up the heads on the engine with light checking springs in place of the valvesprings. Run the lash down to zero and measure the maximum valve lift on the retainer. Be sure to do this on all 16 valves because the lift varies slightly.

Now assemble the heads with the springs you intend to use and duplicate that same test regimen to determine net valve lift. The difference between the two

measurements is the amount of deflection in the valvetrain. For mild street engines this should be minimal, but with springs generating 150 pounds of seat pressure or more, you definitely want to perform this easy check to establish exactly how much deflection is in your pushrods, rocker arms, or rocker studs if you're not using a shaft system. Not only is valvetrain deflection bad from a lost lift standpoint, but some of this deflection (like in the pushrod) reappears at a point where it doesn't belong, such as in a valve toss situation. That's when problems can cause real power loss and/or damage.

in valve weight that the spring does not have to control. Add in a further weight savings with a titanium retainer of 11 additional grams, and your valvesprings are forever grateful.

One area of valvetrain mass that has not received much attention is the spring itself. One way to increase load with a spring is by using a larger-diameter wire. In order to do this, the spring designer must increase the overall diameter of the spring. The typical small-block OE spring diameter is a relatively small 1.25 inches. Most performance cylinder heads bump this up to 1.430 or 1.550 inches. However, this larger diameter also increases the weight of the spring. While the load generated by the spring increases, the spring must also use some of its additional force to control the mass of the spring itself.

This is where the spring engineer begins to really earn his pay. One of

In search of the lightest valvetrain pieces, Manley now makes an ICD Super 7 degree titanium retainer with a scalloped outside diameter for the larger valvespring diameters. Then, the company further lightens it with strategically placed lightening holes designed to introduce oil right at the interface between the spring and retainer.

the latest innovations in spring design addresses this situation. For example, ovate wire springs are becoming increasingly popular. Good valvesprings are made with high strength, very clean chrome silicon alloy steel round wire. Ovate wire is created from the same high-quality steel alloy,

IT'S A SPRING THING

To give you a taste of how springs work, the information provided by this COMP Cams chart should help explain some of what goes on with different valvesprings. This chart plots the amount of valve bounce for three different valvesprings as measured on COMP Cams' Spintron.

As you can see from the chart, no one spring controls the valve the best at all of the engine speeds. While many of the differences are extremely minor, this chart does illustrate how a spring's ability to control valve bounce changes with as small as a 200–rpm difference in engine speed. For example, while Spring 3 looks the best of the three, it's also worst at controlling bounce at both 7,800 and 8,200 rpm. Yet between 7,000 and 8,200 it's the best of the three.

Keep in mind that valve bounce is impossible to see in terms of engine power loss at bounce values of 0.01 inches or less. The main reason for this graph is to show how spring performance changes throughout the RPM

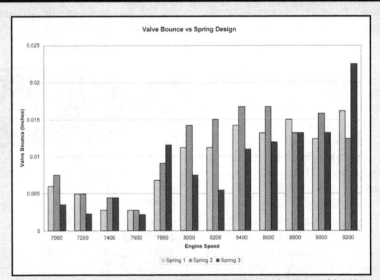

This graph illustrates how a given spring in a given combination reacts. This situation is based on spring dynamics and not merely on engine speed.

range. Also, while this chart illustrates spring performance between 7,000 and 9,200 rpm, this could just as easily be a graph between 5,000 and 7,000 rpm with lighter springs. It's also worth noting that if you change anything, like the cam profile, weight of the valve or retainer, or pushrod thickness, the performance characteristics of the springs would vary dramatically.

SPRING SURGE

All valvesprings surge at a given engine RPM with a certain frequency. This spring surge can be best seen on that COMP Cams graph that reveals a frequency or vibration indicated by a change in load on the load cell. The best description we've heard actually came from COMP Cams valvespring engineer Thomas Griffin. After watching high-speed video of spring surge, he compares the spring to a column of Jello. If you strike this column of Jello with a spoon, you can actually see waves travel from the top of the column to the bottom and be reflected back up toward the top. In a valvespring, these moving waves reduce the total spring force available to control the valve.

If spring surge is a problem with your engine, you might even be able to see it evidenced by a spring bouncing on the seat with the engine at its spring surge RPM. The physical evidence of this is most often confirmed by a broken spring that occurs near the base of the spring since this is where the surge loads concentrate. Surge also creates more heat within the spring, which also weakens the spring and can lead to eventual failure. This is a major reason why it is so important for spring seats to be accurately located on the cylinder head.

Spring surge may not seem like a big problem if you are not experiencing valvespring difficulties. However, surge can be present even if the evidence is much less overwhelming. Evidence suggests that those obscure dips in the torque curve most often blamed on either the intake or exhaust system, might be traced to spring surge. If the spring surge is eliminated with either different springs or a lighter retainer, it's possible for the dip in the torque curve to also disappear.

but is flattened on the upper and lower sides, which allows more valve lift before coil bind. Conical springs are another increasingly popular design approach with spring designers since it benefits from a much lighter and smaller retainer, and generates an incredibly diverse natural frequency that therefore does not require a damper.

Of course all the work on springs and the valvetrain to control valve motion all depends upon keeping the engine under the RPM when this valve float occurs. Anytime the engine experiences excessive RPM, it experiences a point where the springs lose control of the valve. This can happen as a result of a missed shift, a broken drivetrain part, or as is often the case with road racers, a botched downshift where the driver hits first instead of third gear and the engine RPM goes to the moon. Regardless of the reason for the occurrence, significant damage can result from a mistake like this, including bent valves, bent pushrods, and other damaged valvetrain parts. A subsequent result of an over-rev is that the springs become damaged and lose a small amount of force, which reduces their peak RPM operating point.

GRAM SCALE

Component	Weight (grams)
GM 2.00-inch intake valve, LS6	85
GM 1.50-inch exhaust valve, LS6	72
Manley 2.02-inch intake valve, PN 11824	107
Steel aftermarket 2.02-inch valve	123
Valvespring, 1.25-inch single w/ damper	78
Valvespring, 1.430-inch, dual	115
Valvespring, 1.550-inch, dual	138
Valvespring, conical PN 26918	72
Valvespring, conical, GM LS6	69
Retainer, steel, 1.25-inch single	22
Retainer, steel, 1.43-inch dual, 10-degree	29
Retainer, steel, conical spring	11
Retainer, titanium, 1.25-inch	12
Retainer, titanium, 1.43-inch	17
Retainer, titanium, conical	7
Keepers, machined, 7-degree	3
Keepers, machined, 10-degree	6
Lifter, flat tappet hydraulic	97
Lifter, roller, hydraulic factory	122
Lifter, roller, hydraulic	123
Lifter, roller, mech. Crane + 1/2 tie bar	98
Lifter, roller, mech. COMP + 1/2 tie bar	122

THE "CAMLESS" ENGINE

Digital electronics have come a long way from TRS-80 Radio Shack word processors and those early 1980s computers. There comes a time in the not-too-distant future when it's possible that production engines will not require a camshaft at all. Consider the fully digitally controlled electronic valve actuator. A simple solenoid, not much larger than today's existing fuel injectors, is the only valve gear that you need to signal when the valve opens, how long it remains open, and when it closes. This is not a Buck Rogers comic book fantasy. Sturman Industries has already built and operated an over-the-road diesel truck for over 10,000 miles to prove the concept of Sturman's Digital Hydraulic Operating System (DHOS). It's worth looking closer into this concept only because it is so intriguing.

Current technology relies on a dedicated cam lobe to mechanically control when the valve opens, how long it remains open and at what valve lift, and then when it should close. These mechanical devices are subject to a whole host of problems, mostly related to engine speed and control of the valve at high speeds. Even more importantly, the opening and closing points are fixed. Creative types have been experimenting for years with different techniques to alter valve timing, with some success. But mostly these efforts are limited to advancing or retarding entire camshafts. GM designed the Vortec 3500 I-5 inline 5 cylinder, dual overhead cam (DOHC) engine a few years ago that can retard the exhaust camshaft roughly 20 degrees. This was done mainly to control emissions rather than increase power.

Taking this one step further, the ideal move is to have continuously variable opening and closing points along with lift. This allows the engine tuner to create a stable, short-duration valve event for low-speed operation and excellent idle. Merely extending duration and adding a little lift could optimize mid-range power. Finally, wide-open throttle operation would also benefit (throughout the entire RPM band) and power would only be limited by cylinder head flow and engine speed durability limitations.

This means that cam timing would no longer dictate a relatively narrow power band for the engine. With optimized valve timing, the engine would make its maximum power at all engine speeds! Currently, you need to choose the RPM band you want to make power in and compromise the other speeds because of the limitations of the camshaft lobe configuration. With a digitally controlled valve actuator, the cam timing opportunities are almost limitless! This also means that emissions could improve at part throttle and fuel mileage would also not be compromised, which means efficiency would improve as well.

Several years ago at the 2001 Advanced Engine Technology Conference hosted by SuperFlow, Dave Burt, an engineer for Sturman Industries, presented information on the company's digital hydraulic valve actuator, a component that requires no energy to remain open or closed. The only time energy applied to it is when it transfers from one state to the other. Its transient time is very short, which means it requires very little time to move between open and closed. The Sturman application basically locates this hydraulically operated valve (using engine oil pressure) to open, for example, an intake valve. A valvespring would be responsible for helping close the valve.

There's a ton of technology and potential in this idea. Imagine being able to push a button on your steering wheel and reconfigure your computer-controlled small-block to run in any number of different configurations. For example, you're planning a cross-country trip so you hit the optimized fuel mileage cam timing configuration. Next, you want max power for a pass down the drag strip, but you don't have adequate traction at low speeds, so you configure the power output to optimize the launch and then gradually add power as traction allows. The opportunities are astounding.

This may sound a little far fetched, but the reality is that cost appears to be the only real limitation to this becoming a production reality. Of course, the cam companies won't really embrace the coming of this technology since it has the potential to put them out of business, but perhaps the more forward thinking of them will get into this technology in an attempt to modernize. The performance world has generally followed the OEMs in technology innovation, and the word is that Navistar is using this technology in its light-duty diesel truck applications in 2005 with many more and wider spread applications soon to follow. The future is now.

Conclusion

Valvetrain dynamics are perhaps one of the most baffling and least understood actions in a high-RPM race or street engine. Race engine builders are constantly pushing the RPM envelope in an attempt to make more horsepower. As the quality and design of these race components continues to improve, much of that technology has already filtered down to the street performance level to become an affordable resource. The trick to making all this work is to carefully and artfully combine the lightest, strongest, and most durable components to create a powerful engine that also requires only minimal maintenance. Do that, and you've built a winner in anybody's book.

FAT CAM CORES, LESS LOBE LIFT AND HIGH-RATIO ROCKERS

It's interesting to note how engineering eventually catches up with the changes racers contrive and eventually those properly designed parts drive the high-performance marketplace forward. The early small-block Chevy used a flat tappet mechanical camshaft for its initial ventures into high-performance cams. As the accompanying illustration A reveals, the early Chevy "097" (the last three numbers of the Chevy part number) cam used a 1.310-inch diameter base circle and generated a mild 0.263-inch lobe lift to create a theoretical 0.394-inch valve lift for the 250 and 300 hp 327 engines of the early 1960s.

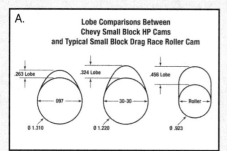

A.
Lobe Comparisons Between Chevy Small Block HP Cams and Typical Small Block Drag Race Roller Cam

.263 Lobe   .324 Lobe   .456 Lobe
097   30-30   Roller
Ø 1.310   Ø 1.220   Ø .923

By the late 1960s, Zora Arkus-Duntov and the Chevrolet Engineering team created the mechanical Duntov 30-30 cam, referenced because of its required 0.030-inch lash specification. This cam reduced the base circle 0.090 inches to achieve 1.220 inches in search of a 0.324-inch lobe lift. The Duntov cam was worth 0.486 theoretical valve lift and employed an advertised duration of 346 degrees at lash (0.050-inch duration was 254 degrees).

Fast forward three decades and drag racers continue to decrease lobe base circle diameters in search of more lobe lift. A typical drag race roller cam of this style employs a 0.923-inch diameter base circle that can generate a 0.456-inch lobe that with a 1.5:1 rocker is worth a theoretical 0.684-inch valve lift. Keep in mind that we say theoretical

since lash must be subtracted from these numbers to come up with static lift numbers at the valve.

Reduced base circle cams are especially in vogue with big-stroke small-blocks because the big end of the rod comes very close to a couple of cam lobes when the stroke is pushed even as little as 3.75 inches, depending on the rods you choose.

The problems with increasingly smaller base circles begin to surface when we plug roller tappets into the equation. All roller tappet followers generate a force vector offset from the direction the lifter is traveling. The interesting point is that this force vector, called a pressure angle, changes with the base circle diameter of the cam lobe. Illustration B reveals how the pressure angle varies from 27 degrees on the smallest 0.801 base circle lobe to a closer to vertical 19 degrees on the 1.060 base circle lobe. Perhaps more importantly, the thrust force generated by the roller follower is radically reduced from 181 to 130 pounds of force, a reduction of 28 percent. As you can see, this should significantly reduce lifter bore wear and stress on the roller tappet while also reducing heat conducted into the oil. This might also be worth a slight amount of power since this is less work required from the valvetrain.

Increasing the cam lobe base circle diameter obviously requires a much larger

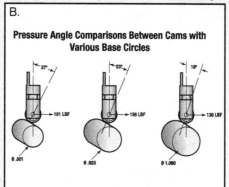

B.
Pressure Angle Comparisons Between Cams with Various Base Circles

27°   23°   19°
181 LBF   156 LBF   130 LBF
Ø .801   Ø .923   Ø 1.060

cam journal, which demands major machine work to the block, as well as custom cam cores. Drag racers and circle track racers have already begun the conversion process. An additional benefit to these larger cam cores is reduced twist and cam timing variations revealed by retarded valve actions comparing the front cylinders with the rear.

Another advantage to large base circle diameters is that actual lifter travel is shortened, which reduces tappet extension out of the bore. This may seem like a small point, but this also reduces lifter bore distortion at the top of the bore.

To complete this scenario, a larger base circle with slightly smaller lobe lift numbers reduces total valve lift, which is counter-productive. These new lobes are also designed with gentler acceleration ramps in anticipation of increased rocker ratios. Small-block rocker ratios from 1.8:1 up to 2.0:1 are now in vogue as race engine builders convert to larger journal cams. The new lobes with less violent acceleration and jerk curves are necessitated by the fact that these movements at the lifter are multiplied now by a more aggressive rocker ratio.

So it appears that those early Chevy engineers were not as far off as many would have believed 20 years ago. Perhaps now we've come, ahem, full circle to appreciate the simplicity of the design and how it works. So beware the backyard engine builder who proclaims that all horsepower ideas for the small-block Chevy have been exhausted. Despite the fact that the little Mouse is now over half a century old, the racing world continues to find ways to make more power to keep this old Mouse running strong.

MATCHING CAMS AND CYLINDER HEADS

Several times throughout this book we have mentioned the concept of using the systems approach when planning and building a performance street engine and/or race engine. This deserves no more emphasis than in this chapter on matching camshafts and cylinder heads, since the integration of camshaft valve timing with the cylinder head is critical if your goal is optimal power. This may seem like flogging the obvious, but plenty of performance enthusiasts are only interested in the appearance of power, rather than achieving a given power level. It's incredibly easy to lean against the fender of your Camaro at a local car show and throw out horsepower numbers with the same gen-

uine enthusiasm that politicians use when promising tax reductions. The classic, "Oh yeah, this motor makes 575 at the crank," sounds an awful lot like, "Read my lips—no new taxes!"

Now that we've got our requisite politician-bashing out of the way, we can get to the guts of this chapter. The number of theories on cylinder head port configuration, valve layout, and flow potential are probably equivalent to the number of small-block Chevy cylinder head manufacturers—a bunch. The simplistic approach is to generate as much flow as you can squeeze in between the head bolt and pushrod holes. The best line we've ever heard was from Pro Stock

racer "The Professor" Warren Johnson. His suggestion is to create the most flow you can get from the smallest port. That tends to fly in the face of suggestions from other sources claiming that size matters—pushing instead bigger ports with the max flow. If that's the case, then why haven't the Ford Boss 302 or the Ford Tunnel Port 429 engines been more successful and longer lasting? Let's look into this a little deeper.

Port Flow

Here comes that theory stuff again, but we try to make it easier on you this time. The plan is that once you under-

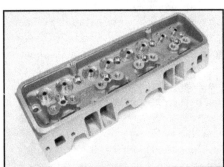

There are easily more small-block Chevy aftermarket heads on the market than for any other single engine in the domestic marketplace. Because of this incredible variety, selecting the right cylinder head and matching it with the right camshaft pays off in power dividends.

For street engines that see more street cruise time than passes down the quarter-mile, a flat tappet hydraulic cam with conservative duration figures matched to a medium-size aftermarket head not only makes great horsepower, but also deliver excellent torque that can make a street engine a ton of fun to drive.

stand the theory behind why some heads work better than others, it makes future engine configurations and concepts easier to generate since you don't have to go through the trial and error process each time. Let's start with cross-sectional area. This is defined as the height times the width of a port at its tightest point. The bigger-is-better theorists suggest that given the choice of several heads, take the biggest, in other words, the one with the largest cross-sectional area. All other considerations being equal, the larger head flows the most air if all we're concerned with is airflow on a flow bench.

However, engine power production is also affected by several other considerations. Just as with choosing a camshaft, we need to know how this engine is to be used to best approach the cylinder head selection process. Let's say that our engine is to be used in a lightweight drag-race car using a deep gear and a 5-speed transmission. This means the engine operates in a very narrow power band at high RPM, which means that a cylinder head with a larger port cross-sectional area would probably work well. But on the other hand, if our small-block is going to be used in a 1932 roadster with a stock torque converter and tall gears, we should be looking for a cylinder head with smaller ports to create good torque and excellent throttle response. This creates a combination that allows this engine to make excellent low-speed torque.

Using a very large cylinder head with a long duration cam in our lightweight street rod produces a very sluggish engine with poor throttle response, and probably won't make decent power until the engine is spinning at very high engine speeds, just like the Ford Boss 302. The reason for this is that a large cross-sectional area requires high engine speeds to create a sufficient inlet air speed. According to GM engineers Ron and Ken Sperry, this speed is generally around 350 feet per second (fps), while other sources place optimal inlet airspeeds higher, at roughly 550 or 600 fps. While these numbers sound impressive and make you sound knowledgeable at your next bench racing session, it's difficult to put into use for a typical street engine builder without reams of compli-

Stock small-block heads generally suffer from weak exhaust port flow for good horsepower. When choosing an aftermarket small-block head, be sure to pay close attention to the exhaust port flow. Raised exhaust ports always flow more air, but they require custom headers to fit a standard Camaro, Chevelle, Nova, or other Chevy chassis.

cated math. The point is that a conservative selection for a cylinder head for most street engine applications may cost a few peak ponies, but also makes more torque in the mid-range where many street machine engines live.

The idea is that the inlet charge has mass and therefore a measurable force (force equals mass times acceleration). Conventional wisdom subscribes to the

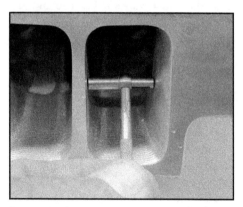

Port volume is the common way ports are categorized, but the figure that has much more effect on port flow is the port's smallest cross-sectional area, as determined by its height times its width. Port volume generally, but not always, follows cross-sectional areas. For the small-block Chevy, the smallest cross-sectional area is almost always where the pushrod intrudes past the intake port. This is why many high-flow heads require offset rockers and lifters to move the pushrod over to leave more room for the port.

notion that as the inlet charge gains speed, it has an inertial force that can be employed to help fill the cylinder. You can think of the inlet charge as a tiny freight train charging down the inlet track. It takes time to get it moving because of its mass, but once underway it wants to continue to move in that same direction, even when presented with obstructions or even pressure building in the cylinder. The cross-sectional area of the port helps determine the inlet air speed. Smaller cross-sectional areas produce higher inlet speeds while larger areas reduce the speed. For example, in the case of a sewer-pipe-sized inlet port, at lower engine speeds, the inlet charge never generates the required inlet speed because of its large area. Conversely, a smaller port can get the inlet charge moving sooner and up to a greater speed sooner, but this same smaller cross-section also eventually limits total mass airflow. As a test of potential velocity and acceleration, have you ever tried launching a spitball from a 2-inch diameter tube? It's much easier to hurl one from a smaller soda straw. This may not be the best analogy, but you get the idea.

It's also good to reinforce the idea that it is ambient atmospheric pressure existing outside the engine that pushes air into the cylinder as it creates a vacuum. Engines don't "suck" air into the port. The air is pushed by atmospheric pressure. This is why your engine makes more power on days with higher atmospheric pressure. While this may seem obvious, it is still worth mentioning.

Our "Mid-Lift Flow" sidebar deals with the concept of concentrating on mid-range flow numbers as a way of helping choose the right cylinder head for a street engine. This builds a case for expanding the research for improving airflow in cylinder heads below the peak lift flow numbers. In fact, research shows that the concept of sacrificing peak lift flow numbers in the hunt for additional mid-lift flow improvements is beneficial. Higher mid-lift flow numbers also tend to support improved mid-range torque (all else being equal), which improves overall acceleration on a street machine with street/strip compromise gears. And that's the ultimate reason we build power, to make the car quicker.

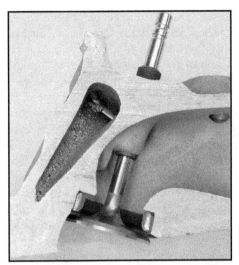

All production small-block Chevy engines and most street performance aftermarket heads use the small-block original 23-degree valve angle. Retaining this valve angle has some flow disadvantages, which is one of the limitations of the small-block's now 50–plus-year-old design.

The Superflow 600 flow bench has become an accepted standard for flow testing performance cylinder heads. This bench can create 28 inches of water test depression for even the largest race heads.

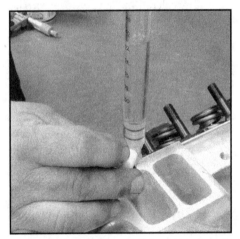

The easiest way to determine port volume is to measure it. Merely install a valve on the seat and position the head so that the port opening is roughly horizontal. Then use a graduated burette to fill the port, using a small plexiglass lid with a hole to fill the port.

Valve size also plays a role in this equation since the transition area just underneath the valve is the critical point where the inlet charge must transition into the chamber. Larger valves can improve flow, as long as the short-side radius transition does not become too sharp. One trick used by most good port designers is to raise the floor of the port just before the bowl area, helping the inlet charge make this change in direction.

Conversely, a head with a flat floor and a sharp transition to the bowl tends to push the inlet charge against the bowl roof on the top side of the valve, reducing flow concentricity around the valve. The idea is to condition the port in such a way so that flow is as equal as possible around the entire circumference of the valve. In reality, this rarely happens, but it is still a goal worth attaining. Many aftermarket cylinder heads have also begun to migrate valve position, promoting a 60/40 valve positioning by moving the intake away from the cylinder wall to improve airflow past the entire valve while also moving the exhaust valve.

Velocity and port flow considerations also pertain to the exhaust side. Because after combustion the cylinder is under high pressure and temperature, the exhaust valve can be roughly 80 percent of the intake valve and still perform well. The flow path is the opposite of the intake tract, but many other port design considerations are still critical. A larger port may work well, but tends to again sacrifice velocity and may hurt mid-lift flow velocity if not sized properly. One idea that certainly improves exhaust port flow is to raise the port exit point on the cylinder head. If you look at all race-style small-block head designs, these castings almost universally raise the exit point in an attempt to reduce the angle that the exhaust gas must traverse in order to escape the cylinder. Unfortunately for street applications, raising the exhaust port also affects header fit in the chassis unless custom headers are used. For this reason, most performance small-block heads are forced to adhere to some version of the stock exhaust port location, although many push the envelope of where "stock" truly resides.

One way to evaluate exhaust port flow is to calculate the exhaust-to-intake (E/I) relationship, expressed in terms of a percentage. By dividing the exhaust flow in CFM by the intake flow at the same valve lift, you can compute this relationship. Generally, most good cylinder heads create an E/I between 70 and 85 percent. Using this formula is a quick way to evaluate the exhaust port's efficiency in relation to the intake. With several ways of looking at this percentage, one important thing to not overlook is that a head with an excellent E/I may in fact be pointing out that the intake port is actually a bit weak, rather than indicating that the head has a killer exhaust port. Comparing that exhaust port flow at the same exhaust valve lift to other cylinder heads with a good exhaust port makes that evaluation easier.

Many theories pick a particular E/I percentage, such as 75 and 80 percent, which are both popular numbers touted as the magic E/I. Before subscribing to any specific number and deciding on a head based on that number, it's best to consider not just the cylinder head but how the head is to be used and what cam you will choose to go with the head. This involves many variables and leads us directly into how to choose a cam that works with your cylinder heads.

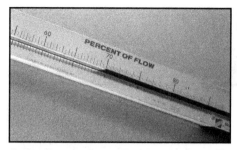

Once the test depression has been established and the proper flow openings have been selected, the inclined manometer on the Superflow bench indicates the percentage of flow based on the known capacity of the selected flow opening. For example, if the opening can flow 300 cfm and the inclined manometer reads 70 percent, then the port flows 210 cfm at that valve lift.

Exhaust port flow is also affected by whether a flow pipe is used. When evaluating exhaust port flow numbers, it's important to know whether a flow pipe was used. Ideally, the test data gives flow numbers both with and without the flow pipe so you have your choice. Generally, mid- and high-valve lift values benefit the most from using a flow pipe.

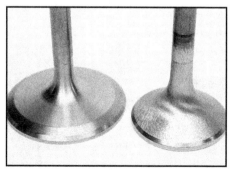

High-quality stainless steel valves are almost a necessity today in any respectable performance engine. If you are in the market for a quality valve, also remember that weight is always a factor and larger valves weigh more.

Accurate flow testing also requires ensuring that the valve lift numbers are correct. The easiest way to do this is with a dial indicator. Several companies make fixtures that locate a dial indicator and a valve actuator to create the required valve lift.

Cams and Cylinder Heads

From Chapter 10, we already know a few basics for choosing a cam and how duration, overlap, and lift all interrelate. Now we take that information and use it to help us decide how to build an engine based on cylinder-head flow.

Let's take a mild small-block street engine as our first example. With 355 cubic inches, many small-block engine builders on a budget are forced to use stock iron production cylinder heads. In our dyno test chapter, we address a 350 H.O. style crate engine with Vortec heads, but let's choose instead a set of pre-Vortec iron production heads such as a set of 441 heads. This number is the last three numbers of the casting number, using 1.94/1.50-inch valves and a 76-cc combustion chamber. These heads flow acceptable intake flow numbers for a stock head, but suffer greatly from a weak exhaust port. They're not as bad as early Ford small-block heads, but close. To address this weakness, our engine builder has done some mild pocket porting work and back-cut the exhaust and intake valves to improve the low-lift flow.

The smart move is to wait and choose the cam only after selecting all the other components in the engine. This way the engine builder can match the cam more accurately to the entire engine. The rest of the engine features 9:1 compression, an Edelbrock Performer intake manifold along with an Edelbrock Performer 600–cfm carburetor, and a set of

1–5/8-inch headers. The application is in a little 1964 Chevy Nova with a TH–350 transmission and a stock 10-bolt with 3.08:1 gear with a limited slip.

Several pieces on this engine point us toward a conservative cam selection. First of all, the stock heads, mild Performer dual-plane intake, and the small carburetor all indicate that great part-throttle torque is where this engine is headed. Perhaps a few "bottom-of-the-page" enthusiasts still want to prescribe a big cam to be lumpy and impressive, so it's worth it to look a little closer at why this isn't such a good idea. First of all, a long duration cam, like a COMP Cams Magnum 292H (244/244 duration at 0.050, with 0.501/0.501-inch valve lift) automatically dictates a very late closing intake with lots of overlap. This would sacrifice low- and mid-range torque, the engine would be lazy off idle and would not begin to make decent power until 3,500 or even 4,000 rpm.

This scenario has several problems. Let's start with the Performer intake, which maxes out in flow potential around 5,000 rpm, just about the time the cam really starts to work. Add in the single-pattern cam that doesn't help stock heads with a weak exhaust port, and an intake port that probably won't flow any more air at 0.500 inches than it does at 0.450-inch valve lift, and we're working on a lame engine. Sure, it still makes decent peak power, around 335 hp or even 350 hp at around 5,800 rpm. But the torque curve is very weak and this combination's part-throttle performance is dismal.

Now let's take the same engine and plug in a much milder cam. First of all, for simplicity's sake, let's pick a flat tappet hydraulic cam family that uses dual-pattern design so we can crutch our weak exhaust port. Let's look for a cam that offers around 10 degrees or so of additional advertised duration to give the motor a fighting chance at higher engine speeds. Next, with the mild intake and small CFM carburetor, there's no need to employ a cam with more than 220 degrees of duration at 0.050-inch tappet lift. Several companies have dozens of cams that fit this bill, but this book narrows it down to a choice between a

FLOW BENCH BASICS

Since flow bench numbers constitute an important tool in selecting a good cylinder head, it's worth spending time to understand how a flow bench works and what it tells you. Most flow benches work by creating flow across a cylinder head, either by creating low pressure inside the bench to move air through the intake port, or pushing air out through the exhaust port. Most benches use several large vacuum cleaner motors to create this airflow, although we've seen home-built benches that also use a large electric motor to spin a 6-71 supercharger that moves some serious air!

Once we have a cabinet built that houses and moves the air, we need a couple of air measurement devices. These are called manometers and are basically clear plastic or glass tubes filled with colored water. The first manometer is mounted vertically alongside the test bench with its height marked off in inches, which measures the test depression. For most flow-bench testing, the accepted test depression standard for cylinder heads is 28 inches of water. That means the depression (differential in pressure) created by the electric motors creates a standing column of water 28 inches tall.

Before we mount our cylinder head on the top of the bench, find the large hole through which all this air passes. This orifice must be calibrated so that we know how much air flows through this hole at a given test depression. SuperFlow benches supply plates calibrated to flow a given volume of air, expressed in cubic feet per minute (cfm) at a given test depression. This is used as the standard that the flow through the cylinder head is compared. This measurement is accomplished by using a second, inclined manometer usually mounted on the vertical back of the bench at an angle. This manometer is calibrated in percentage of

flow. This means that if we place a restriction (the cylinder head intake port) over the opening to the flow bench, there is a reduction in airflow compared to our calibrated standard. Let's say our standard flow is exactly 300 cfm at 28 inches of water. Once the head is bolted in place, we measure only 50 percent on the inclined manometer. That means that the head flows 150 cfm at 28 inches of water. For a SuperFlow 600 bench, for example, it's a bit more complicated than this because six holes (SuperFlow calls them "Ranges") can be selected, based on the volume of air flowing through the cylinder head. The reason for these different-sized flow orifices is that we want to more closely match the flow volume through these orifices to the flow in the head so that our inclined manometer is more accurate. In other words, we have a better chance of creating accurate data when working with volumes that place the inclined manometer above 70 percent instead of around 20 or 30 percent.

SuperFlow lists the actual calibrated flow numbers for each of the six flow ranges. Those numbers are listed in the accompanying chart pulled from an actual SuperFlow 600 bench. These numbers change slightly from one machine to another, which is why the numbers are listed in plain sight right on the front of the machine. For example, Range 4's actual flow number is 207 cfm for the intake and 217 cfm for the exhaust.

Once we know how much air flows through these calibrated orifices at a given depression, we can now place our cylinder head on the top of the bench and carefully clamp and seal the head so there are no leaks. Then we use a fixture with a dial indicator to accurately open the valves a precise amount. Once all that is arranged, we have included a spark plug in the head, and there

are no other leak passages (like an EGR port in an exhaust port), we can begin to measure the airflow at each valve lift. Placing the intake valve lift at 0.200 inches, let's say we measure 85 percent flow for Range 3, which is 149 cfm. To determine actual flow at this test depression at this valve lift, all we have to do is multiply the actual range number of 149 by 85 percent to come up with a flow number of 126 cfm.

After we've measured the entire flow curve for the intake port, we can reverse the airflow path on the flow bench and now test the exhaust port. This is basically performed the same way as the intake. It's important to note that for best results, flow bench airflow numbers should be corrected for temperature, since the longer you run the bench, the hotter the air becomes. This is especially true when testing the exhaust side. This is an extra step that few flow bench operators perform, but it has a significant effect on the actual flow numbers. There are other variables as well, such as the bore size the head is tested on and whether the head is accurately centered over the bore fixture. These variables, along with a few more, are the reason why flow numbers vary so much between flow benches and even between flow bench operators. This is why it's not completely accurate to compare flow numbers on cylinder heads tested on difference benches since not everyone performs their tests in the same manner.

Flow Range Numbers

	Intake	Exhaust
Range 1	35.7	42.2
Range 2	71.3	81
Range 3	149	158
Range 4	207	217
Range 5	448	476
Range 6	598	625

COMP Cams Xtreme Energy 262 and a Crane PowerMax 272. The Crane might seem to be much larger than the Comp grind, but let's take a look at the 0.050-inch tappet lift numbers.

The Comp XE262 specs out at 218/224 degrees of duration at 0.050 with 0.462/0.469 inches of lift and a lobe separation angle of 110 degrees. The Crane PowerMax 272 offers 216/228 degrees of

duration at 0.050-inch tappet lift with 0.454/0.480 inches of lift with a lobe separation angle of 112 degrees. Keep in mind that Crane uses 0.004-inch tappet lift for its advertised duration figures, while Comp uses 0.006-inch. This accounts for some of that 10-degree difference in the advertised numbers between the two cams since the 0.050-inch tappet lift duration numbers between the two cams are only two degrees apart. In fact, these cams are very similar when this difference in seat timing is taken into account. For mild cams like these, you can figure on a ballpark figure of two degrees per 0.001 inches of change in duration. This is a significant number, but it makes sense since the lobe acceleration is very mild at these checking points just off the base circle.

To investigate this further, let's see what happens when you look a little closer at the timing cards for each cam. Both cam companies indicate intake closing at their advertised duration measuring points. You might expect that two cams within 2 degrees of each other in duration at 0.050-

One quick way to improve low- and mid-lift flow is with a 30- to 33-degree back cut on the inboard side of the 45-degree seat angle. This back cut establishes a gentler radius as the inlet air transitions between the seat and the valve. However, be aware that back cuts can often hurt high-lift flow.

inch tappet lift specs would also have very similar intake closing specs. But the reality is that the Crane cam offers an intake closing of 63 degrees ABDC checked at 0.004-inch tappet lift. The COMP Cams grind checks the advertised duration numbers at 0.006-inch tappet lift, which means the intake closing number should occur a little earlier than the Crane. That's exactly what we see with the Comp XE262 cam intake closing point with a much earlier 57 degrees ABDC. This is a difference of 6 degrees. Given our 0.002-inch-per-degree rule of thumb, this places the advertised opening and closing points now within a degree of each other when both the opening and closing points are combined.

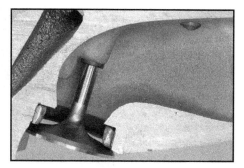

Since air and fuel do not like abrupt changes in direction, a good 23-degree small-block Chevy head incorporates a slight port floor rise to create a smoother transition from horizontal flow into the intake bowl area and out past the valve.

We also need to look at other differences including the 110-degree lobe separation angle for the COMP Cams compared to the 112-degree lobe separation angle for the Crane cam. While we could probably dissect these two cams for a few more paragraphs with interesting delineations, the point is, again, that the more you know about the cam you choose, the better your selection is bound to be. Overall, these cams are very similar, with the most significant difference being the small lift advantage given to the COMP.

Both these cams combine with our mildly ported stock heads and conservative induction system to make good torque and decent power. With no big corks in the intake or exhaust systems, you could expect this engine to make 325 to 340 hp with a wide power band. This would make an excellent street engine that would be incredibly durable, reliable, and fun to drive.

Perhaps more readers would be interested in a much more aggressive combination, so let's look at a 383-ci small-block with good heads and a bigger cam. The 383 is a simple stroker combination that retains the 4.030-inch bore but adds a 3.750-inch stroke crank from a 400-ci small-block. In this particular combination, we used a static 9.5:1 compression ratio combined with a set of Trick Flow Specialties (TFS) 200cc 23-degree valve angle Duttweiler Signature heads along with an Edelbrock Performer RPM Air Gap dual plane intake manifold, a 750-cfm carburetor, and a set of 1-5/8-inch primary pipe headers used to pump up the torque.

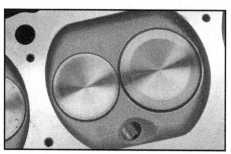

Small-block head development doesn't stop with the intake or exhaust ports in the head. It also extends to the combustion chamber. Note how the new chamber (top) has a kidney or heart-shaped configuration, which is an attempt to push the combustion process toward the exhaust valve side of the chamber. This improves cylinder scavenging. In comparison, the other chamber is a big-block Oldsmobile chamber.

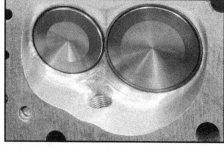

Many new aftermarket small-block heads are actually changing the position of the intake and exhaust valves, moving these heads to what the head companies call a 60/40 relationship. This is done mainly to unshroud the intake valve from around the cylinder bore to improve flow.

From this collection of parts, it would appear that the engine builder was aiming at maximizing the torque curve, even if this meant sacrificing a bit of peak horsepower. Building torque is evidenced by the use of conservative 200-cc heads, 9.5:1 compression, the dual plane intake, and the smaller 1-5/8-inch headers.

Based on the rest of these parts, we don't want to slide an oversized cam in the middle of this setup, since like the above combination, a too-large cam would only sacrifice torque and slide the peak torque curve up beyond the operating parameters of the intake and headers. With this in mind, the engine builder came up with a COMP Cams XR282H hydraulic roller cam. The advantage the roller offers is more lift with a more aggressive velocity curve on the opening flank to generate a 0.510/0.520-inch lift with 1.5:1 rockers complemented with 230/236 degrees of duration at 0.050-inch tappet lift with a 110-degree lobe separation angle. On the dyno, this engine made a solid 501 ft-lb of torque at 4,400 rpm while also making a respectable 490 horsepower at 5,600. This gives the engine a decent power band of 1,200 rpm while still making almost 500 hp at a durability-enhancing peak engine speed. In addition to its peak power potential, this 383 can grunt out 422 ft-lb at a tight converter speed of only 2,400 rpm.

Some may question why the engine builder chose to run such a "small" camshaft for this 383, but the focus again was an emphasis on a milder street engine that would still run strong without having to resort to deep gears and a high stall speed converter. To hammer this home, we fit this into a heavier car of around 3,700 pounds with a TH350 automatic and a mild torque converter. Here, an important question is how much slippage you're willing to put up with on the street, since a higher stall just launches the car harder. With a 2,800-rpm converter and a 3.73:1 rear gear, this conservative cam and head package pushes a heavy Chevelle certainly into the high 11s at 116 to 118 mph on a good density altitude day with excellent traction. That's going through the traps at just over peak horsepower, which is perfect.

If you still think that a bigger cam is warranted, then that's when we have to change our combination to regard not only to the engine, but also with the car. If we plug in a cam with 15 degrees more duration, then we'd want to add a single plane intake, a larger carburetor, and bigger headers. That would work best if we converted to a mechanical roller rather than a hydraulic. We might even want to step up to 220–cc port heads with a larger

MID-LIFT FLOW

Selecting a cylinder head based on flow bench numbers can be fun. You have a column of flow numbers for a couple of different heads and you just pick out the head with the biggest number at max lift. Unfortunately, the selection process isn't quite that easy. Dozens of variables affect a cylinder head's ability to make power, but let's take a look at just one. Most enthusiasts take the flow numbers generated by a flow bench and take the simplistic approach of evaluating only the maximum valve lift flow numbers, judging the head based solely on those numbers. To show how misdirected this can eventually become, some enthusiasts choose a head based on flow numbers at valve lifts that even their own "bottom of the page" camshafts can never attain.

The first point is to limit your flow-bench evaluation to achievable valve lift numbers. If your cam can only punch up 0.500-inch lift, there's no reason to be concerned with flow numbers at 0.600-inch lift. To take this example further, it would seem beneficial then to spend more time evaluating the low- and mid-lift flow numbers. While 0.100-inch valve lift may not be crucial, certainly flow numbers at 0.200, 0.300, and 0.400 inches become increasingly important.

There are several excellent reasons for paying close attention especially to mid-lift flow. To begin with, the valve achieves max lift only once in the curve, but achieves 0.400 inches, as an example, twice in the curve—once on the opening side and then again on the closing side. But even more importantly, consider what is going on in the cylinder, especially on the closing side of the valve lift curve. It's relatively accepted that the column of air that begins in the plenum area of the intake manifold and extends all the way into the cylinder has had time to generate signifi-

cant speed and momentum as intake duration nears the end of its lift curve. As the valve is closing, the piston is also nearing the top of the cylinder. A long-duration, later closing intake valve allows the piston to get closer to TDC before the valve closes. So it would make sense that a port with good mid-lift flow numbers would be able to fill or pack a cylinder with more air and fuel than a port with poor mid-lift numbers.

According to engine theorist Jim McFarland, his discussions on this subject with Smokey Yunick and the legendary Zora Arkus-Duntov uncovered separate-yet-similar conclusions from both men who emphasized concentrating on and improving port flow efficiencies in the range of 65 to 70 percent of maximum valve lift. Given a camshaft with 0.600-inch lift, improving flow numbers in the 0.390- to 0.450-valve lift would be of significant benefit.

It's worth a closer look at why this occurs. As the piston approaches TDC, flow velocity in the intake port has already peaked. Also, cylinder volume is decreasing and pressure is rising. However, if the flow velocity with its attendant energy is sufficient, the inlet tract can continue to pack the cylinder with additional fuel and air, increasing the volumetric efficiency. At a given point, the valve closes and the engine makes more power based on an improved mid-lift flow capability. As you may have surmised, this means there is a definite connection between inlet flow velocity and actual cfm flow potential. Combine the two, and you begin to see why all the accomplished engine builders in the country are right on target when they recommend choosing a cylinder head with the smallest port and the biggest flow numbers.

cross-sectional area to complement this higher engine speed combination. Then in respect to the car, we'd have to add a higher stall speed converter than could launch the car at a higher engine speed, closer to the higher peak torque along with a deep-

er rear gear and more tire. Of course, all that also means the car is much less streetable. But it delivers perhaps a low 11-second e.t. even in this heavy car. It all depends on how much you're willing to compromise the car's manners.

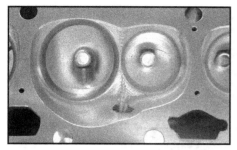

The relative merits of iron vs. aluminum heads have stirred much conversation. While aluminum is lighter and easier to repair should the head be damaged, the performance advantage of an iron head is probably minimal. Often a minor chamber shape revision can be worth more than the difference between iron and aluminum in horsepower.

The area within a 1/2 inch of either side of the valve seat is the area where you can gain the most in terms of flow improvements. Minor pocket-porting work here to smooth out any sharp angles can be worth significant gains, especially when working with stock production iron heads.

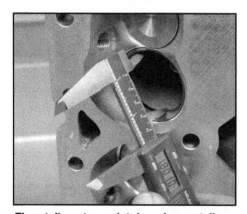

Throat diameter vs. intake valve seat diameter has several "theories." Most of these seem to hover between 80 and 85 percent. A throat diameter of more than 90 percent often only results in intake flow degradation, so don't get greedy.

CURTAIN AREA

One of the terms often used when referring to cylinder head flow is "curtain area." This refers to the flow area defined as the valve's circumference multiplied by valve lift. If you think of the area between the valve seat and the bottom of the valve at a given lift with a curtain around this entire area, then you get the idea.

Computing this flow curtain area is very easy. The definition of circumference is diameter times Pi (3.1417) times the valve lift, which makes the curtain area formula:

Curtain Area = Valve Dia. x 3.1417 x Valve Lift

Let's say we have a 2.08-inch intake valve with a valve lift of 0.600 inches. To be as accurate as possible, we're going to compute circumference based on the valve diameter at the seat, which makes the actual diameter 2.05 inches. Now let's do the math:

Curtain Area = 2.05 x 3.1417 x 0.600

Curtain Area = 3.86 square inches

Now, when you run across the term again, you not only know what it means, but you also know how to compute its value.

PORT VOLUME

The most popular way to categorize cylinder heads is by port volume. This is done for reasons of expediency, but it is also somewhat misleading. Let's start this explanation by looking at a simple pipe. Let's make it a 2-inch inside diameter pipe that's 4 inches long. If we measure its volume, we discover that it has a volume of 12.5 ci or 206 cc. Now, let's measure how much air flows through this pipe at a given test depression. If we were to double the length of the pipe, this would double the volume and there would probably be a slight reduction in air flow through the pipe, but barely enough to measure. The point here is that an increase in port volume does not automatically mean an increase in flow.

The more accurate way of comparing cylinder heads is by rating ports by their smallest intake port cross-sectional area. This has also been called the intake port's choke point. While port configuration, its bowl shape, valve size, and dozens of other details all help define how well an intake port performs, perhaps the single most important point is still any intake port's cross-sectional area.

Nowhere is this more important than if you are attempting to compare cylinder heads of different families. For example, let's say you wanted to evaluate the relative flow performance of both a small-block Chevy head and a small-block Ford head, or perhaps the flow performances of a GEN I versus a GEN III head. If the port cross-sectional areas were identical, or even close, you would have a valid test. But if you used port volume as your scale for comparison, this would be less than accurate.

Is there a relationship between ultimate flow and cross-sectional area? Engineers with much more training and math background have created what are called flow coefficients. They can help you determine a given intake port's efficiency based on its flow and its cross-sectional area. The math gets a bit complicated, but it is possible to do. We'll save that discussion for our book on small-block Chevy cylinder heads.

You can spend time gasket matching the intake port to the intake manifold, but unless the port is smaller than the intake port or creating a ledge, there are minimal performance gains (if any) to be had by porting this end of the head.

Dart Machine has created its own custom-built wet flow-bench that is already helping the company develop better cylinder heads. The concept is that there could be modifications to the head that don't improve airflow but do result in better mixture quality introduced into the cylinder. That results in more power, possibly across the entire power band.

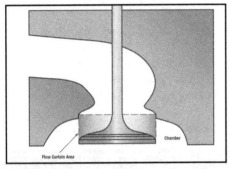

Valve curtain area is the square inches of area defined by the circumference of the valve times the valve lift.

Some of the best small-block heads on the market are the Airflow Research (AFR) heads. AFR offers heads ranging from 180 to 227 cc in the standard 23-degree valve angle. These heads flow exceptionally well and also make excellent torque at a decent price.

WET FLOW

The latest buzz in cylinder head development is the wet flow-bench. The concept is an attempt to duplicate or at least simulate what happens to the fuel in an intake port and how this liquid reacts to changes in direction, pressure, and velocity as it travels through the intake port and into the cylinder. Certainly this work has been on-going in the OEMs for years, but this is relatively new to the aftermarket. The first company to develop a working aftermarket bench was Joe Mondello.

Since then, Dart has been the first of the aftermarket cylinder head companies to address this situation with a complete system that takes up a large portion of a good-sized room. If you think about this, the idea makes perfect sense. Fuel has much more density compared to air and therefore is more drastically affected by abrupt changes in direction than air. Unlike a flow bench that merely measures airflow volume, the wet flow-bench concentrates more on the quality of airflow coming out of the intake valve and how that airflow affects the wet flow pattern into the cylinder. There has been considerable discussion about swirl and tumble into the cylinder from the intake valve which is way beyond the scope of this chapter. However, all this does affect how well the air and fuel mixes in the cylinder. As the homogeneity of this mixture improves, it allows tuners to run a slightly leaner air-fuel mixture to make more power without causing engine damage.

We'll go out on a limb and predict that this study of the effects of wet flow has a drastic affect on future cylinder head design. The net result of combining what the industry learns about improving cylinder filling with increasing mixture motion without air-fuel separation begins bearing fruit in terms of increased horsepower and torque.

Conclusion

We've actually spent as much time proscribing entire engine combinations as we have looking at combining heads and cams in this chapter. That was intentional since the key to any successful engine is the entire combination as opposed to just heads and cams. Clearly, we've only scratched the surface of what is attainable. If you've never built a small-block before, we'd suggest erring on the conservative side and at least interview three or four engine builders or enthusiasts with combinations that you think are successful. If you're truly interested in performance, ask to see their e.t. slips. Better yet, witness the performance first hand. Then you know for sure.

VALVE ANGLE

Certain restrictions are placed on production-based engines and cylinder heads. One of the biggest restrictions, besides port layout, is the stock small-block valve angle of 23 degrees. This is the angle that both the intake and exhaust valves form in relationship to the piston and deck of the engine. This was established way back when the small-block was first created in 1955. Since then, small-block race engine builders have discovered that standing the angle up (or making it smaller) and moving the valve centerline closer to true vertical in relation to the piston improves flow. This is basically done to soften the change in direction the inlet charge must make in order to enter the cylinder. Since bringing the inlet charge straight into the cylinder isn't possible, the next step is to make this angle as close to vertical as possible.

NASCAR race engine builders began pushing this envelope many years ago with the factory-supplied 18-degree head that was quickly followed by the 15-degree head. Later, these heads were superseded first by the SB2 and later by the SB2.2 heads. These latest heads not only change the inlet valve angle, but also completely change the port layout of the small-block to eliminate the siamesed or pair exhaust ports in the middle of the head, which tends to build heat in an endurance or circle-track engine. Around this same time, Chevy introduced the splayed valve head, which looks very similar to a small-block version of the Rat motor head, with intake valves at 16 degrees, but also tilted (or splayed) an additional 4 degrees. The exhaust valves are at 11 degrees also with a 4-degree tilt. Generally, these heads also come with very small

chambers. The splayed valve head comes with 45 cc chambers, intended to increase compression without requiring domes on pistons, which both shroud the combustion process, but also increase piston weight.

While all this sounds good—and it is—for a pure race engine, these specialty heads also require a shopping cart full of dedicated parts. The list begins with custom pistons to handle the new valve angles, along with a new intake, complete new valvetrain to accommodate the different valve angles, plus valve covers, and custom headers.

It is possible to purchase Nextel Cup cast-off cylinder heads for much less money than buying new, but beware that a good deal on the heads may sound alluring, but be sure to price all the other accoutrements before making a decision.

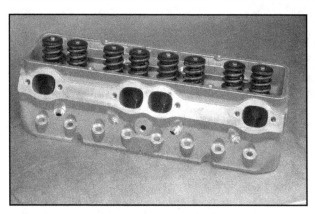

Trick Flow Specialties (TFS) builds an 18-degree valve angle head for a small-block Chevy that still requires an 18-degree intake, headers, and valvetrain, but TFS claims the head flows over 330 cfm at 0.600-lift!

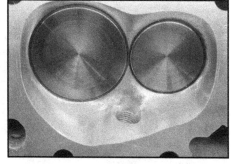

Don't overlook the potential power in a CNC-machined and profiled combustion chamber. Remember that all the work you put into cramming that cylinder full of air and fuel needs to be combusted efficiently in order to extract the maximum power from the induction system.

This is a Chevy SB2.2 head used on Ken Duttweiler's 287 ci turbo charged Comp Eliminator engine. Note how GM Racing changed to a symmetrical port layout that looks similar to a Ford head, but the ports flow an amazing amount of air. Add a pair of turbos and it's no wonder this little 287 makes 1800 hp!

DYNO TESTS

Dyno testing has progressed from the old days when companies merely bolted an engine to a stand with the controls all in the same room. Today, sophisticated cells now cost tens of thousands of dollars to build and use monster fans to move air quickly through the cell to optimize power.

cylinder heads is available; camshaft, intake, and exhaust components to make the power level you want to achieve. One way to get an idea of what works is to evaluate different engine combinations.

By now, perhaps you can predict where we're going with this. The idea, once again, is to not merely look at the peak values of toque and horsepower, but also look closely at the entire curve. To this end, we've included average torque and horsepower numbers along with peak horsepower per cubic inch (hp/ci) and torque per cubic inch (ft-lb/ci) evaluations as well as a broader perspective on what power really represents. As we mentioned in the chapter on power adders, these components also radically pump up the torque curve. Especially with regard to nitrous, adding 100 ft-lb of torque or more is huge and also the main reason why a car with a mild 100 hp shot of nitrous can improve the e.t. by a full second or more. It's not the peak 100 hp that improves the acceleration as much as the radical torque improvement throughout

The ultimate goal of this book is to lay the valvetrain foundation for a powerful small-block Chevy. So at some point, we have to pull our noses out of theory books and get our hands dirty building an engine or two. If you are in quest of knowledge to help with your first engine, you are on the right track. For a first attempt, a mild street engine teaches you volumes about what works and those moves that would best be avoided. For those who have more experience, a limitless selection of different combinations of

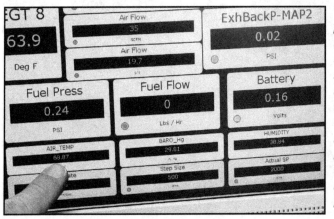

Temperature, barometric pressure, and the amount of water in the air (called vapor pressure) are the three major atmospheric conditions that affect engine power. The combination of high atmospheric pressure, low temperature, and low vapor pressure creates optimal conditions to make best power.

More sophisticated dyno cells also use an air turbine to measure the amount of air entering the engine. This number can be deceiving since an engine may not necessarily use all the air that it ingests. But generally, more air into the engine usually results in more power.

the entire RPM band that substantially improves the car's acceleration. This is also the reason why nitrous is such a kick in the pants when you hit the button; that's the torque bump you're feeling.

This is our way of promoting why it's so important to pay close attention to the engine's torque curve. The plan should be to create the combination that raises the engine's entire power curve. That's the challenge and what makes effective power building so difficult. Conversely, it's easy to build a peaky engine that has a needle-point power curve.

An engine can be tested on the dyno several different ways. By excluding the accessory drive and air filter, and by using a less restrictive exhaust system than is used in the car, the power numbers can be significantly higher compared to the power the engine makes in the car.

Now that we've set some guidelines, look at the following combinations and evaluate their overall power curve. Generally, the wider the RPM band between peak torque and peak horsepower, the more stable the power curve and easier it is to put this power to the ground. Engines with wider power bands make excellent street powerplants because they demand less gear ratio and generally a lower RPM stall speed torque converter. This improves drivability and doesn't heat up the transmission fluid due to excessive slippage. Of course, at some point, excessive torque becomes very difficult to manage from a traction standpoint. This level is generally above the 500 ft-lb of torque point. If you look at the accompanying engine packages, only the 454-ci small-block exceeds this torque level for the majority of its power curve. Even at this power level, you could still use a 26 x 10.5-inch wide sticky street tire like a Mickey Thompson ET Street tire or Hoosier gumball and hook the car, assuming decent track preparation. On the street, this might be more difficult.

The overall point is maximizing the entire power curve as opposed to just the peak horsepower point. Much like how a roller lobe increases lift earlier in the lobe profile compared to a flat tappet design, maximizing torque in the mid-range is one of the magic buttons you can push to improve e.t. and speed. This way you do not have to resort to high-RPM power with deep gears that make an otherwise reasonable car less fun to drive on the street. Combine a very wide power band with excellent torque and good horsepower and you have an engine that is fun to drive, pulls like gangbusters, and is generally a kick in the pants to drive, no matter what the situation. Build an engine that performs like that, and consider yourself a winner.

Engine 1
The Iron Mouse
355ci

To begin our dyno section, we thought we'd evaluate a conservative small-block that makes excellent horsepower and torque, but also could be affordably built. We started with a basic

one-piece rear main seal, hydraulic roller cam style 2-bolt main block, cast crank, and hypereutectic flattop pistons with 5/64-inch rings. In keeping with the budget theme, the GMPP Vortec iron head is the best iron cylinder head for the price. Even better, you can buy a head reconfigured for more lift from Scoggin-Dickey or one of several other GMPP dealerships that have modified these heads to accept additional valve lift for under $600 for a pair of complete heads. The heads come with 1.94/1.60-inch valves, but do require a special Vortec-style intake manifold.

For the valvetrain side of things on this particular small-block, we decided to keep with the GMPP theme and add the Hot cam and kit also from Scoggin-Dickey. This cam was originally designed as a performance upgrade for the LT1/LT4 engines, but is also an outstanding street performance hydraulic roller grind. With 279/287 advertised duration, 218/228 degrees at 0.050-inch tappet lift, and 0.525-inch lift on both the intake and exhaust with a 112-degree lobe separation angle, this cam offers a great blend of torque and horsepower potential. For the intake, we used the ubiquitous Edelbrock Performer RPM Air Gap along with a Holley 750-cfm carburetor and a set of 1-5/8-inch headers pumping exhaust pressure through a set of DynoMax 2-1/2-inch mufflers.

Note that this engine makes at least 400 ft-lb of torque between 3,200 and 5,000 while cranking out a peak of 428 ft-lb of torque at 4,200. In fact, the engine averages 401 ft-lb between 2,600 and 6,000 rpm. The peak horsepower point is also relatively conservative with a 401 peak horsepower point of 5,600 rpm. That's an impressive 1,400-rpm-wide power band that supports the car's acceleration curve nicely. Also, note that the engine maintains more than 99 percent of peak torque, 425 ft-lb, all the way down to 3,600 rpm. That's almost a pool-table-flat curve from 3,600 to 4,600. If you accept that 425 is not much different than 428 ft-lb, this expands the power band between peak torque and peak horsepower out to an outstanding 2,000 rpm. This is excellent power for a set of stock iron port heads, which points out just how well these Vortec iron castings really flow air.

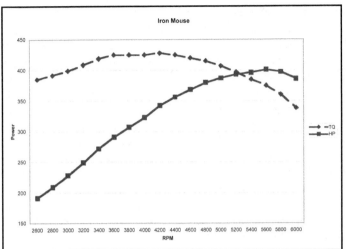

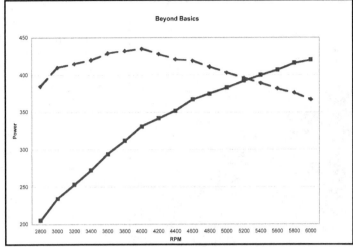

RPM	TQ	HP
2600	385	191
2800	392	209
3000	399	228
3200	409	249
3400	419	272
3600	425	291
3800	425	307
4000	425	323
4200	428*	342
4400	425	356
4600	420	368
4800	415	380
5000	407	387
5200	397	393
5400	385	396
5600	375	401*
5800	360	397
6000	338	386
Peak	428	401
Avg.	401.6	326.4

1.20 ft-lb/ci
1.13 hp/ci

Engine 2
Beyond The Basics
355ci

The idea of a conservative street engine is to create a powerplant with sharp throttle response, strong torque, good drivability, and yet still impressive horsepower numbers. This may seem like a contradiction, and therein lies the compromises that must be addressed for a street engine. The classic approach is to stuff a big cam in an engine with underwhelming heads and hope for the best. The excuse usually has something to do with budgets. But let's turn that around and invest in a smaller but strong set of heads like a set of the AFR 180-cc aluminum heads fitted with a set of 2.02/1.60-inch valves. The small-block's compression is a very conservative 9:1 so that you could even run 87 octane gas for part-throttle cruising.

To maintain that very conservative approach, the engine builder matched these smaller, high-velocity heads with a conservative COMP Cams XE262 flat tappet hydraulic cam with 218/224 degrees of duration at 0.050-inch tappet lift, along with 0.462/0.469-inch lift using 1.5:1 roller rockers and a set of matching COMP single springs with a damper. On top, the builder also spec'd one of AFR's matching Street Pro-Flow RPM dual plane intakes along with a 750-cfm Holley mechanical secondary carburetor. This particular dyno test was run with 1–5/8-inch headers and an open exhaust, but the power curve would probably not change much with a set of full-flow mufflers.

In a similar test with a longer-duration XE268 cam, that combination only made slightly more horsepower and lost considerable torque below 4,000 rpm. In our experience, these 180–cc AFR heads have such a strong exhaust port that this XE268 intake lobe, matched with a single pattern cam where the exhaust duration is the same as the exhaust, is a better combination that makes more power below peak torque, and yet would make a little more horsepower above peak torque. Theory suggests this cam probably over-scavenged the cylinder, pulling a small amount of incoming charge right out the exhaust at engine speeds above peak torque. However, this engine still makes excellent power even if you merely duplicated this combination. Note that the XE262 combination offers an outstanding 2,000 rpm-wide power band that extends from 4,000 to 6,000 rpm and makes an excellent 410 ft-lb of torque at 3,000. True, it makes "only" 420 hp at 6,000. But the overall power this engine makes is very impressive for a 355–ci Mouse with a small cam. This engine averages 420 ft-lb of torque between 3,000 and 5,000 rpm and averages 405 ft-lb for the entire curve! That's stout for a "little" 355 with a tiny cam. The key is matching the conservative cam with a high-flow, high velocity set of heads.

RPM	TQ	HP
2600	370	183
2800	385	205
3000	410	234
3200	415	253
3400	420	272
3600	429	294
3800	432	312
4000	435*	331
4200	428	342
4400	421	352
4600	419	367
4800	411	375

5000	403	383
5200	396	392
5400	389	400
5600	382	407
5800	376	416
6000	367	420*
Peak	435	420
Avg.	405	330

1.22 ft-lb/ci
1.18 hp/ci

Engine 3
Torque 400s
383ci

The 383 small-block has become incredibly popular in the small-block Chevy market. This is especially because

Many dyno shops use an electric water pump on an engine, mostly just for convenience. But add a water pump, complete accessory drive, and a large mechanical engine-drive fan and the difference in power could easily be 15 to 20 hp on a high-winding small-block. That's one reason that electric fans have become so popular.

the cranks are virtually no more expensive than a standard stroke 350 crank. The only expense increase is in the material choice, from cast to 4340 and on up the food chain. This particular motor actually displaced 385 inches with a 0.040–over bore to match the 3.75-inch stroke. Using a steel 4340 Scat crank and Scat 6.0-inch rods to help the rod-length-to-stroke ratio, the engine builder used a set of SRP forged pistons that help create 9.2:1 compression since the engine was intended to run strictly on pump gas. It's possible that with the cam, the engine could have run without detonation problems with as high as 10:1 compression with the aluminum heads given the cam's late closing intake. With a stock block and some judicious grinding to clear the block, the lubrication

THE DYNO-SHELL GAME

Virtually every month, the big performance car magazines deliver at least one engine dyno test. This type of engine performance testing is very useful to evaluate different engine combinations, and the small-block Chevy has probably had more tests run on it than any engine in the history of internal combustion engines. On the surface, these tests may appear to be very similar, but take it from us—they are not. Unlike the test parameters established by the Society of Automotive Engineers (SAE) that dictate the way an engine must be run to create the power numbers for new cars (which has changed over the years), no established guidelines exist for the high-performance industry.

The main problem lies in how the engine is configured. It is rare that an engine is dyno tested in exactly the configuration that it runs in the vehicle. Most often, the dyno operators do this out of expediency. Almost everyone who brings an engine to be dyno tested for the first time omits many essential components. So the dyno shop most often runs its own accessories because it is expedient to do so. As an example, most dyno shops prefer to test with an electric water pump so that

they can eliminate the hassle of bolting on accessory drive pulleys and belts that many first-time engine builders forget to bring.

Also, many dyno rooms are not big enough to permit using a complete car-style exhaust system. Some are so cramped that they cannot even accommodate mufflers, so engines must run with open headers. Even worse, many chassis-style headers do not clear the test stand that mounts the dyno absorber. Many dyno shops then resort to sprint-car-style headers that make more power than a typical chassis header even if the lengths of the primary tubes and the collector diameters are the same. Finally, most dynos run with at least an air turbine hat to measure inlet airflow or nothing above the carburetor as opposed to the air cleaner assembly that you run on the street.

Include corrected power into this equation and a typical dyno session can spit out some pretty impressive power numbers that may not be even close to what you see in the car. Let's begin with the front of the engine and the accessory drive. A typical street car at least runs an alternator, which draws very little power even at max amperage output. But add a steel flex fan to that mechanical

water pump and we've seen dyno tests where the fan and water pump can eat as much as 15 hp. Add additional components like power steering and air conditioning and the hp price tag begins to add up.

No self-respecting streeter runs without an air cleaner, but only the best designs reduce the power cost to a negligible level. We've seen a poorly designed air cleaners cost 10 hp on a 500 hp small-block. Look for an air cleaner with a gentle radius leading into the carburetor. On the exhaust side, not all headers are created equal, so be careful when choosing headers since inexpensive sets can cost 20 ft-lbs of torque compared to a quality set with a good collector design. Mufflers don't make horsepower, but a poorly constructed exhaust system with more than 2 psi of back pressure costs horsepower, and with engines making over 500 hp, you'd better be looking at a mandrel-bent 2-1/2 or 3-inch system to make sure you maintain power in the car.

The point of all this is that just because the dyno says your engine made 550 at the crankshaft, that rarely equates to the same power level in the car, unless you test your engine on the engine dyno exactly the way it runs in the vehicle.

system was finished with a Milodon kickout oil pan and windage tray followed up with a standard Mellings oil pump.

The power-producing parts list began with a set of TFS aluminum Kenny Duttweiler signature 195–cc street heads that come from Trick Flow, with a set of stainless 2.02/1.60-inch valves in a 64–cc CNC-profiled combustion chamber. The heads were also equipped with a set of dual-wound 1.460-inch diameter valvesprings and 7/16-inch studs to handle the matching roller cam. For the cam timing, the engine builder spec'd a COMP Cams mechanical roller with an Xtreme Energy XT274 cam with 236/242 degrees of duration at 0.050-inch tappet lift along with 0.603/0.608-inch lift using 1.6:1 COMP roller rockers. The COMP valvesprings spec out with 155 pounds of seat pressure installed at 1.850 inches while delivering 419 pounds at 1,250 with a spring rate of 441 lbs/in.

For the induction side of things, the builder chose a very typical Edelbrock Victor Jr. single plane and topped it off with a Holley HP 750 carburetor with the radius inlet into the carb main body. On the exhaust side, while a 1-3/4-inch header would probably have created an even stronger peak horsepower number, the engine builder went with smaller 1–5/8-inch headers to make torque and completed with a 2-1/2-inch set of Flowmaster mufflers. In a Camaro with a set of 3.73:1 gears and a 2,500-rpm stall speed converter in front of a TH-350 transmission, the car has gone 12.50s, but the owner feels that with the proper tuning the car has more.

RPM	TQ	HP
2600	425	210
2800	434	231
3000	439	251
3200	445	271
3400	459	297
3600	466	319
3800	468	339
4000	468	357
4200	470*	376
4400	468	392
4600	464	406
4800	461	422
5000	460	438
5200	448	443
5400	437	449
5600	426	454
5800	414	457
6000	397	454
6200	377	445
Peak	470	457
Avg.	443	369

1.23 ft-lb/ci
1.19 hp/ci

Engine 4
Juice Roller 490
383ci

This is a very streetable 383 that started out as a post-1988 one-piece rear main seal small-block configured to use a hydraulic roller cam. These blocks are probably more numerous now in bone yards than two-piece rear main seal engines. This allows you to use a performance hydraulic roller camshaft and either used factory hydraulic roller tappets, or less expensive new factory-style tappets

on the cam. These blocks are also equipped with a hardened cam retainer plate, so you don't need to mess with a roller cam button.

Because this was a 383ci stroker motor, the engine builder decided to go with a larger set of Trick Flow Specialties 215–cc aluminum 23-degree heads to take full advantage of the increased displacement. When it came time for the camshaft, the builder decided on a COMP Cams Xtreme Energy 282 dual pattern hydraulic roller with 230/236 degrees of duration a 0.050-inch tappet lift and 0.510/0.520-inch lift ground with a 110-degree lobe separation angle. He also used a set of 1.5:1 roller rockers to actuate the valves. Since this engine was aimed at mostly street duty, the Edelbrock Performer RPM Air Gap was a simple choice since so few manifolds can match its combination of torque and horsepower. With another nod toward useable street power, he also went with a set of 1–5/8-inch Hedman chassis headers plumbed with a pair of 2–1/2-inch pipes leading to a set of Flowmaster mufflers.

As you can see, the engine makes great torque with a peak of 501 ft-lb at a streetable 4,400 rpm. The power band is slightly narrow with the 490 peak horsepower coming in at a relatively low 5,600 rpm, but this just means that the valvetrain will not be overly taxed even shifting at 6,000 rpm. What's impressive is that this engine never falls below 420 ft-lb of torque throughout its entire power curve from 2,400 to 6,000, and averages an amazing 470 ft-lb of torque over that same band. Frankly, this makes this combination a stout package that really pulls almost anywhere you want to stab the throttle! In a 3,200-pound Camaro and excellent traction, this could ideally be

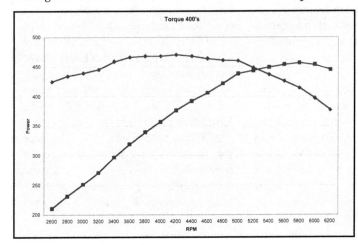

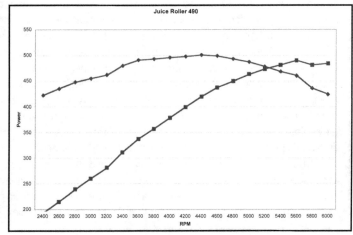

worth 11-teens at 120 mph on a good day. That's what torque does for you.

RPM	TQ	HP
2400	422	193
2600	435	215
2800	448	239
3000	455	260
3200	462	281
3400	480	311
3600	491	337
3800	493	357
4000	496	378
4200	498	399
4400	501*	419
4600	499	437
4800	493	450
5000	487	463
5200	478	473
5400	468	481
5600	460	490*
5800	436	481
6000	424	484
Peak	501	490
Avg.	470	376

1.31 ft-lb/ci
1.28 hp/ci

Engine 5
Mechanical 529
383ci

While 383s are as common as street urchins who claim they can run 10s, the reality is it takes a manly small-block to make 500 hp. It takes even more to make 529 hp, especially when the motor is only spinning 6,400 rpm. Starting with a good steel Scat

crank and 4340 forged rods, this small-block relies on a set of SRP pistons with 10.5:1 compression, just enough squeeze to make good power on pump gas without undue concern about detonation. It helps when the engine builder decided on a set of CNC-ported Dart Pro-1 215–cc heads sporting 2.05/1.60-inch stainless valves and an excellent combustion chamber design.

To match these heads with the proper camshaft for respectable power, the engine builder chose a Crane mechanical roller with 294/302 advertised duration for this stormin' Mouse. The 0.050-inch tappet lift numbers equal 240/248 degrees with 0.543/0.561-inch valve lift actuated by a set of Crane 1.5:1 Gold Race rockers. Completing the induction path includes an Edelbrock Super Victor and a Barry Grant 775–cfm Race Demon carburetor. On the high-temperature side of things, the spent gases find their way by way of a set of 1–3/4-inch headers through a pair of Flowmaster 2–1/2-inch mufflers.

Peak torque occurs at a reasonable 4,800 rpm, and with a 1,600–rpm power band the peak horsepower is still below 6,500. Shift this runner at 6,800 and this is more than enough power to shove a 3,400–pound Camaro to 11.20s at just over 120 mph using a 3,000 rpm converter in front of a TH350 automatic and a 3.90 gear spinning 28-inch tall tires.

RPM	TQ	HP
3000	449	256
3200	456	278
3400	445	288
3600	451	309
3800	450	325
4000	448	341
4200	461	369
4400	488	409
4600	500	438
4800	504*	460
5000	499	475
5200	491	486
5400	488	502
5600	478	509
5800	472	521
6000	450	514
6200	445	525
6400	434	529*
Peak	504	529
Avg.	467	418

1.31 ft-lb/ci
1.38 hp/ci

Engine 6
Torque Tank
406ci

Not too long ago, a 406–ci small-block was considered big. Today, it's strictly a middle-of-the-road Mouse as 434-ci and 454-ci small-blocks become increasingly common. This upper middle-class Mouse is a 10:1 compression small-block sporting a set of excellent 210–cc Airflow Research (AFR) heads with 2.08/1.600-inch valves and 1.5:1 Crane Gold Race rocker arms. A Crane mechanical roller cam actuates those rockers with 236/244 degrees at 0.050-inch tappet lift with 0.525/0.543-inch lift with a 112-degree lobe separation angle. This conservative camshaft is one reason for the engine's strong torque curve along with the selection of an Edelbrock Performer RPM Air Gap intake and Hooker 1-3/4-headers. The carb is a Barry Grant 750 Race Demon

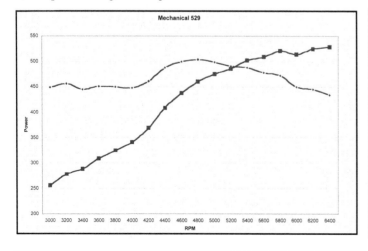

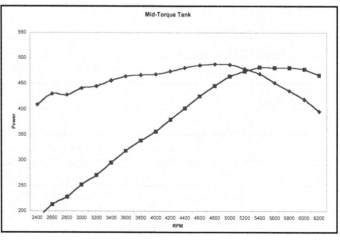

that offers an excellent fuel delivery curve. With an average of 453 ft-lb of torque across the entire power band and a peak horsepower point of only 5,400 rpm, this is another torque-generating small-block despite its "small" displacement. Certainly the triumvirate of 210-cc intake ports with a conservative Crane roller and dual plane intake are three good reasons for the engine's excellent torque characteristics. Even with a mild 2,600-rpm stall speed converter, this would make an outstanding and fun street engine.

RPM	TQ	HP
2400	409	184
2600	430	213
2800	428	228
3000	441	252
3200	445	271
3400	456	295
3600	464	318
3800	467	338
4000	468	356
4200	474	379
4400	481	402
4600	486	425
4800	488*	446
5000	487	464
5200	479	474
5400	469	482*
5600	452	481
5800	436	481
6000	419	478
6200	395	466
Peak	488	482
Avg.	453	371

1.20 ft-lb/ci
1.19 hp/ci

Engine 7
Maximum Cubes
454ci

This is the big daddy of small-blocks, at least as far as standard deck height Mouse motors is concerned. This is one of World Products' 454 crate engines configured slightly differently from the engine that *Hot Rod* magazine tested, which made 610 hp. This small-block still features its signature 4.250-inch bore and 4.00-inch stroke to create the same dis-

placement as its ubiquitous big-block relative. The motor spins 10.1:1 static compression using 20 cc dished pistons pushing against a set of aluminum World Products Motown 220-cc heads that employ massive 2.125/1.60-inch valves in a 64-cc chamber. The cam is a Crane flat tappet mechanical cam with 252/260 degrees of duration at 0.050-inch tappet lift with 0.560/0.554-inch valve lift and a 112-degree lobe separation angle. The engine also employs Harland Sharp 1.5:1 roller rockers and work against a set of Crane 408 lb/in dual valvesprings with 120 pounds of seat pressure at a 1.875-inch installed height. For the induction side, the 454 relies on a World Products single plane 4150 style intake with a Holley 850–cfm HP carburetor. For headers, the test used a set of Hooker 1–3/4-inch

primary pipe Camaro headers along with a complete 3-inch exhaust using a pair of Flowmaster Super 40 mufflers.

Of course, with 454 inches, you would expect this Rat in Mouse clothing to crank out some serious torque. As you can see, it never makes less than 475 ft-lb of torque throughout its entire curve. In all fairness, that number is a bit deceiving since the test starts at a higher 3,600 rpm rather than at a lower 2,600 rpm. This engine does have a somewhat narrow power band of 1,400 rpm, but that's easy to overlook because it makes such serious power. This also points out how a larger displacement accommodates a larger cam and still creates a strong torque curve. This 252 at 0.050 duration cam would be very peaky in a 355–ci engine. But add an additional 100 cubic

ROCKER RATIO CHANGES

Another quick way to "tune" your camshaft is with rocker ratio changes. It's common knowledge that increasing rocker ratio from a standard 1.5:1 to 1.6:1 ratio adds lift. Generally, a 0.10 of a ratio increase (from 1.5:1 to 1.6:1 for example) bumps the lift by around 0.030 inches, but the only way to know for sure is to multiply the cam lobe lift by the actual rocker ratio. If you know the valve lift figure but don't know the cam lobe lift, you can divide the valve lift by the old rocker ratio to get lobe lift. Then multiply the lobe lift by the new rocker ratio to get the new valve lift figure. As an example, let's take a cam with 0.530-inch valve lift using a 1.5:1 rocker ratio creates a lobe lift of 0.3533 (0.530 / 1.5 = 0.3533). If we wanted to know what valve lift a 1.6:1 ratio rocker would create, merely multiply 0.3533 x 1.6 = 0.565.

Beyond modifying lift, a rocker ratio change also affects valve duration as well. While the opening and closing points remain the same, an increase in rocker ratio accelerates the valve open and closed at a faster rate, which means the effective duration at the valve with

lifts of 0.050, 0.100, 0.200, and 0.300 inches also increases. As a basic rule of thumb for every half-point of rocker ratio gain is that duration increases by one degree. This means that if you increase the rocker ratio from 1.5:1 to 1.6:1, a cam with 248 degrees at 0.050 now measures 250 degrees at the same 0.050-inch checking point. Conversely, reducing rocker ratio subtracts effective duration by the same amount.

When changing rocker ratio, it's best to keep in mind that an increase (or decrease) in power may be partly due to the lift changes, but could also be due in part to the effective duration change as well. This makes the evaluation process a bit more critical and not nearly as easy as you might have previously thought. Plus, the added acceleration rate of the valve may also push the valvetrain into valve float at an earlier RPM, even if you didn't have problems before the rocker ratio change. As a system, the rocker plays a big role and you have to think about the entire system and not just one component when making a change.

inches with a half-inch more stroke, and this cam works well. This cam is the big reason why the horsepower is so impressive, and also why this engine is not the torque-per-cubic-inch king of the engines in this section since the torque curve moves up in the engine speed range slightly with peak torque occurring at a rather high 5,000 rpm. Regardless, this is still impressive power for a normally aspirated small-block.

In a 2,600–pound Camaro with a good suspension, but with only a 3.37:1 gear and sticky 10-inch wide rear tires and a 2,600–rpm stall speed converter, this stout 454 small-block could easily push a combination like this deep in the low 11s at over 120 mph without too much trouble. The biggest challenge would be sticking all that torque to the pavement.

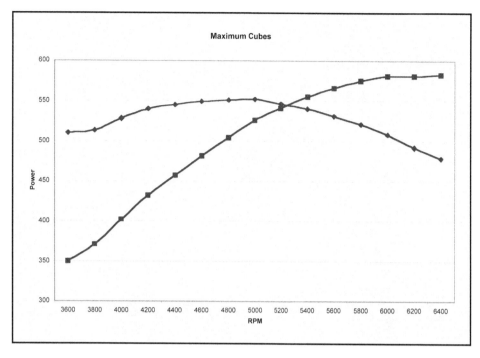

RPM	TQ	HP
3600	510	350
3800	513	371
4000	528	402
4200	540	432
4400	545	457
4600	549	481
4800	551	504
5000	552*	526
5200	546	541
5400	540	555
5600	531	566
5800	521	575
6000	508	581
6200	492	581
6400	478	583*
Peak	552	583
Avg.	527	500

1.21 ft-lb/ci
1.28 hp/ci

Engine 8
Twin-Turbo Terror
287ci

Just for fun, we thought we'd include Ken Duttweiler's mini-displacement Competition Eliminator small-block. With a bore of 4.080, the crank only moves the pistons a scant 2.750 inches of stroke. It also sports one of the old Pro Stock Truck short-deck blocks

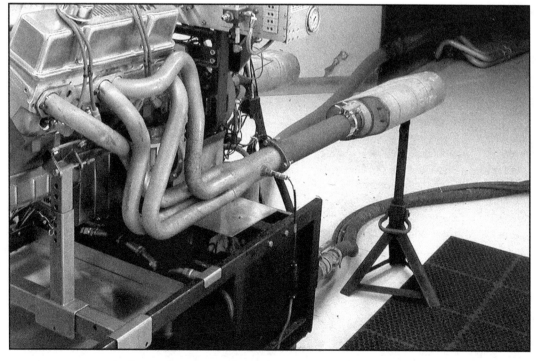

A barely streetable 3-inch exhaust system versus a more conservative 2-1/2-inch system can also make a big difference when testing "muffled" on the dyno. Any engine making over 500 hp should be considered a candidate for a 3-inch system.

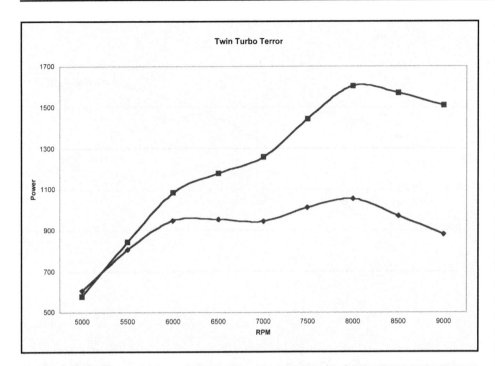

Twin Turbo Terror

CORRECTION FACTORS

All internal combustion engines are directly affected by the atmospheric conditions that exist at the time of the test. Comparing two engines tested on different days with vastly different atmospheric conditions requires a correction factor that takes the three most important variables that affect power into account. Carburetor inlet air temperature, atmospheric pressure, and vapor pressure (humidity) are the most critical to engine performance, and these are the factors that contribute to the correction process.

Most performance dyno shops use the standard "hot rod" correction factor, which uses a standard of sea level air pressure of 29.92 inches of mercury, 60-degree F air temperature, and zero vapor pressure. This means that the "corrected" air is very dense with a high

atmospheric pressure, relatively cool with no humidity. These three factors combine to create a very good power number. Obviously, it is rare that these three factors ever combine in the real world. That's why the Society of Automotive Engineers (SAE) has changed their correction factor to one with lower atmospheric pressure, higher inlet air temperature, and a given amount of water vapor. This reduces the "corrected" power number but is closer to a real-world situation for the engine.

When you see horsepower and torque numbers quoted by the new car manufacturers, their numbers were corrected to this SAE standard, which is generally considered to be about 5 percent lower than the "hot rod" correction factor. At 400 hp, that's a difference of 20 hp, so it's worth noting.

that were also built for Trans Am racing to take advantage of the diminutive stroke. Clearly, the low back-pressure turbochargers spinning 33 psi are the main power motivators, but the Mouse also employs a set of GM splayed-valve heads with massive titanium intake 2.150– and steel 1.625-inch valves. The solid roller cam uses 260/263 degrees of duration at 0.050-inch tappet lift with 0.770-inch gross valve lift and a T&D shaft rocker system with a 1.7:1 rocker ratio. Hogan supplied the sheetmetal aluminum intake while a Motec ECM manages the spark and fuel. This includes a complete coil-on-plug ignition system to ensure rock-solid timing accuracy with individual cylinder timing control. Intercoolers also play a part in this effort with the outlet temperatures from the turbos dropping as much as 100 degrees. Just before this book went to press, Duttweiler pushed this little small-block to 1,833 hp—an awe-inspiring 6.3 hp/ci!

RPM	TQ	HP
5000	606	577
5500	805	843
6000	948	1083
6500	953	1179
7000	944	1258
7500	1011	1444
8000	1054*	1605*
8500	970	1570
9000	881	1510
Peak	1054	1604
Avg.	908	1228

3.67 ft-lb/ci
5.59 hp/ci

SOURCE GUIDE

A

Automotive Racing Products
(ARP)
531 Spectrum Circle
Oxnard, CA 93030
800/826-3045
805/278-RACE (7223)
www.arp-bolts.com

Airflow Research (AFR)
10490 Ilex Ave.
Pacoima, CA 91331-3137
818/890-0616
www.airflowresearch.com

Audie Technology
Philadelphia, PA
610/630-5895
www.audietech.com

B

Billet Fabrication
649 Easy St., Suite F
Simi Valley, CA 93065
877/424-5538
805/584-0428 Tech
www.billetfab.com

Brodix, Inc.
301 Maple St.
Mena, AR 71953
479/394-1075
www.brodix.com

Bullet Racing Cams
8785 Old Craft Rd.
Olive Branch, MS 38654
662/893-5670
www.bulletcams.com

C

Cam Craft Performance Cams
357 Black Dog Alley
Easton, MD 21601
410/822-2122
www.camcraftcams.com

Cam Motion
2092 Dallas Dr.
Baton Rouge, LA 70806
225/926-6110
www.cammotion.com

Cloyes Gear and Products, Inc.
P.O. Box 287C
Paris, AR 44094
501/963-2105
www.cloyes.com

COMP Cams
3406 Democrat Rd.
Memphis, TN 38118
901/795-2400
800/999-0853 Cam Help
www.compcams.com

Competition Products
280 W. 35th Ave.
Oshkosh, WI 54902
920/233-2023
800/233-0199 ORDERS
www.competitionproducts.com

Crane Cams
530 Fentress Blvd.
Daytona Beach, FL 32114
386/258-6174 Tech
386/258-6167 Tech FAX
www.cranecams.com

Crower Cams & Equipment
3333 Main St.
Chula Vista, CA 91911
619/422-1191
www.crower.com

CV Products
42 High Tech Boulevard
Thomasville, NC 27360
800/448-1223
336/472-2242
www.cvproducts.com

D

Depac Dyno Systems
201 Mill St.
Rome, NY 13440
315/339-1265

E

Edelbrock
2700 California St.
Torrance, CA 90503
310/781-2222
800/416-8628 Tech
www.edelbrock.com

Endura-Tech
1325 Remington Rd.
Suite W
Schaumburg, IL 60173
847/843-7277
www.endura-tech.com

Engle Racing Cams
1621 12th Street
Santa Monica, CA 90404
310/450-0806
www.englecams.com

Erson Cams
550 Mallory Way
Carson City, NV 89701
775/882-1622
www.mrgasket.com

F

Federal-Mogul Corporation
P.O. Box 1966
Detroit, MI 48235
810/354-7700
www.federal-mogul.com

Ferrea Racing Components
2600 NW 55th Court
Suite 238
Ft. Lauderdale, FL 33309
888/733-2505
954/733-2505
www.ferrea.com

Ferry's Aluminum Repair
710 Quietwood St.
Dallas, TX 75253
972/557-3565
972/286-6199

H

Howards Cams
280 W. 35th Ave.
Oshkosh, WI 54902
920/233-5228
www.howardscams.com

I

Integral Cams
212 E. County Rd. 1
Dundas, MN 55019
507/645-9308
www.integralcams.com

Iskenderian Racing Cams (Isky)
16020 S. Broadway St.
Gardena, CA 90248
323/770-0930
www.Iskycams.com

J

Jesel
1985 Cedarbridge Ave.
Lakewood, NJ 08701
732/901-1800
www.jesel.com

K

K-Motion Valve Springs
2831 North 24th St.
Lafayette, IN 47904
800/428-7891
765/742-8494

L

Lazer Cams
2839 Sanderwood Dr.
Memphis, TN 38118
901/795-6000
www.lazercams.com

Bo Laws
BLP Products
1015 W. Church St.
Orlando, FL 32805
407/422-0394
800/624-1358
www.blp.com

Lunati Cams
Holley Performance Products
1801 Russellville Road
Bowling Green, KY 42101
270/781-9741
800/HOLLEY-1, 8530 (465-
5391) for nearest dealer
901/365-0950 Lunati Tech
www.holley.com

M

Manley Performance Products
1960 Swarthmore Ave.
Lakewood, NJ 08701
732/905-3366
www.manleyperformance.com

Manton Pushrods
558 Birch St., Ste. 4
Lake Elsinore, CA 92530
951/245-6565
www.mantonpushrods.com

Milodon
www.milodon.com

P

PBM Performance Products
7301 Global Dr.
Louisville, KY 40258
800/588-9608

Powerhouse Products
3402 Democrat Rd.
Memphis, TN 38118
800/872-7223 ORDERS
901/795-7600
www.powerhouseproducts.com

R

Rev Racing Engine Valves
4704 NE 11th Ave.
Ft. Lauderdale, FL 33334
800/398-6348
www.revvalves.com

S

Schubeck Racing
4160 S. Cameron St.
Bldg. D
Las Vegas, NV 89103
702/252-0677
www.schubeckracing.com

Scoggin-Dickey Performance
Center
5901 Spur 327
Lubbock, TX 79424
800/456-0211 Parts Center
806/798-4013 Parts
806/798-4108 Tech Line
www.sdpc2000.com

SI Industries
4477 Shopping Lane
Simi Valley, CA 93063
800/564-8258
www.sivalves.com

Harland Sharp
Custom Speed Parts, Mfg.
19769 Progress Dr.
Strongsville, OH 44149
440/238-3260
www.harlandsharp.com

Stealth Engineering and Technologies
1489 Cedar St.
Hold, MI 48842
800/854-4545
www.stealth-engineering.com

T

T&D Machine Products
4859 Convair Drive
Carson City, NV 89706
775/884-2292
www.tdmach.com

Titan Speed Engineering
13001 Tree Ranch Rd.
Ojai, CA 93023
800/308-4826
805/525-8660 Tech
www.titanspeed.com

W

Del West
28128 W. Livingston Ave.
Valencia, CA 91355
800/990-2779
www.delwestusa.com

X

Xceldyne Technologies
Division of CV Products
42 High Tech Blvd.
Thomasville, NC 27630
800/448-1223
www.xceldyne.com

MORE GREAT TITLES AVAILABLE FROM CARTECH®

CHEVROLET

How To Rebuild the Small-Block Chevrolet* (SA26)
Chevrolet Small-Block Parts Interchange Manual (SA55)
How To Build Max Perf Chevy Small-Blocks on a Budget (SA57)
How To Build High-Perf Chevy LS1/LS6 Engines (SA86)
How To Build Big-Inch Chevy Small-Blocks (SA87)
How to Build High-Performance Chevy Small-Block Cams/Valvetrains SA105)
Rebuilding the Small-Block Chevy: Step-by-Step Videobook (SA116)
High-Performance Chevy Small-Block Cylinder Heads (SA125P)
High Performance C5 Corvette Builder's Guide (SA127)
How to Rebuild the Big-Block Chevrolet* (SA142P)
How to Build Max-Performance Chevy Big Block on a Budget (SA198)
How to Restore Your Camaro 1967–1969 (SA178)
How to Build Killer Big-Block Chevy Engines (SA190)
How to Build Max-Performance Chevy LT1/LT4 Engines (SA206)
Small-Block Chevy Performance: 1955-1996 (SA110P)
How to Build Small-Block Chevy Circle-Track Racing Engines (SA121P)
High-Performance C5 Corvette Builder's Guide (SA127P)
Chevrolet Big Block Parts Interchange Manual (SA31P)
Chevy TPI Fuel Injection Swapper's Guide (SA53P)

FORD

High-Performance Ford Engine Parts Interchange (SA56)
How To Build Max Performance Ford V-8s on a Budget (SA69)
How To Build Max Perf 4.6 Liter Ford Engines (SA82)
How To Build Big-Inch Ford Small-Blocks (SA85)
How to Rebuild the Small-Block Ford* (SA102)
How to Rebuild Big-Block Ford Engines* (SA162)
Full-Size Fords 1955–1970 (SA176)
How to Build Max-Performance Ford FE Engines (SA183)
How to Restore Your Mustang 1964 1/2–1973 (SA165)
How to Build Ford RestoMod Street Machines (SA101P)
Building 4.6/5.4L Ford Horsepower on the Dyno (SA115P)
How to Rebuild 4.6/5.4-Liter Ford Engines (SA155P)
Building High-Performance Fox-Body Mustangs on a Budget (SA75P)
How to Build Supercharged & Turbocharged Small-Block Fords (SA95P)

GENERAL MOTORS

GM Automatic Overdrive Transmission Builder's and Swapper's Guide (SA140)
How to Rebuild GM LS-Series Engines* (SA147)
How to Swap GM LS-Series Engines Into Almost Anything (SA156)
How to Supercharge & Turbocharge GM LS-Series Engines (SA180)
How to Build Big-Inch GM LS-Series Engines (SA203)
How to Rebuild & Modify GM Turbo 400 Transmissions (SA186)
How to Build GM Pro-Touring Street Machines (SA81P)

MOPAR

How to Rebuild the Big-Block Mopar (SA197)
How to Rebuild the Small-Block Mopar* (SA143P)
How to Build Max-Performance Hemi Engines (SA164)
How To Build Max-Performance Mopar Big Blocks (SA171)
Mopar B-Body Performance Upgrades 1962-1979 (SA191)
How to Build Big-Inch Mopar Small-Blocks (SA104P)
High-Performance New Hemi Builder's Guide 2003-Present (SA132P)

OLDSMOBILE/ PONTIAC/ BUICK

How to Build Max-Performance Oldsmobile V-8s (SA172)
How To Build Max-Perf Pontiac V8s SA78)
How to Rebuild Pontiac V-8s* (SA200)
How to Build Max-Performance Buick Engines (SA146P)

ENGINE

Engine Blueprinting (SA21)
Automotive Diagnostic Systems: Understanding OBD-I & OBD II (SA174)

SPORT COMPACTS

Honda Engine Swaps (SA93)
Building Honda K-Series Engine Performance (SA134)
High-Performance Subaru Builder's Guide (SA141)
How to Build Max-Performance Mitsubishi 4G63t Engines (SA148)
How to Rebuild Honda B-Series Engines* (SA154)
The New Mini Performance Handbook (SA182P)
High Performance Dodge Neon Builder's Handbook (SA100P)
High-Performance Honda Builder's Handbook Volume 1 (SA49P)

INDUCTION & IGNITION

Super Tuning & Modifying Holley Carburetors (SA08)
Street Supercharging, A Complete Guide to (SA17)
How To Build High-Performance Ignition Systems (SA79)
How to Build and Modify Rochester Quadrajet Carburetors (SA113)
Turbo: Real World High-Performance Turbocharger Systems (SA123)
How to Rebuild & Modify Carter/Edelbrock Carbs (SA130)
Engine Management-Advanced Tuning (SA135)
Designing & Tuning High-Performance Fuel Injection Systems (SA161)
Demon Carburetion (SA68P)

DRIVING

How to Drift: The Art of Oversteer (SA118)
How to Drag Race (SA136)
How to Autocross (SA158P)
How to Hook and Launch (SA195)
How to Drift: The Art of Oversteer (SA118P)

HIGH-PERFORMANCE & RESTORATION HOW-TO

How To Install and Tune Nitrous Oxide Systems (SA194)
Custom Painting (SA10)
David Vizard's How to Build Horsepower (SA24)
How to Rebuild & Modify High-Performance Manual Transmissions* (SA103)
High-Performance Jeep Cherokee XJ Builder's Guide 1984–2001 (SA109)
How to Paint Your Car on a Budget (SA117)
High Performance Brake Systems (SA126P)
High Performance Diesel Builder's Guide (SA129)
4x4 Suspension Handbook (SA137)
How to Rebuild Any Automotive Engine* (SA151)
Automotive Welding: A Practical Guide* (SA159)
Automotive Wiring and Electrical Systems* (SA160)
Design & Install In Car Entertainment Systems (SA163)
Automotive Bodywork & Rust Repair* (SA166)
High-Performance Differentials, Axles, & Drivelines (SA170)
How to Make Your Muscle Car Handle (SA175)
Rebuilding Any Automotive Engine: Step-by-Step Videobook (SA179)
Builder's Guide to Hot Rod Chassis & Suspension (SA185)
How To Rebuild & Modify GM Turbo 400 Transmissions* (SA186)
How to Build Altered Wheelbase Cars (SA189)
How to Build Period Correct Hot Rods (SA192)
Automotive Sheet Metal Forming & Fabrication (SA196)
Performance Automotive Engine Math (SA204)
How to Design, Build & Equip Your Automotive Workshop on a Budget (SA207)
Automotive Electrical Performance Projects (SA209)
How to Port Cylinder Heads (SA215)
Muscle Car Interior Restoration Guide (SA167)
High Performance Jeep Wrangler TJ Builder's Guide: 1997-2006 (SA120P)
Dyno Testing & Tuning (SA138P)
How to Rebuild Any Automotive Engine (SA151P)
Muscle Car Interior Restoration Guide (SA167P)
How to Build Horsepower - Volume 2 (SA52P)
Bolt-Together Street Rods (SA72P)

HISTORIES & PERSONALITIES

Fuelies: Fuel Injected Corvettes 1957–1965 (CT452)
Yenko (CT485)
Lost Hot Rods (CT487)
Grumpy's Toys (CT489)
Woodward Avenue: Cruising the Legendary (CT491)
Rusted Muscle — A collection of junkyard muscle cars. (CT492)
America's Coolest Station Wagons (CT493)
Super Stock — A paperback version of a classic best seller. (CT495)
Rusty Pickups: American Workhorses Put to Pasture (CT496)
Jerry Heasley's Rare Finds — Great collection of Heasley's best finds. (CT497)
Street Sleepers: The Art of the Deceptively Fast Car (CT498)
Ed 'Big Daddy' Roth — Paperback reprint of a classic best seller. (CT500)
Rat Rods: Rodding's Imperfect Stepchildren (CT486)
East vs. West: Rods, Customs Rails (CT501)
Car Spy: Secret Cars Exposed by the Industry's Most Notorious Photographer CT502)

*Workbench® Series books featuring step-by-step instruction with hundreds of color photos for stock rebuilds and automotive repair.

CarTech®, Inc. 39966 Grand Ave., North Branch, MN 55056. Ph: 800-551-4754 or 651-277-1200 • Fax: 651-277-1203
Brooklands Books Ltd., PO Box 146 Cobham, Surrey KT11 1LG, England. Ph: 01932 865051 • Fax 01932 868803
Brooklands Books Aus., 3/37-39 Green Street, Banksmeadow, NSW 2019, Australia. Ph: 2 9695 7055 • Fax 2 9695 7355

Visit us online at
www.cartechbooks.com for more info!

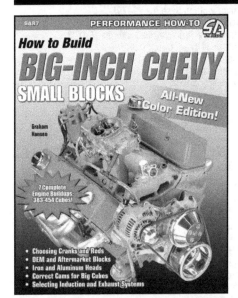
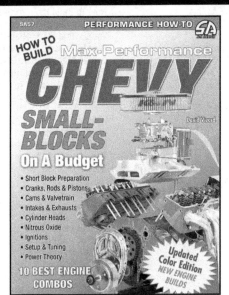
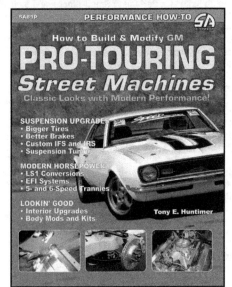

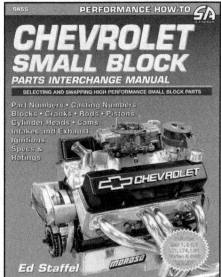

CPSIA information can be obtained
at www.ICGtesting.com
Printed in the USA
BVHW011121230220
R10673800001B/R106738PG572818BVX4B/3